Washington Times and Trails

★★★★★★★★★★★★★★★★★★★★★★★★

by **Joan** *and* **Gene Olson**

"What do we want of this vast, worthless area, this region of savages and wild beasts, of shifting sands and whirlwinds of dust, of cactus and prairie dogs? To what use could we ever hope to put these great deserts or these great mountain ranges, impenetrable and covered to their base with eternal snow? What can we ever hope to do with the western coast, a coast of three thousand miles, rockbound, cheerless and uninviting, and not a harbor on it? What use have we of such a country? Mr. President, I will never vote one cent from the public treasury to place the Pacific Coast one inch nearer Boston than it is now."

—*Senator Daniel Webster*

WINDYRIDGE PRESS

Library of Congress Catalog Card Number: 75–83521
ISBN: 0-913366-01-3

PUBLISHED BY

WINDYRIDGE PRESS
780 OXYOKE ROAD
GRANTS PASS, OREGON

PRINTED IN THE UNITED STATES OF AMERICA

Table of Contents

Acknowledgments

The gratitude of the authors must go to Walter and Clarice Foelker; Wendell C. Allen, Office of State Superintendent of Public Instruction; Frank Arnich; Jean Badten, Office of State Superintendent of Public Instruction; James Bracken, Spokane *Spokesman-Review;* W. Ray Carder; Art Chipman; Leo Clark, U.S. Soil Conservation Service; Robert E. S. Clark, Fort Vancouver National Historic Site; Martin Cole; R. S. Duter, U.S. Bureau of Public Roads; Jesse Ebert, Ebert-Aerolist Photographers, Inc.; Barbara Elkins, Oregon Historical Society; Margaret Felt, State Department of Natural Resources; Lt. L. F. Ficca, Puget Sound Naval Shipyard; Lambert Florin; Ed Garrison, Port of Tacoma; Sam Gilluly, Montana Historical Society; Frank Green, Washington State Historical Society; M. Jeanne Gulick, Whitman College; Howard Hansen, Southern Oregon State Bank; Dorothy Hanson, International Paper Co./Long-Bell Division; Edna May Hill, Josephine County Library; Anna M. Ibbotson, Washington State Historical Society; John T. Jensen; Margaret Knispel, National Education Association; John and Clara Knoll; Priscilla Knuth, Oregon Historical Society; Alfred T. McCallum, Office of State Superintendent of Public Instruction; Lucile McDonald; Robert D. Monroe, University of Washington Libraries; Robert W. Olsen, Jr., Whitman Mission National Historic Site; Bernard A. Ossey, U.S. Army Corps of Engineers; Mary Pfeiffer; Douglas W. Polivka, U.S. Army Corps of Engineers; Don M. Richardson, State Department of Commerce and Economic Development; Rhoda Ritzenberg, U.S. Department of the Interior; Lee Ryland; Lorena Sample; John C. Sherman, University of Washington; P. W. Stafford, Great Northern Railway Company; Carl and Leona Thomas; Mabel Turner, Eastern Washington State Historical Society; Celiene F. Wentworth, Eastern Washington State Historical Society; Jim and Lillian Wilson, Northwest Air Photos; Paul W. Wiseman, State Employment Security Department; William L. Worden, The Boeing Company.

The authors thank the following publishers for permission to quote from their published titles:

Doubleday & Company, Inc.; THE WOBBLIES; Patrick Renshaw; 1967.

Duell, Sloan and Pearce; VISION; Harold Mansfield; 1956.

Alfred A. Knopf, Inc.; JAMES J. HILL; Stewart H. Holbrook; 1955.

Quotes from THE STORY OF AMERICAN RAILROADS by Stewart H. Holbrook © 1947 by Crown Publishers, Inc. Used by permission.

Material about Spokan Garry reprinted by permission of the publishers of Chief SPOKAN GARRY, by Thomas E. Jessett, T. S. Denison & Company, Inc. Publishers.

Material quoted by permission from ONE MAN'S GOLD RUSH, A Klondike Album, by Murray Morgan, photographs by E. A. Hegg, © 1967 by the University of Washington Press.

Material quoted by permission from THE OLYMPIC RAIN FOREST, by Ruth Kirk, with photographs by Johsel Namkung and Ruth Kirk, © 1966 by the University of Washington Press.

Photo Credits:

Chapter One ★

Early Exploration
SAILS IN THE OFFSHORE MIST

To find fascination in Washington history, one needs only to start at the beginning of the record with a wild tale by an old sea dog who proudly bore two unlikely names.

The wrinkled sailor's real name was pure Greek music: Apostolos Valerianos. On the Rialto in Venice one fine day in the year of 1596, Apostolos Valerianos chanced to meet an Englishman, Michael Lok, who owned a pair of receptive ears.

Then as now, sailors liked nothing better than to spin fanciful tales of wonders they had glimpsed beyond the watery horizons of the world. And so it was that a listener expected to hear yarns, fables, the entertaining products of an overstimulated imagination.

But the story told by Valerianos knocked Lok for a loop. When the Englishman recovered the cool facade expected of a British consul, he wrote:

"When I was in Venice, Italy, haply there arrived there an old man about sixty years of age, of the Island of Cephalonia, by profession a mariner and an ancient pilot of ships. He was a Greek by birth, by the name of Apostolos Valerianos, but better known by his Spanish name of Juan de Fuca.

"He stated that in 1592 he sailed in a small caravel from Mexico in the service of Spain, along the Mexican and California coasts, until he came to the latitude of 47 deg., and there finding that land tended north and northeast with a broad inlet of sea, between the latitudes of 47 deg. and 48 deg., he entered therein, sailing more than twenty days and passing divers islands in that sailing.

"And at the entrance to the said strait, there is on the northwest coast thereof, a great headland or island, with an exceedingly high pinnacle or spired rock like a pillar thereon; that he saw some people on land clad in skins and that the land is very fruitful and rich in gold, silver, and pearls . . ."

Michael Lok was convinced that the old sailor had actually made a voyage much like the one he had described. There were exaggerations and elaborations, of course; no sea dog worth his salt would leave them out. For instance, Valerianos probably hadn't sailed all the way east to the Atlantic Ocean as he claimed. At the time, America was considered a relatively slim continent, measured east-west, but surely it wasn't so slim that Valerianos could sail across it in 20 days in a caravel!

What particularly interested Lok was that Juan de Fuca, as he had chosen to call himself, wanted to go to sea again. The old man was willing to sign on as pilot of a British ship and sail it along the course he had followed four years earlier.

Lok published an account of Juan de Fuca's story in England, hoping to stir up government interest. He failed. The English were not interested in financing an expedition based on no more than the senile memories of a Greek sailor who may or may not once have served aboard exploring ships for the Spanish.

After all, asked the men in government, if this silly old man named Valerianos, or de Fuca, had once served the Spanish on the seven seas, why was there no record of such a person in the archives of the Spanish navy? If de Fuca had made such a discovery, why hadn't the Spanish rewarded him properly and claimed the Northwest coast of America as their own, with all its riches?

The questions could not be answered by Michael Lok, nor by anyone else. The flurry of excitement faded; Juan de Fuca made no more voyages. The patriotic crusade of Michael Lok ended in failure.

★

Gold, silver and pearls . . .

The reported treasures of the New World caused greedy licking of lips among rulers of the Old World, particularly among the Spanish, but it was another prize which had stimulated Michael Lok: the treasure of the Orient.

Trade with Asiatic countries had reached fabulous proportions, but the violent voyages from any European port around Africa, thrusting prows of wooden ships into the demonic storms lurking hard by the Cape of Good Hope, had become a hair-graying experience that seafaring men wanted to talk about only in fearful whispers.

Surely there was a better route. Of course: the Northwest Passage.

The Northwest Passage became an article of faith among the men of the sea and the governments which supplied their ships and provisions; a sea route simply had to exist between the Atlantic and Pacific coasts of North America. The country which first discovered this quick, easy path to the riches of the Orient could soon rule the world. If America turned out to be larger and wealthier than expected, this was merely a bonus.

Lok and many other Englishmen were convinced that the fabled water passage would connect the Northwest American coast with Hudson's Bay, then with an Atlantic Ocean ruled by an English fleet. And this is why Lok had listened so carefully to the old sailor in Venice.

★

The English and Spanish governments may have forgotten the Greek known as Juan de Fuca but the sea roamers had not. The story of the Greek's voyage colored their dreams and outlined their ambitions.

Almost a century later, in 1787, an English fur trader named William Barclay discovered a broad strait leading inland, within a degree of where Juan de Fuca said it was. A year later, another English fur trader, John Meares, ruddered his ship into the same wide opening in the wooded coast and on his charts gave it a name: "Juan de Fuca Strait."

It was not the Northwest Passage. Instead it was the waterway which flowed into Puget Sound, the passage which made it possible for Seattle, Tacoma, Everett, Olympia, Bremerton, Bellingham and a dozen more towns facing saltwater beaches and gentle tidewater to become the population centers of modern Washington.

There are historians who still insist that Apostolos Valerianos was no more than an entertaining liar. But the salty men who roved the seas in search of wealth and adventure named the wide, stormy strait after Juan de Fuca and no other.

So it is today and so it is likely to remain.

GREED AND THE PREVAILING WINDS

Human greed is blamed for a lot of human misery, and rightly so, but it also should be credited with a fair amount of human achievement.

As an example, consider the first seaborne explorations of the Washington-Oregon coasts. The Spanish, greatest explorers of the Old World, were as greedy a band of pirates as ever sailed the seven seas. They were also vigorous, brave and intelligent.

Once the Spaniards had the exploitation of Mexico well underway and the royal houses in Europe were ringing with the happy cries of the rich getting richer, they could wander north along the coast. In the process of looking for the mythical passage to the Atlantic, they managed to conquer and for a time control a vast empire including modern Mexico and Central America, plus much of what is now the southwest U.S.

For a period of about 20 years starting in 1774, Spanish, British and American explorer-traders made frequent voyages along the Northwest Coast. Occasionally one of them stiffened his back and stepped ashore. If he wasn't immediately wiped out by waiting Indians, more likely than not he planted his country's flag and claimed a large section of real estate for king and company. The widespread belief among the nations of the white race in those days was that if land wasn't owned by whites, it was up for grabs, no matter how many members of other races there might have been living on it.

Among the remembered Spanish names of the early exploring years were Perez, Heceta and Bodega. In 1778, Captain James Cook, an Englishman, sailed past the Strait of Juan de Fuca after dark, saw nothing, and concluded there was nothing there.

About 10 years later, Barclay and Meares came to a more sensible conclusion. In 1788, the Americans finally got into the act when Robert Gray and James Kendrick sailed onto the scene.

In 1789 and 1790, the Spanish returned and Manuel Quimper sighted the snow-capped bulk of Mt. Baker and no doubt wished he could buy a picture postcard to send back to San Blas, the Spaniard's base on the west coast of Mexico.

In 1792, the Britisher, George Vancouver, explored and named Puget Sound and many of its islands, harbors and mountains. In the time-honored way, he took possession of the entire Pacific Northwest for Great Britain while quite possibly standing within what are now the city limits of Everett, Washington, U.S.A. (Moral: it is one thing to plant a flag, quite another to keep it planted.)

The American, Robert Gray, also returned to the scene in 1792 and discovered the coastal irregularity now called Grays Harbor and a legendary and still-fantastic river called "Columbia" after Gray's ship, *Columbia Rediviva*.

Then the day of the exploring sailors came to a close. The overland

Crossing the Columbia bar could be a hair-raising experience, as depicted here by an early artist.

adventure was about to begin with America's Louisiana Purchase in 1803 and the Lewis and Clark expedition of the following year. But the curtain shouldn't be drawn over the seagoing exploits of the Spanish, English and Americans without a cryptic quote which causes one to wonder if the Northwest Coast hadn't seen many more explorers than the record shows:

"Seventy-five Oriental junks are known to have been found adrift or ashore on the American side of the Pacific up to the year 1875."

Was the much-sought easy route to the Orient a two-way street?

INTO THE SHINING MOUNTAINS

Think of frontier exploration and the Lewis and Clark expedition of 1804–1806 immediately comes to mind. This fabulous adventure was a trek through largely unexplored wilderness between St. Louis, Missouri, and Astoria, Oregon. Before the party returned to so-called civilization, the Lewis and Clark Trail had been stretched out for almost 8000 miles.

Eight thousand miles.

Merely 13 hours in a jet plane. (The food and drink will be great but the in-flight movie will be a hardship.) Sixteen days in a modern automobile. (Cold? Turn up the heater. Hot? Turn on the air-conditioning. Still hardships, though. One might occasionally be battered by boredom or a poor motel bed.)

The Lewis and Clark party made the trip by keelboat, by canoe, astride horses and afoot. They departed in May, 1804, and returned in March, 1806. They lived off the land, mostly; they saw no movies; they alternately froze and roasted and nearly drowned; they were seldom bored and they had no problems with poor beds. No beds. They slept on the ground much of the time and one patch of ground is much like another when it comes to sleeping.

President Thomas Jefferson, perhaps the most far-seeing of early Americans, pulled the trigger which fired the Lewis and Clark expedition into the western wilderness. In the President's mind was a grand design— a United States of America which stretched from the Atlantic to the Pacific. If the Lewis and Clark expedition failed or arrived too late at the mouth of the great River of the West, the unexplored vastness west of the Rocky Mountains might be claimed by Great Britain and would be forever British, not American.

Jefferson instructed his 29-year-old secretary, Captain Meriwether Lewis, to "explore the Missouri River, and such principal streams of it as

. . . may offer the most . . . communication across this continent."

An intelligent, intense and rather a brooding man, Captain Lewis chose as co-leader a jolly comrade with whom he had shared experience in the Indian Wars: Lieutenant William Clark, 33.

On May 14, 1804, a keelboat carrying the party of 32 on the great adventure was poled away from a St. Louis wharf and turned into the current of the Missouri River.

The group was soon joined by one of its most interesting members, Sacajawea, a teen-age Indian girl. The decision may have saved the party from destruction months later, when it had to leave the rivers and face a crossing of the monstrous Shining Mountains. Without horses, the party was likely to perish on the slopes. They had been told that Shoshone Indians in the mountains would give them horses but where were the Shoshones?

Less than a calendar page away, winter threatened. The towering rock wall had to be conquered before the heavy snows fell or it would not be conquered at all and the dream of President Jefferson would die.

Sacajawea was a Shoshone by birth, although she had been living among Minnetarees, who had kidnapped her. Sacajawea insisted that the Shoshones were there, hiding in the foothills of the mountains, and soon, when they felt safe enough, they would show themselves.

Then, in one of the most unlikely episodes of Western history, the first contact of the party with Shoshones was with a band led by Cam-me-ah-wait, Sacajawea's brother!

And so another crisis passed. The Shoshones supplied horses and the mountains were conquered. The Lewis and Clark party, riding Shoshone ponies and with an old Shoshone brave as guide, came down the Lolo Trail, then set off in Indian canoes on the last leg of the terrible trek, the relatively easy journey down the Columbia River to the ocean. The fort they built near the modern town of Astoria, Oregon, was called Fort Clatsop. (A reconstruction of the fort is now a popular national memorial and one of the outstanding landmarks of the Lewis and Clark trail.)

Much has been written about Sacajawea; less has been said about a giant man whose only name was "York." York was Clark's servant but long before the expedition reached the mouth of the River of the West, he had gained a position in the party far above servant. York proved himself

➡

In a Mandan village on the way west, curious Indians try to rub the black off York of the Lewis and Clark band. Charles M. Russell painted the scene.

resourceful and dependable, a tower of strength during bad moments . . . and there were many bad moments.

In another of history's many ironic twists, York became one of the party's outstanding assets because of what was then—and is now—a personal liability: his skin was black.

Yes, York was a Negro. At many points along the way, Indians who might have been hostile were put off by the great size and uncommon color of York.

At a village of Arickara Indians, Clark said, "The natives all flocked around and examined him from top to toe." York enjoyed the situation immensely. "He carried on the joke himself and made himself more turribal than we wished him to doe." (You may have noticed Clark was not the world's best speller.)

York told the Indians he was a wild animal Clark had captured and tamed. "A horde of little boys followed him at a safe distance wherever he went. York loved it. He would turn and bare his teeth or growl and the small fry would scatter screaming, only to gather again immediately when he turned his back."

It was not unusual for an Indian to shuffle cautiously close to York, moisten a finger and try to rub the black off his skin. York always submitted patiently to the test.

★

In September, 1806, Captain Lewis reached St. Louis and immediately wrote a message to President Jefferson: "In obedience to your orders we have penetrated the Continent of North America to the Pacific Ocean and sufficiently explored the interior of the country to affirm that we have discovered the most practicable communication which does exist across the continent."

Thus ended one of the most important and most difficult journeys of exploration ever attempted. Now Americans could understand what Thomas Jefferson had pulled off with his Louisiana Purchase; he had bought nothing less than a new empire, one of the world's richest, a golden land which would give America space in which to flex its young muscles.

Lewis and Clark, York, Sacajawea and the others had made the value of the far-reaching land a matter of record.

After his return from the West, Captain Lewis posed in St. Louis for this painting by St. Memin.

Poor Meriwether Lewis . . . the expedition was the high point of his life; thereafter his trail led toward the abyss in the dark of night. Among other honors, he was appointed governor of Louisiana Territory but the busy, nervous, indoor life of an important politician did not set well with him. He needed solitude and was much happier in the wilderness.

Only three years after his return from the West, he was travelling on official business along the Natchez Trace, the fabled, fearsome trail which led north from the mouth of the Mississippi River. On the night of October 10, 1809, somebody shot him through the head at Grinder's Stand, an overnight station along the trail. At death, Lewis was only 35 years old.

The Grinders, man and wife, had none too savory a reputation. Predictably, they insisted that Governor Lewis had committed suicide.

Maybe yes; maybe no. Pressures of his job might have driven him to kill himself, but if so, what happened to the substantial sum of money he carried? Mystery surrounds the macabre episode and probably always will.

William Clark, jolly and gregarious, fared much better. He occupied himself with much gusto and popularity as a brigadier general in charge of Indian affairs for Louisiana Territory, then was named governor of Missouri Territory. He died in 1838.

It is believed that York is buried somewhere in Missouri, not far from Clark's grave. In the time-honored way, no one considered it important to mark the site. York may have been a valued member of the historic expedition but he was, after all, a Negro, and only a servant Negro, at that.

Along the Oregon Trail, pioneers buried their dead, then drove wagons repeatedly over the unmarked graves to obliterate them, lest Indians or wolves or coyotes dig up the remains. History has deep-buried many American Negroes and wiped out the traces with wagon tracks. Now that we have learned that history can be a seed-bed of self respect for a race or a nation, we are trying to uncover some of those graves. In too many cases, we are finding only dust. An unguarded heritage can be stolen, or it can merely slide away into oblivion, leaving nothing but faint, tantalizing traces.

It appears that the United States intends to remember Lewis and Clark and the dangerous trail they carved across an unknown land. Most of the historic route has been marked by 11 states; eventually access roads will allow those who care to do so to seek out the original trail along most of its length. The work has been spearheaded by the Lewis and Clark Trail Commission established by the U.S. Congress in 1964.

The Lewis and Clark medallion was struck to commemorate the epic journey of exploration.

There is the town of Clarkston, where the expedition first entered what is now the state of Washington on October 11, 1805. Near Pasco is Sacajawea State Park. Close to the mouth of the Columbia on the Washington shore is Lewis and Clark Campsite State Park, the point from which the explorers first saw Pacific breakers. Two miles east of Ilwaco is Fort Canby State Park. On November 18, 1805, the expedition reached the ocean at this point. A monument at Long Beach marks the northernmost point of a side trip of exploration made while the party was encamped near the mouth of the Columbia. Stones in the monument were

14

contributed by communities along the trail.

Fort Lewis near Tacoma commemorates the co-leader of the expedition. The fort, now the second largest permanent army post in the nation, was established as Camp Lewis on 62,000 acres of land donated by Pierce County in 1917.

Lewis and Clark wrote detailed journals of their fantastic trip, as did other members of the party. These make up some of the most fascinating, racy and uninhibited records ever written of frontier exploration. The spelling occasionally was atrocious but the subject matter triumphed over all.

Would you care to know how it was to face a giant grizzly bear on a wilderness trail, with the nearest doctor and hospital many hundreds of miles away? A bear, mind you, so big and strong that a few bullets fired into his fur caused him only to blink his eyes? Clark wrote about it thusly: ". . . these bear being so hard to die rather intimedates us all: I must confess that I do not like the gentlemen and had reather fight two Indians than one bear."

Say again that courage is not the absence of fear, but the ability to overcome fear. Explorers striking out into the wilderness certainly were brave, but they were anything but fearless.

Lewis, Clark, Sacajawea and York weren't fearless; they merely had courage. Lewis and Clark will be remembered; Sacajawea's position in history is more than secure, as is York's.

Which leads one to hope that Scannon will some day emerge into plain view through the mists of history. But Scannon was nothing but a dog, a Newfoundland bought for $20 by Captain Lewis. Scannon made the journey and earned his keep by catching game and bringing it back to his master. Who knows where Scannon is buried?

GEOGRAPHY CAN BE DANGEROUS

The first man to put Washington on the map—literally—was an Englishman. This Englishman was the first person to travel the hazardous Columbia River from its source to its mouth. He took a half-Indian wife at age 29 (she was 14) and kept her at his side throughout a very long life. He has been called the greatest English land geographer of his day, perhaps of any day. Maps that he drew of remote Canadian regions over a century ago are still being used today.

Does the name of this illustrious figure pop into mind?

Probably not. His skin was suitably white but he was the sort of quiet soul who constantly hid his light under a bushel. History has followed suit.

David Thompson was his name but Indians along the meandering course of the great river called him "Koo-Koo-Sint," or "Man Who Watches Stars." If Hudson's Bay Company hadn't objected to his eternal star-gazing, he might have died completely unknown.

Certainly his beginning in London was unpromising. His Welsh father died when David was two years old. At age seven, he was turned over by his hard-pressed mother to the Grey Coat Charity School for Boys.

Seven years later, Hudson's Bay Company in Canada asked for apprentices to serve seven-year terms. David Thompson and another boy were signed up but the other boy, faced with a fearsome journey across a stormy ocean to an unknown land, ran away. David was forced to launch his new life alone.

Its first chapter would have discouraged almost anyone. He was stationed at an Arctic post where fuel was so scarce that fires could be built only to cook morning and evening meals. He might have frozen to death that first winter if some inventive soul hadn't decided that the thing to do was to soak the four inches of frost inside their log cabins with water, thus turning it into ice which provided a little insulation against the killing cold.

The other seasons at the Churchill River post weren't much better. The 15-year-old recorded in his diary: ". . . summer, such as it is, comes at once and with it myriads of tormenting mosquitoes; the air is thick with them and there is no cessation day or night of suffering from them."

Between the orphanage in London and the bleak post in the Arctic tundra, David Thompson was being prepared well for the life of physical hardship which lay ahead. He learned to shoot and trap; he developed great physical stamina. For proof, consider that Hudson's Bay, no coddler of children, sent him to York Factory and insisted that he provide his own food and shelter along the way. David was 15 years old at the time; York Factory was 150 miles away from the post on the Churchill. David Thompson survived the trip.

He worked for Hudson's Bay until 1797, when a superior told him that there was to be no more star-gazing. Young David thought it over, then folded his pack and headed south. Six hundred hard miles later, he took a job as surveyor with Hudson's Bay Company's arch-rival, North West Company. The mold of his life was set. David Thompson had found his place doing work he loved: roaming the wilderness and recording on

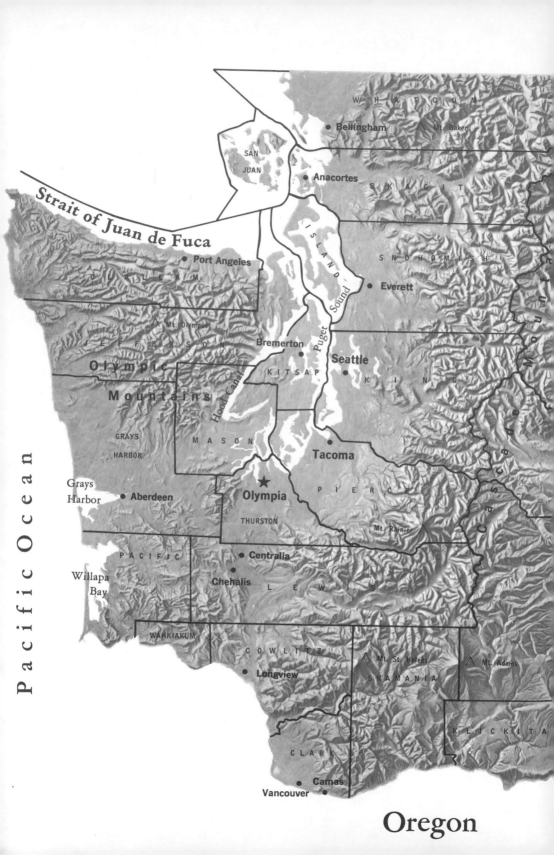

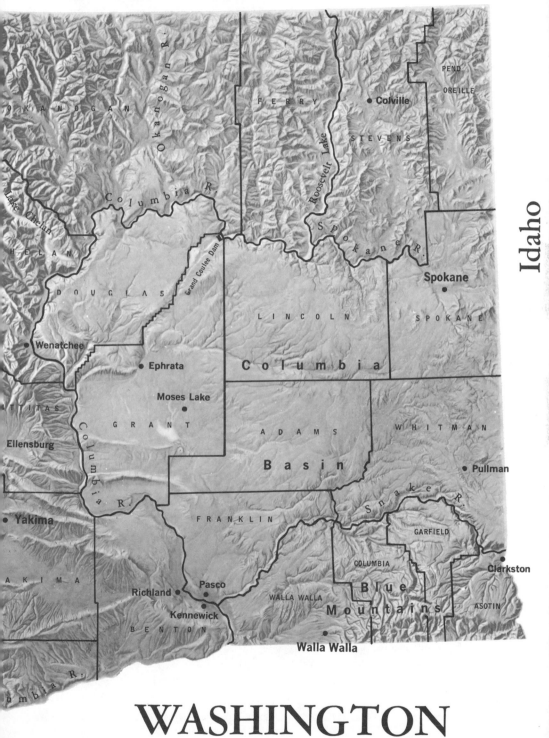

British Columbia

OKANOGAN

FERRY

Colville

PEND OREILLE

STEVENS

Idaho

Roosevelt Lake

Okanogan R.

Columbia R.

Lake Chelan

CHELAN

DOUGLAS

Grand Coulee Dam

Wenatchee

Ephrata

Moses Lake

GRANT

Spokane R.

Spokane

SPOKANE

LINCOLN

Columbia

TTITAS

Ellensburg

Columbia R.

ADAMS

Basin

WHITMAN

Pullman

Yakima

FRANKLIN

Snake R.

GARFIELD

AKIMA

Richland

Pasco

Kennewick

BENTON

COLUMBIA

WALLA WALLA

Blue

Mountains

Walla Walla

Clarkston

ASOTIN

WASHINGTON

umbia R.

paper the length and breadth of the land, registering its heights and its depths and marking the wandering of its streams and pinpointing its lakes. At last the new country had met the man who would take its measure, record the measurements scientifically and transmit the information to those who might be lured to follow.

But always in the back of his mind—and in the minds of his employers—lurked the River of the West, the fabled Columbia. Somehow that great watercourse had carved a path from the interior of the continent to the western coast; the fur company which found it first could avoid the slow treks through the cruel mountains with trade goods and furs. The Columbia could be nothing less than a water highway to the sea. In addition, the country which first established a permanent post at its mouth would have a strong claim to the entire Northwest. And so the mission was clear: trace the Columbia.

North West Company bet all its chips on its star gazer.

★

David Thompson knew that he had been on the great river in his travels but he had not been able to puzzle out its course. The Columbia had to flow generally south and west to get where everyone said it went. He had been on a stream which might well have been the fabled river but it flowed north; how could this be?

Anyone who looks at a modern map of Canada can understand his puzzlement. The Columbia flows north from its source in Canada, then swings sharply south until it crosses the border. In Washington, it flows south, north and west in wild convolutions. To say nothing of east, before and after Richland-Pasco-Kennewick. Then it takes the bit in its teeth and bores straight west to the sea. Well, not straight exactly. Being the Columbia, it does turn north a bit, then west again, before emptying into the ocean. In speed of flow, the Columbia is one of the quickest rivers in the world but the ground it gains on the straightaways, it loses in the corners.

In midwinter of 1811, David Thompson committed himself to his destiny. Early in January, he wrote in his journal: "Many reflections came on my mind. A new world was in a manner before me and my object was to be at the Pacific Ocean before the month of August. How were we to find provisions and how many men would remain with me, for they were dispirited. Amidst various thoughts, I fell asleep on my bed of snow."

After crossing the continental divide in the Canadian Rockies, the party reached the Canoe River and traced it down to the Columbia, which promptly swung into a big bend and turned south, thus solving the puzzle of long standing. Here David Thompson and his party, at a place called Boat Encampment, built a 25-foot canoe. Then at last Thompson was ready to seek out the secrets of the Columbia.

Unfortunately, most of his men weren't. Only three of his party of 24 were brave enough, or foolish enough, to risk the wild ride down the uncharted river.

Thompson knew that chancing the river without a sizeable party was foolhardy. He would have to paddle back upriver and recruit.

Only after much persuasion was he able to find 11 men, including two San Poil Indians, with enough courage to accompany him.

Then he wrote: "After praying the Almighty to protect and prosper us on our voyage to the ocean, early on the third of July, we embarked."

A few days later, he inscribed: "We set off on a voyage down the Columbia River to explore this river in order to open out a passage for the interior trade with the Pacific Ocean."

Did David Thompson set out to reach the river's mouth before the Astor party because by doing so he would add strength to Britain's claim to the Pacific Northwest? Or was he merely looking for an easier path for the fur trade? Historians still argue the point. Perhaps he wanted both. David Thompson was a complex man.

Unlike most rivers, the Columbia, fed by melting snowfields and glaciers, tends to run high in summer, so David Thompson's party could race along. They canoed deep into present Washington and the river gave them little trouble but in south central Washington, rattlesnakes did.

Thompson wrote: "On going ashore, our custom always was to throw part of our paddles on the grassy ground and although we think we can see everything on the short, scanty grass, yet by doing so we are almost sure to start one of these snakes that we did not see. Every morning we rose very early, while the dew was falling, and tied up our bedding as hard as we could. These were two blankets or one with a bison robe, and when we put up for the night did not untie them until we lay down, by which time they (the snakes) were all withdrawn into their holes in the sands, for they always avoid dew and rain and they are fond of getting on anything soft and warm.

"One evening, seeing a convenient place and a little wood, we put up rather early and one of the men undid his blankets and laid down. The fish was soon boiled and we called him to supper. He sat up but did not dare to move. A rattlesnake had crept in his blanket and was now half erect, within six inches of his face, threatening to bite him. He looked the very

20

image of despair. We were utterly at a loss how to relieve him but seeing several of us approaching, the snake set off and left us."

★

Events of ensuing days put mere snakes out of their minds. The snow-capped presence of Mt. Hood reared up to the south. With great interest, they watched Indians fishing in the river with nets and from dugout canoes 36 feet long.

And here it was that David Thompson heard the news which may have crushed him: John Jacob Astor's ship *Tonquin* had arrived at the mouth of the Columbia. Now the Thompson party could only take second place to the Americans.

But David Thompson had little time to fret about losing the race. Near The Dalles, the river squeezed down into a basalt-walled channel only 60 yards wide.

He wrote: "Imagination can hardly form an idea of the working of this immense body of water under such compression, raging and hissing as if alive."

Wisely, they portaged around the rapids. David Thompson recorded: "Trees are once more in sight, a most agreeable change from the bare banks and monotonous plains. Snow covered mountains lie ahead."

Finally, after portaging around another series of rapids known as the Cascades, they approached journey's end. They had lost the race, but they remained proud Englishmen. Said Thompson: "According to custom, the men put on their banners and ribbons and hoisted the Union Jack to leave no uncertainty as to the country represented."

As expected, when they arrived at the mouth of the Columbia, the Astor party was already established there. David Thompson had not accomplished the mission set for him by his company and his country but he may well have completed the job he had set for himself. Again, from his diary:

"Next day in my canoe with my men, I went to Cape Disappointment, which terminates the course of this river, and remained until the tide came in. Thus I have fully completed the survey of this part of North America from sea to sea, and by almost innumerable astronomical observations have determined the positions of the mountains, lakes and rivers, and other remarkable places in the northern part of this continent."

The roaming years were over; David Thompson returned to his old haunts in Canada. Now he wanted to produce a piece of work of which he

A mural in the University of Washington's Suzzalo Library pinpoints historic places in early Washington.

had long dreamed: an accurate, detailed map of the Northwest wilderness. In 1813 and 1814, he did this enormous job, then turned the map over to the North West Company.

Between 1816 and 1826, he surveyed the boundary line between the U.S. and Canada. The government paid him what he was worth, a good deal of money, and when he was through with his meticulous work, he was considered wealthy by the standards of the time.

But he was not to remain wealthy for long. He loaned $10,000 to a church and the church could not repay; then several of his many sons used his money to establish businesses which failed; always a man of honor, David Thompson settled their debts.

Finally, at age 70, he tried to go back to surveying to escape poverty but his eyesight failed. He wrote of his experiences in the wilderness but couldn't find a buyer. Washington Irving was interested but he and Thompson couldn't get together.

So the great man died poor in 1857, at age 87. His half-breed wife, mother of his seven sons and six daughters, died three months later. Their graves were unmarked.

A many-sided man, David Thompson may have been the greatest of the early explorers; certainly he was the best mapmaker; without doubt he was a thoroughly decent man, a loving husband and father. In his case, a brief eulogy is easy—"Koo-Koo-Sint: Man Who Watches Stars."

David Thompson was a Britisher in a day when Britishers weren't overly popular in the Northwest but he is remembered, as he ought to be, in modern Washington. A state highway marker north of Ruby in Pend Oreille County puts it plainly enough:

"In the historic race between British and American fur traders for control of Columbia River trading, David Thompson, a partner of North West Company, was first to travel the Columbia from source to mouth. Energetic explorer, surveyor and mapper, he founded Kootenay House in Canada, the first trading post on the Columbia, in 1807; Spokane House in 1810, and first mapped the Pend Oreille, Snake, and other rivers in the Columbia Basin, claiming the entire region for Great Britain."

The good name also lives on in David Thompson Junior High School, Colville, Stevens County. ★

History, which is nothing more nor less than the record of the past, breeds heritage, and a heritage lays a foundation for a future. Each generation, like it or not, must build on the groundwork left by previous generations. We are, partly, what our ancestors were.

Like it or not, we need to know those ancestors.

"Life must be lived forward," said Soren Kierkegaard, Danish philosopher, "but can only be understood backward."

SUGGESTED READING

Bakeless, John Edwin; THE ADVENTURES OF LEWIS AND CLARK; Houghton Mifflin; 1962.

DeVoto, Bernard; JOURNALS OF LEWIS AND CLARK; Houghton Mifflin; 1953.

Frazier, Neta Lohnes; FIVE ROADS TO THE PACIFIC; McKay; 1964.

McDonald, Lucile; SEARCH FOR THE NORTHWEST PASSAGE; Binfords and Mort; 1958.

Salisbury, Albert and Jane; TWO CAPTAINS WEST; Superior; 1950.

(The authors have discovered two comprehensive bibliographies of supplementary material. One, A BIBLIOGRAPHY OF THE PACIFIC NORTHWEST, was compiled by the Washington State Library Association under the supervision of the Office of State Superintendent of Public Instruction. It lists a large selection of audio-visual materials as well as hundreds of books. The second is THE PACIFIC NORTHWEST IN BOOKS, by Ebbert T. Webber, published by Lanson's, Inc., of Portland, Oregon.)

Dr. John McLoughlin, giant on the horizon of Northwest history.

Chapter Two ✭

Government
THE PUZZLE OF JOHN McLOUGHLIN

The motto emblazoned on the blue pennants of the Hudson's Bay Company, mightiest merchandisers of the New World, was *Pro Pelle Cutem.* Translation: "Skin for Skin."

The intention of the unfortunate motto was to indicate that the British company believed in fair dealing in the fur trade. But in the light of what happened to Dr. John McLoughlin, chief administrator for Hudson's Bay in the Pacific Northwest, one might translate the Latin in another way: "What's good for Hudson's Bay Company is good for the Northwest and if you dare to disagree, we'll nail your hide to the wall."

It is conceivable that no one could have made the Northwest fur trade more profitable than did McLoughlin, the tall, white-haired chief factor of Fort Vancouver, Hudson's Bay headquarters on the Columbia.

Yet Hudson's Bay forced him out of its employment after more than 20 years of service.

It is conceivable that no single individual did more to help American settlers get established in the Oregon Country (which then included what is now the state of Washington) than did John McLoughlin.

Yet American settlers, after McLoughlin had left Hudson's Bay and had become an American citizen, pressured the U.S. Congress into taking away much of his property and let him go embittered to his grave, with the work of a lifetime apparently buried in the ashes of failure, with his enemies in full cry defiling his name.

He remains the most controversial figure in Washington history. Was he mostly hero, a man who fed and clothed and financed American settlers out of the goodness of his heart and who became an American citizen because he believed in the principles of democracy? Was he a victim of circumstances beyond his control? Did he truly live up to his noble Indian name, "White-Headed Eagle"?

Or was he mostly villain, a cunning, money-grubbing servant of hated Hudson's Bay Company who became an American citizen only to secure his grip on one of the choicest pieces of real estate in the Oregon Territory? Should his Indian name have been "Black-Hearted Vulture"?

Or . . . was he both eagle and vulture?

History supplies clues to the puzzle, but the individual student of history must arrive at his own answer. The history of Dr. John McLoughlin is shot through with clues. So let's examine the man . . .

★

John McLoughlin earned his license to practice medicine and surgery at age 18, in Quebec, Canada. This was in 1803. A muddy street and a pretty girl intervened, or so the story goes. The incident, unimportant in itself, might shed some light on the developing character of the man.

Young Dr. McLoughlin was out walking with a young lady. They were forced to cross a muddy street on planks. A British officer, drunker than he should have been, staggered along the plank walk and forced the young lady into the mud.

As heroes always do in stories like this, McLoughlin, already a husky giant, picked up the officer and threw him into the goo.

British citizens simply did not do that to British officers, drunk or sober.

McLoughlin wisely left Quebec soon thereafter for the empty spaces of upper Canada. The influence of his uncle had gotten him an appointment as medical attendant for the North West Company, British fur trading concern which was a fierce competitor of Hudson's Bay Company. Young John McLoughlin quickly proved himself to be more than a doctor; he had a head for business.

About 1811, he married Marguerite, the part French, part Indian widow of Alexander McKay. She was a woman of striking beauty, intelligence and even temperament. John McLoughlin, in a lifetime of profitable business dealings, would never make a better bargain.

In 1814, North West Company took McLoughlin in as a partner. In 1821, North West Company and Hudson's Bay Company decided to stop cutting each other's throats; they would combine and monopolize the fur trade in the New World, hoping thereby to cut everyone else's throats.

Leaders of both companies took passage for London in 1820 to work out a merger. The sour relationship of the two companies was demonstrated clearly in a dialogue recorded by Colin Robertson of the Hudson's

Bay Company. "Wine went around freely and subscriptions were opened for the ship's hands. Our friend, the Nor'wester, Dr. McLoughlin, put down his name. I took the pen to put mine down, but seeing Bethune, the other Nor'wester, waiting, I said to Abbé Carriere, 'Come Abbé, put down your name, I don't want to sign between two Nor'westers.'

" *'Never mind,'* said the Abbé, *'Christ was crucified between two thieves.'*

"McLoughlin flew into a dreadful passion, but being a good Catholic, he had to stomach it."

In spite of the enmity, the companies were consolidated in London. George Simpson, age 29, of Hudson's Bay, was put in charge of company affairs in the field. This gave Simpson authority over McLoughlin at Fort Vancouver. Simpson being the aggressive, ambitious man that he was, McLoughlin's doom may have been sealed at that early moment.

McLoughlin was given the title of chief factor and placed in charge of the department of the Columbia, which included all territory west of the Rocky Mountains. McLoughlin's intelligence and knowledge had impressed the Hudson's Bay kingpins. Here, obviously, was a strong man. A dangerous man, as well? Possibly. They might have reasoned thusly: "Let's send this strong and perhaps difficult person as far from London as we can. The department of the Columbia, that's the place for him. We'll bury him in the wilderness."

Those men in London couldn't have known then, but they were sending this tall young man who may already have learned to believe in liberty, equality and fraternity to a place where a crude but pure democracy was about to burst out of the ground and flower in a frontier garden. It was sheer coincidence, an accident of history, a simple case of the right man happening to be sent at the right time to the right place. The place prospered; the man experienced a historic tragedy.

★

Colorful French-Canadian *voyageurs,* sweeping their long, slim canoes down the wild rivers of the West toward the great ocean called Pacific, carried John McLoughlin and his family toward his new home, toward his last home, toward his place in history. The year was 1824.

McLoughlin and Simpson decided to establish headquarters at a place called by the Indians *"Skit-so-to-ho"* or "The Place of the Turtle." The French-Canadians called it *"Jolie Prairie."*

Simpson wrote of the location: "I have rarely seen a gentleman's seat in England possessing so many natural advantages and where ornament

and use are so agreeably combined."

Certainly it was beautiful. Three snow-capped peaks—Hood, Adams and St. Helens—towered over the place. The Columbia River lapped the prairie's lower edge. Above the gradual slope of open farmland near the river (where the city of Vancouver now stands) rose great forests of fir and cedar. Low hills formed the western horizon across the river. Beyond the hills lay the Tualatin Valley and south of them the Willamette Valley, thousands of acres of well-watered, fertile soil begging for the bite of the settler's plow.

Ornamental it was, without a doubt, but George Simpson was as dazzled by the site's commercial prospects as by its natural beauty. Three great fur trails converged here, the Willamette from the south, the Cowlitz from the north and the Columbia from the east. In addition the site could be reached easily from the sea.

Jolie Prairie, indeed . . .

The stage was set, the lights up, the actors in place. The dramatic puzzle of John McLoughlin was taking shape.

★

Under McLoughlin's firm direction, Hudson's Bay business prospered at Fort Vancouver. The chief traders twice a year led their brigades, laden with trade goods, into the interior and usually returned with a full quota of furs. These, along with casks of salt salmon, were loaded onto ships for London delivery. Lumber from the Hudson's Bay sawmill was shipped to the Sandwich Islands (Hawaii). Wheat grown in the Willamette Valley, not far from Fort Vancouver, was sold in quantity to the Russians who controlled the fur trade in Alaska.

Dr. McLoughlin reigned over this far-reaching enterprise with strength and wisdom and occasional arrogance, when his quick temper blew up a storm and he lashed out at whoever had provoked him. But in a moment of crisis, he usually managed to be the coolest person in the room.

He worked hard and expected hard work from others . . . and some of these learned to hate him for it. Most often his wrath was directed at someone he considered lazy or careless or stupid. During the course of his long working days, he had to deal with a great variety of individuals, persons of many nationalities, of greatly varying degrees of civilization.

In this drawing of Fort Vancouver about 1853, large building to left of road is a Catholic church. Stockade and main buildings are at center right near the river. Officers' quarters are on the hill.

Fort Vancouver, after all, was the only strong outpost of order and discipline in a wild land.

Early during his working day, he might have to vent his wrath on a Kanaka (Hawaiian) caught sleeping in the morning sun against an east-facing wall; an hour later, he might have to sugar-talk an Indian chief whose last fur shipment had been marked down on quality. The *voyageurs,* creatures of the wild, presented problems all their own during their *"regales"* (sprees) as they rested between their long, hard journeys with the fur brigades.

In addition to personnel problems, he had the responsibility for daily, quarterly and annual accountings of Hudson's Bay business to his demanding employers in London. Figures leaped into place before his eyes and spoke of profits gained and yet to be gained. There was a sawmill to run and a grist mill, too; there were incoming shipments and outgoing shipments, loans to be made to Willamette Valley settlers, punishments to be meted out and rewards to be offered—a thousand details crying out for decisions. And McLoughlin was the decision-maker, the complete administrator, often making rules to fit new situations which demanded action now, action which couldn't be postponed until precise instructions from London had slogged for months across the thousands of miles of ocean separating the new land surrounding Fort Vancouver from the old world.

In 1830, new Fort Vancouver quarters closer to the river and a good water supply were ready for occupancy. (This is the location of the present Fort Vancouver National Historic Site.)

White, American civilization had begun to roll, ride and walk west. Americans were discovering the fabulous land which lapped the Pacific shore. In the East, those who had been to the West laid it on thick.

America's destiny, they said, lay in that vast land of milk and honey watered by the Willamette and in the fertile, wooded plains ringing Puget Sound. They drew an eye-popping picture of easy valleys where trees stayed green year around, where the camas root served for bread, where the rivers foamed with salmon and trout demanding to be hooked, where endless woods teemed with wild game begging to be welcomed to a feast.

"And they do say, gentlemen," one of the speakers always remembered to mention, "that out in the Oregon Territory pigs are running around under the great acorn trees, round and fat, and already roasted with knives and forks sticking in them, so that all you have to do is to cut off a slice when you are hungry."

No one believed that, of course. But still, just in case . . .

They came by the hundreds, then by the thousands. The businessmen came, the farmers came, the housewives came. The children came, too, most of them having the time of their lives on the trail despite the hardships.

For Dr. McLoughlin at Fort Vancouver, the westward surge of Americans presented both problems and opportunities. Hudson's Bay Company was the only established general store and finance company in the entire area. Hudson's Bay sold everything to the settlers from soup to nuts and if they couldn't pay immediately, they could buy now and pay later, plus six per cent interest. With every new wave of settlers, Hudson's Bay business boomed.

Many of the settlers, in addition to buying what Hudson's Bay had to sell, produced what Hudson's Bay wanted to buy. Wheat, for instance, to ship to the Russians. (Always, of course, at a profit to Hudson's Bay.)

The main problem for Dr. McLoughlin was simply this: If too many Americans moved in and prospered, chances were good that the Oregon country would eventually become a part of the United States. Dr. McLoughlin's London employers didn't care for this at all, because an Oregon country which had gone American would certainly kick out Hudson's Bay Company.

If ever there was a man in American history caught between a rock and a hard place, Dr. McLoughlin was that man. Forced to a choice between hard, cold, ambitious, autocratic George Simpson and his new American friends, he would finally choose his American friends.

Whereupon his new American friends would kick him in the teeth . . .

★

Much of the trouble went back to 1824, when something called a "joint occupancy treaty" was puttied into place by the Americans and the British. It simply decreed that Americans and British could settle in the

➡

This outstanding diorama at the visitors' center of Fort Vancouver National Historic Site shows Dr. John McLoughlin (white hair, right), James Douglas and Dr. William Tolmie welcoming the Whitman missionary party to Fort Vancouver. The man in the checked coat is J. K. Townsend of Hudson's Bay Company; he partially conceals the figures of Narcissa and Dr. Whitman. To the left of Townsend are Eliza Spalding, Rev. Henry Spalding and Dr. William Gray. Pierre Pambrun and John McLeod of Hudson's Bay, who have escorted the Whitman party up from the river, stand at rear.

Oregon Country and could trade there but could not acquire title to land. In plain words: "Until we have a war to settle the ownership of this rich land, both sides may pick it clean if they can."

There was an alternative to war—compromise. Hudson's Bay and England had decided early on that they would compromise at the Columbia River. The land north of the great watercourse would be British forever; the Americans could have what is now the state of Oregon, south of the river.

And Dr. McLoughlin was the man caught in the middle . . .

He admired the Americans and their democratic philosophy, but he owed allegiance to his employers, Governor George Simpson and Hudson's Bay Company. Hudson's Bay had fattened his pocketbook; thanks were due. The Americans, on the other hand, had warmed his soul and gladdened his heart; they had something coming, too.

In addition, the Oregon Country had captured him completely. In this majestic, pine-scented land next to the world's greatest ocean he wanted to live what remained of his life and here he wanted to die.

The decision was made for Dr. McLoughlin in 1845, when George Simpson and Hudson's Bay cut his territory and slashed his salary. The rulers of Hudson's Bay seemed to feel that he had helped American settlers too much, that he was no longer sufficiently dedicated to the cause of making the rich Hudson's Bay people in London richer.

John McLoughlin was a proud man. When it became plain that Hudson's Bay no longer trusted his judgment, he retired and moved to Oregon City on the Willamette River (just a few miles south of Portland) and cast his lot with the many Americans who had settled in the area. The Scotch-Irish Canadian, the man who had always thought of himself as a Britisher, became an American. Or tried to . . .

This was the man who had written to Hudson's Bay: "Gentlemen, you complain of me for having supplied the first wants of Americans on their arrival in this country and that by doing so, I have enabled them to occupy for agricultural purposes a country to which we have hitherto looked for fur-bearing animals. I admit that our interests as a fur company, and my personal interest, could not thus be promoted and that they have even suffered by my doing so. But, what else could I do as a man having a spark of humanity in my nature? I did not invite the Americans to come. To be frank, I greatly regretted their coming, but they did come, covered with the dust of travel, worn out by fatigue, hardships and dangers incident to a very long and perilous journey. They came without food or raiment. I fed them and clothed them. The Bible tells me that if my enemy is hungry I must feed him, if naked, I must clothe him, but these destitute men and helpless women and children were not my enemies, and I am sure that God does not require me to do more for my enemies than for these."

★

The Willamette Valley settlers had brought the issue to a boil in 1843 by voting in an earthshaking meeting at Champoeg on the Willamette to form a "provisional" government. The vote was breathlessly close and history suggests that loud, brash Joe Meek, one of the really delightful characters of the territory, won the day for the Americans. The provisional government leaned toward the United States.

Mere existence of the government was a terrible blow to Great Britain's ambitions, for until that lovely day in May on the spring-green Champoeg prairie, Hudson's Bay Company, British through and through, had been the only force for law and order in the wild land, which strengthened the British claim on the country.

The provisional government was needed because many Americans and French-Canadians had settled in the Willamette Valley and people, in their timeless way, created problems they couldn't solve singly; government action was necessary. First, though, there had to be a government.

For instance, the rich American, Ewing Young, had died and there had to be a legal disposition made of his considerable property. Hudson's Bay was well aware that Dr. McLoughlin had helped many of those troublesome settlers get established. Inevitably Hudson's Bay began to wonder whose side Dr. McLoughlin was on. Perhaps because Dr. McLoughlin apparently wondered, too . . .

Retired in Oregon City at age 61, John McLoughlin, still ambitious and energetic, set about building a house (which still stands as a National Historic Site), developing the town and fighting off the scavengers who wanted part or all of his valuable land claim along the Willamette River, which included the great water power potential of Willamette Falls.

In 1846 the long-festering boundary controversy was settled. Great Britain, faced with revolt in some of its colonies, and the United States, on the verge of war with Mexico, put first things first and decided not to fight each other over this western wilderness of doubtful value. The boundary was established at the 49th parallel, the present friendly, unfortified dividing line between Canada and the state of Washington. (The Americans had asked for a boundary much farther north, at 54 degrees and 40 minutes, which gave rise to the famous war cry: "Fifty-four forty or fight!")

On August 14, 1848, during the last few hours of a session of the U.S. Congress, the Oregon Country, including the present state of Washington, became a territory of the United States.

In 1849, the U.S. Congress passed a donation land law. Section 11 read: "And be it further enacted that what is known as the Oregon City land claim, excepting the Abernethy island, which is hereby confirmed to the legal assigns of the Willamette Milling and Trading company, shall be set apart and be at the disposal of the legislative assembly . . . provided, however, that all lots and parts of lots in said claim sold or granted by Dr. John McLoughlin . . . shall be confirmed to the purchaser . . ."

In other words, if McLoughlin said he owned it, it was taken from him. But if McLoughlin had sold it to somebody else, that was all right; the new owner had a good title. In still other words, the U.S. Congress took everything from McLoughlin but his underwear.

From the bitterness of his soul, Dr. McLoughlin cried: "By British demagogues I have been represented as a traitor. For what? Because I acted as a Christian, saved American citizens, men, women and children from the Indian tomahawk and enabled them to make farms to support families. American demagogues have been base enough to assert that I had caused American citizens to be massacred by hundreds of savages . . . To be brief, I founded this settlement and prevented a war between Great Britain and the United States, and for doing this peacefully and quietly I was treated by the British in such a manner, that from self respect, I resigned my situation in the Hudson's Bay Company's service by which I sacrificed $12,000 per annum, and the Oregon land bill shows the treatment I received from Americans."

The disappointment and frustration took its toll. McLoughlin became ill, went into seclusion in his home and died on September 3, 1857. He was buried in Oregon City. His grave draws many visitors even today.

In 1862, three years after Oregon became a state, the legislature felt pangs of conscience and restored ownership of most of Dr. McLoughlin's land claim to his family. Almost a century later, in 1957, the Oregon legislature was still trying to square accounts; in that year it named Dr. McLoughlin "Father of Oregon."

But the man remains in history a tragic figure, who was left to die in bitterness.

◀

Olympia has always been capital of Washington. The site of the capitol building on a bluff overlooking the southernmost arm of Puget Sound surely is one of the most attractive anywhere.

PIGS, VEGETABLES, WAR AND GOVERNMENT

Before we giggle our way into one of the most ridiculous episodes of American history, in which Great Britain and the United States almost went to war over a pig (not a herd of pigs; just one hungry, wandering porker), we ought to try to sort out the confusing pattern of the early gropings toward government in what is now the state of Washington.

How did the confusion arise? Well, there was an "Oregon Territory" which contained what is now the state of Washington. At a later period, there was an "Oregon Territory" which did *not* contain what is now the state of Washington. There was a "Washington Territory" which included part of what had once been "Oregon Territory." When Easterners spoke of the "Oregon Country," they meant the whole Pacific Northwest, including what is now the state of Washington.

Is that confusing enough?

At present, of course, there is a state of Oregon and a state of Washington, and they are anything but two peas in a pod. Oregon is much larger in land area; Washington has much the greater population. Both sprang from the same geologic conditions, began their development in much the same way, then parted company along about the turn of the century. Until then, Oregon had been dominant, both economically and politically.

Then the Alaska gold rush gave Washington a hard push to the front. Washington went on to thriving health and robust, lively government, while Oregon settled back into quiet enjoyment of its rocking chairs, roses and Republicanism.

★

Spurred by the horrifying news of the Whitman tragedy at Waiilatpu, Congress in 1848 surprised everyone by biting off a great chunk of land and officially declaring it Oregon Territory. The new territory sprawled grandly over what is now Oregon, Washington, Idaho and part of Wyoming and Montana.

In fact, the first Oregon Territory was so big that it was unmanageable, with the inland portions populated mostly by coyotes and jackrabbits.

Puget Sound settlers grew more and more unhappy with the arrangement. The capital of the territory, Oregon City, was too far away, for one thing. They began to feel like neglected stepchildren.

In 1853, a bill which would create a "Territory of Columbia" was thrown into the hopper in Washington, D.C. A Congressman from Kentucky knocked out "Columbia" and inserted "Washington." On March 2, 1853, the Territory of Washington burst into official flower with great fanfare around Puget Sound, while everyone tried hard not to notice that this great new section of civilized America consisted mostly of elbow room.

The first head count showed 3965 white settlers and they rattled around in a territory including what is now the state of Washington, plus northern Idaho and Montana as far east as the Rocky Mountain summit.

Oregon beat Washington to statehood by a good many years. Congress took Oregon into the Union in 1859; Washington didn't make it until 1889, which hardly seems fair. One big reason for the delay, though, was that eastern Washingtonians weren't sure they wanted to ride in the same boat with western Washingtonians, so each rowed in different directions and statehood paddled around in circles in Congress. (No question but what a fair share of this feeling remains today. The Cascade Mountains, both in Washington and in Oregon, seem to operate somewhat like a spite fence.)

So, finally, Oregon was Oregon and Washington was Washington and the only remaining confusion had to do with a place called Washington, D.C., and that may never be cleared up. (It wouldn't have helped if that Kentucky congressman had left well enough alone, either; "D.C.," remember, stands for District of Columbia.)

Now let's turn back to pigs and wars and the everblooming idiocy of mankind.

★

The pig was on San Juan Island and it belonged to an Englishman, Charles Griffin by name. The pig liked to munch on vegetables.

An American, Lyman Cutler, also lived on San Juan Island. He liked to munch on vegetables, too, and didn't particularly care to have English pigs (or any pigs, for that matter) chewing their way through his garden.

One day Mr. Cutler shot Mr. Griffin's pig. Dead.

The Englishman reported the whole sordid affair to British authorities and demanded that they arrest the American. The American immediately requested protection from the government of the United States.

This neighborhood squabble over a dead, vegetable-stuffed pig threatened to explode into full scale war between the United States and Great Britain.

The year was 1859. The trouble over the pig had roots growing back to 1846, when a treaty mentioned previously in this chapter established a sea boundary between Vancouver Island (Canada) and mainland U.S. The sloppy treaty language referred to a line in "the middle of the channel."

Trouble was, more than one channel existed. The U.S. claimed that the treaty meant Haro Strait but the British said Rosario Strait and the interesting result was that both countries claimed the San Juan Islands. American and English settlers moved in willy-nilly and brought their pigs and planted their vegetables. Trouble was inevitable. (No one yet has managed to teach a pig the difference between an American and an English vegetable, nor perhaps has even tried.)

But let's jump back to 1859, with the score: one pig dead, one American in big trouble.

A company of the 9th U.S. Infantry under George E. Pickett of Civil War fame rushed to the scene. Unfortunately for the American cause, the British garrison consisted of 2140 soldiers and they had five warships for support. It was plain that the British had every intention of backing up the grazing rights of British pigs.

While the Americans hesitated in the face of such overwhelming force, General Winfield Scott arrived, sized up the situation quickly and came to an agreement with a British admiral on the scene. The silly season closed; the Pig War had taken its place among history's near-tragic guffaws.

The agreement stipulated that each country would be allowed 100 troops on San Juan Island until the boundary dispute could be settled. In the years that followed, the American and English garrisons, freed of the necessity of killing each other, gave parties and banquets for each other. (No doubt the tension rose whenever roast pig was served.)

In 1872, Emperor William I of Germany, who had been asked to arbitrate, awarded the San Juan Islands to the U.S., whereupon the British withdrew.

(During this period, the Olympia town baseball team was practicing for its big game at Victoria, B.C. Just as the team was about to leave for Victoria, a telegram from Emperor William I posted on the bulletin board of the Capitol building announced that the baseball game would decide the issue. Olympia won the game. Unromantic citizens insisted that practical jokers had trumped up the telegram, but there were Olympians who believed as long as they lived that the baseball team had secured the islands for the United States.)

In 1966, the U.S. Congress approved a bill to establish an 1800-acre national historical park at the site. The only buildings remaining are at

English Camp, a blockhouse and two one-story buildings. A cannon used in the Pig War was displayed by the Washington State Historical Society in Tacoma for many years.

★

Major Isaac Stevens, the first governor of Washington Territory, was a man who liked to keep busy. He asked President Pierce to appoint him superintendent of Indian affairs, too, which the president promptly did.

There was a long trail to be ridden between Washington, D.C., and Washington Territory and rather than just kill the time in aimless travel, Stevens took over command of an exploring expedition headed west in 1853. (The route he laid out on this trip was eventually used by the Northern Pacific railroad.)

Governor Stevens was a man of great energy. His inclination was to assault a problem headon, then rush along to the next. Partly as a result of this headlong, hurry-up method, his career as leader of the new territory was short and stormy. His handling of the Indian treaties and ensuing bloody wars caused President Pierce in 1856 to appoint Joseph Lane as the new governor but the U.S. Senate refused to confirm Lane and Stevens hung on until he became territorial delegate to Congress in 1857. He was re-elected in 1859, decided not to run in 1861 and died fighting for the Union Army at the Battle of Chantilly in 1862.

Elisha P. Ferry, a Republican, was elected the first governor of the new state in 1889.

Olympia, the territorial capital, was retained as state capital. The site of the capitol building, a tree-draped bluff overlooking the southernmost inlet of Puget Sound, may well be more attractive than that of any other state.

The buildings in the main capital group were completed between 1911 and 1935. Olympia has many lovely old buildings but one of the most striking is the old state capitol on 7th Avenue downtown. With its tall towers and arched windows, the great stone structure has the glowering aspect of a feudal castle.

Considering the high standing of Washington's present-day school system, it's hardly surprising that an early Washington legislature passed a measure called the "Barefoot Schoolboy Law." It was the first attempt to equalize educational opportunity among the state's counties. Until then,

This blockhouse remains as a landmark of the Pig War at English Camp on San Juan Island.

rich counties had schools; poor counties didn't. Sponsor of the law in 1895 was John R. Rogers, a member of the Populist party who later served as a firm, effective state governor.

Many of Washington's early political parties and politicians leaned away from the rich and powerful and tilted toward the underdog. Perhaps the pattern was set way back in 1853, when Isaac Stevens, first governor of Washington territory, rode a horse into Olympia to take over his post. It was raining, as it does to this day in Olympia, and the governor was soggy and muddy. When he entered the dining room of the little town's hotel, he was told to go elsewhere because an official banquet was being prepared.

Stevens protested that he was tired and hungry, so a cook took pity on him, ushered him into the kitchen and fed him scraps . . . or so the story goes.

Later, outside the hotel, Stevens heard a man complain that the new governor was late for his ceremonial banquet.

"Sir," said Stevens, "I am the new governor."

Finally someone believed him but the new governor of Washington Territory couldn't enjoy his banquet; he was full as a tick from eating kitchen scraps.

FUN AND POLITICS

The structure of Washington's modern government, on paper, offers few surprises. In general, the state organizes and conducts its public business in much the same way as its sister western states.

But while the organization is routine on paper, it doesn't seem to work out that way in practice. There has always been a certain fascinating flair to government in Washington that is often lacking elsewhere. Perhaps the enthusiasm and effervescence of youth have something to do with it; with statehood coming as late as 1889 (only eight states are younger), Washington, relatively speaking, is hardly dry behind the ears.

Those who have kind feelings for the state express it this way: "Washington has always been receptive to new ideas."

Some less sentimental souls put it another way. James Farley, Democratic party bigwig in the 1930s, once snapped, "There are the 47 states, and then there is the Soviet of Washington."

Governor Isaac I. Stevens as he looked in 1853.

Where politics was concerned, Farley had no sense of humor.

In the early 1930s, with economic depression clamping a grim lid on the land, the state of Washington decided to get some entertainment out of government. Instead of earning the thanks of a gloomy nation, the state was accused of turning government into a circus for the amusement of the masses.

What was the evidence supporting such a serious charge?

Well, for one thing, they pointed to good ol' Vic Meyers, Seattle orchestra leader, who ran for lieutenant governor in 1932. Meyers had once run for mayor of Seattle with the promise that if elected, he would put hostesses on all of the city's streetcars. Good ol' Vic, everybody's friend, was elected lieutenant governor.

In the same year, a man was chosen as attorney general who hadn't practiced law in 15 years. A newly-elected member of the legislature had one difficulty in assuming his seat: he lacked the price of a ticket to Olympia. Another new legislator might have managed the transportation but for another small fact: he was in jail.

In 1935 the state adopted something called the "blanket primary," which in effect abandoned party distinctions and let anybody run for anything. One pursed-lip critic grumbled that only in Washington was it possible for a person "to vote at the same primary for a Republican as the nominee for governor, for a Socialist as the nominee for attorney general, for a Democrat as the nominee for state treasurer, for a Communist as the nominee for sheriff."

Somehow government in Washington survived. The state began to grow and prosper and to turn respectably conservative; if some of the fun went out of its politics, considerable joy emerged from its booming economy.

For the record, Washington has a governor as chief executive with a lieutenant governor to step in if needed. The governor appoints the heads of about 20 major departments in the state bureaucracy and also appoints judges when vacancies occur. He can veto legislation (but the legislators can override the veto with a two-thirds vote) and call special sessions of the legislature. The governor can reprieve and pardon criminals. He is commander-in-chief of the state's military units and can call out the National Guard. (These last functions, as you can imagine, don't exhaust the governor's energy.)

The governor's powers on paper are one thing; his powers in person are another. A strong, intelligent governor who can get most of what he wants from a friendly legislature can change the face of the state in a single term. It is said that we have a government of laws, not of men, but in practice, law provides only the launching pad; men and women in government, with their enthusiasm, energy and political skill, supply the rocket fuel.

In addition to the governor and lieutenant governor, Washington elects a secretary of state, state auditor, state treasurer, attorney general, insurance commissioner, commissioner of public lands and superintendent of public instruction.

There are 49 legislative districts in the state with approximately the same population in each. Each district elects a senator to a term of four years. Members of the House of Representatives—99 of them—serve two-year terms. Sessions of the legislature are conducted in each odd-numbered year. Sixty days is the legal limit for a single session but the governor can extend the session if necessary; in recent years, as government grew to meet demands made upon it, extension of the session has come to seem normal.

There are also commissions, departments and boards in state government, dealing with activities as varied as horse racing and veterans rehabilitation, or health and liquor control.

GREENE TO THE RESCUE

Washington's recent respectability in government had begun to bore some of the state's more adventurous citizens, which is why they greeted with glad little cries the race for land commissioner in 1968. Suddenly politics in Washington was fun again.

All of which was due to Richard A. C. Greene, a fat, bald and mustachioed young man who reluctantly filed as a candidate for the Republican nomination for land commissioner in the primary election, then promptly moved to Hawaii.

It was permitted; he maintained legal residence in Washington. He had been a classics professor at the University of Washington; he became a teacher of Latin and Greek at the University of Hawaii. Much of his campaign planning was done as he lay in beefy splendor on a rubber mattress in the ocean off Oahu.

To his consternation, Greene, then 30 years old, won the primary nomination by 88,500 votes without casting a ballot for himself. (Instead, he kept it as a souvenir.) He beat out three other candidates, including an Indian chief. Whereupon he drew up a program to protect Indian fishing rights, an issue which was causing much stir in the state.

No fisherman, he proclaimed, would be allowed to catch more than four Indians and any Indian under five feet, one inch must be thrown back.

He was also deeply concerned about use of land in the state. "Land should be used," Greene announced forthrightly, "gently but firmly."

The candidate had other ideas. A Boeing aircraft plant near Seattle was to be turned into a wilderness area. All of eastern Washington, Greene promised, would be handed over to Idaho, "including the fearful town of Yakima." If he lost in the general election, the candidate threatened, he would have his teeth capped and run for governor. If he were elected as land commissioner, Greene promised, he would go right out and fearlessly commission the land. (First, though, in the event of victory, he would demand a recount.)

Running in the general election against Bert Cole, who had been land commissioner for almost as long as anyone could remember, Greene lost. But in the process, he offered modern Washingtonians a taste of how it used to be when politics in Washington had a maximum content of hilarity and a minimum content of pomposity.

SUGGESTED READING

Burger, Carl; BEAVER SKINS AND MOUNTAIN MEN; Dutton; 1968.
Hart, Herbert M.; OLD FORTS OF THE NORTHWEST; Superior; 1963.
Johnson, Enid; GREAT WHITE EAGLE: THE STORY OF DR. JOHN McLOUGHLIN; Messner; 1954.
Olson, Joan and Gene; OREGON TIMES AND TRAILS; Windyridge; 1965 (Joe Meek).

Chapter Three ★

The Indians
GARRY: MIGHTY BOWLEGGED MAN

The scene was burned into the mind of Lucius Nash, a white boy living in a little eastern Washington town then called Spokane Falls. Many years later, he wrote:

"An army tent with a marque stretched was put up with rough folding chairs and a wood table for the commission and staff and army blankets spread on the ground for the chiefs and sub-chiefs of the two tribes.

"All were present except Garry, the chief of the Spokanes. The commissioners were plainly annoyed and impatient at his tardiness. This was feigned and done for a purpose by this wily and, by and large, a great chieftain, although historians do not accord him this, his proper rank . . ."

Nash was describing the first meeting of the Dawes Commission, which had been sent by the federal government in 1882 to hold meetings at the site of present-day Spokane. The commission's announced purpose was to convince the Spokane and Coeur d'Alene Indians that they would be snug and happy on reservations. Translation: *Get the Indians out of the hair of the white farmers and miners and politicians who are frothing to take over the rich Indians lands. Do it fast. Don't let Garry stall any longer.*

The opening session was conducted outdoors at a site west of Monroe Street in full view of the falls and the flooding river. The children of the town flocked around; such entertainment was rare. There was a flurry among them when a mounted Indian approached. Lucius Nash reported:

"He appeared on a milk-white horse, clad in paper white buckskin, handsomely embellished with porcupine quills, the Indian insignia of his rank. He wore them proudly as much so as our soldiers and sailors who won their ribbons on foreign duty, conspicuous for gallant service. Magnificent eagle feathers adorned his war bonnet. His big war bow encased in

beautifully beaded buckskin across the horn of his saddle. A full quiver of arrows slung over his shoulder with flint chip arrow-heads and feathered with red pinions of high-hole woodpecker. He disdained the blanket spread for him as he never dismounted. The fact was, he was rarely seen on foot . . ."

Even hero-worshipping Lucius Nash noticed.

"He was so bow-legged it was a deformity," wrote Nash. "He was big and heavy from the waist up, with short legs . . ."

This was the man the Dawes Commission had been waiting for. This was the man the Dawes Commission had been warned against.

This was Spokan Garry.

★

In 1825, stern, strong Governor George Simpson of Hudson's Bay Company decided to educate two Indian boys at a company school near what is now Winnipeg, Canada. The school was operated by the Church of England—Episcopalians.

Two boys were chosen, one the son of a Kootenai chief, the other a son of a Spokane chief. According to Alexander Ross, a chief trader at the company's post, Spokane House, "They were about ten or twelve years old, both fine promising youths . . ."

Apparently the Spokanes and the tribes who lived around them were eager at this time for a new religion. The old ways had lost their potency. They had seen the white men and were curious about their magic. When Ross told the Spokanes that the two Indian boys would go to a minister of the white man's religion to learn how to serve the white man's God, a Spokane chief said that he might have "hundreds of children in an hour's time."

But Governor Simpson wanted only two. On the day of departure for the chosen pair, an old chief, Illim-Spokanee, made a little speech to Simpson and Ross:

"You see, we have given you our children, not our servants, or our slaves, but our own. We have given you our hearts—our children are our hearts—but bring them back again before they become white men. We wish to see them once more Indians, and after that you can make them white men if you like. But let them not get sick or die. If they get sick, we

Spokan Garry was a man of good heart who was caught betwixt and be-tween.

get sick; if they die, we shall die. Take them; they are yours."

Both boys were named by Hudson's Bay; logically enough, both were named after Hudson's Bay officials, preceded by tribal names to mark their origin.

One, a Kootenai, was called "Kootenai Pelly."

The other was named "Spokan Garry." He was 14 years old.

★

Garry returned to his homeland to stay in the spring of 1831. The youngster had his work cut out; the Episcopalians of Hudson's Bay expected him to pave the way for Christianity among the Spokanes, Nez Perce and Kootenais.

It was a large order, but at first it appeared that Garry could fill it. During the week he was a school teacher; his subjects were English, agriculture and Christianity. In winter, when the tribes weren't roaming in search of salmon or buffalo, his enrollment sometimes reached 100, adults as well as children. On Sunday mornings, he rang the bell in front of the tule mat building he had constructed across the river from Spokane House and an eager crowd hurriedly gathered. Garry was young, only 18, but apparently he had impressed his elders with his knowledge of the white man's language and religion. Many of the old rituals had worn out their welcome; now this young man of the Spokane tribe had suddenly returned from the distant Red River with new rituals that seemed fresh and interesting and potent.

Among those who listened to Garry was a Spokane named Curley Jim, who said, "He told us of a God above. Showed us a book, the Bible, from which he read to us. He said to us, if we were good, that then when we died, we would go up above and see God."

It was a good time for Spokan Garry; perhaps he would never see such a good time again. (Incidentally, Garry always spelled it "Spokan," without the final "e." Later there were those who wanted to spell the name of the town this way, too, but the advocates of the "e" won out.) Garry had planned to return to Red River in 1832 for further study but his life along the river was too good. He decided to remain in his homeland, then married a girl from the San Poil tribe and named her Lucy, a name he remembered fondly from his Red River days.

The good years came and passed in golden splendor. But in 1836, Dr. Marcus Whitman and his wife, Narcissa, established a Christian mission in the Walla Walla country at Waiilatpu. The tide was turning, but no one felt its warning pull.

Three years later, two missionary families, one named Walker, the other Eells, settled at Tshimakain, near the present Ford, Washington, deep in the heart of Spokane country.

It became plain almost immediately that now there were too many cooks in the kitchen.

In the tule mat lodge across the river, Garry had taught his flock a simple kind of Christianity based on the Ten Commandments. The Indians had responded well; the new teachings of Garry gave them something fresh but didn't change many old habits or snatch away many old pleasures.

But such a comfortable, old-shoe approach didn't satisfy the white missionaries. They said that the Ten Commandments were fine, as far as they went, but they didn't go nearly far enough. To become a Christian with a stamped and certified passport to Heaven, cried the white missionaries, the Indians would have to give up smoking and drinking and dancing and gambling and horse racing—and what's more, a man could marry only one woman at a time.

In short, the Walkers and the Eellses were demanding that the Indians make drastic changes in their life pattern. In the way of missionaries the world over since time began, these whites at Tshimakain were insisting that Spokanes become not only Christian, but *their* kind of Christian.

Then, as if the situation weren't muddy enough, along came two energetic, dedicated Catholics, Father Blanchet and Father Demers. They preached very effectively that *their* way was the only way. The listening Indians, quite naturally, drew back in confusion.

The Spokanes who had sat for years at Garry's feet began to drift away. Sunday services at the lodge across the river from Spokane House drew smaller and smaller groups of worshippers.

Disgust crept into Garry. Finally he gave up teaching and preaching entirely. Pressed for his reason, he said simply that the Spokanes "jawed him so much about it."

Garry cast aside his white man's clothes and again donned Spokane garb—a tunic reaching to the knees, deerskin leggings and moccasins, the whole costume liberally decorated with colored beads. When the cold blasts of winter swept across the hills, he donned a blanket or buffalo robe.

The star pupil of the Episcopal school along the Red River in white man's country had become an Indian again. He lived and dressed in the Indian way, ate Indian food and amused himself as an Indian did, by gambling. Garry had preached against gambling, but now he gambled.

And in 1841, it embarrassed him . . .

Garry, dressed in the Indian way, was gambling in a Spokane tent when word came that an important visitor wanted to see him.

When Garry heard who it was, he refused to leave the tent. Finally he was persuaded to come out. When he did, he had to face Governor George Simpson of Hudson's Bay Company, the man who had arranged for a 14-year-old Indian to get a white man's education 16 years earlier.

The effect on Simpson was powerful. Completely dismayed at the sight of his protege, he later wrote that Garry had "relapsed into his original barbarism, taking to himself as many wives as he could get."

It was true that Garry had taken a second wife, a Umatilla girl whom he called "Nina." (Again, a Red River name.) But it was also true that Simpson didn't have much room to complain. In 1830, the stern Hudson's Bay governor had thrown off his half-breed wife and four children and married an English woman. (Even in those days, there were those who preached: *Don't do as I do; do as I say.*)

☆

Garry was Indian again and it was a life style he enjoyed again. When autumn laid its golden mantle on the rolling hills of Spokane country, he led his people east into the mountains to hunt among the thundering herds of buffalo. When the wind drove snow into their faces, they rode with burdens of dried meat into the lowlands to sit out the winter around the fires in the villages.

Garry, with little to do in the winter, began to appear at the Tshimakain mission, where he did a little teaching and preaching again. At Tshimakain, he could practice his English, too. The Walker and Eells families seemed glad to see him but he did not feel comfortable among them.

He was Indian—but he could never be completely Indian again.

He was partly white, too, by training and inclination, but he was not white enough.

He was a man confused and often miserable in his mind. His highest moments of happiness seemed to come when he worked on his rich farm along the Spokane River, with Nina. His horse herd grew to satisfying numbers and among the Spokanes, horses were riches equal to gold among the whites. Horses and land . . . Garry had both. By Spokane standards, without a doubt, Garry was wealthy. The Spokanes did not listen to his sermons any more but they respected him as a man of property.

A turning point came in 1847. In that year, angry Cayuses rose up and killed the Whitmans at Waiilatpu.

Garry and the Spokanes were not involved directly but they were certainly affected, as was almost everyone in the Northwest at the time. The white missionaries fled in fear toward the safety of Oregon's Willamette Valley. This event had the effect of giving Garry an audience again; his importance swung sharply upward when the Walkers and the Eellses left Tshimakain.

In the tense days following the massacre, some Indian leaders urged that the blow be followed up. They argued that the whites were frightened and falling back; more hard blows quickly struck might smash them forever, might halt the terrible flow of white-topped wagons across Indian lands which had carved ruts into the buffalo country and which now threatened to wipe out an ancient Indian way of life.

Garry was foremost among those leaders who tried to cool the hotheads. Always he talked for peace and argued with those who screamed for a fight to the death.

Garry had been to the land of the whites; he had seen their strength and knew that the Indian was only a pebble in the flood stream of the white advance.

To Garry, the choice was plain: they could stall and bargain and plead their friendship and thereby live out their lives holding onto some of what they had treasured . . . or they could commit suicide.

In a war to the death, Garry knew better than most of the leaders, it would be mostly Indians who died.

★

In the eyes of white government, there were only two possible solutions to the Indian problem: (1) the Indians could go on reservations; (2) the Indians could be exterminated.

It was seldom put so bluntly but this was the policy, with all its raw edges showing. In addition—and this was very important—whites were to choose the boundaries of the reservations. As it usually worked out, Indian reservations were composed of land on which one could look farther and see less than anywhere else on earth—the barren, bleak, godforsaken, far reaches of nowhere. The best Indian reservation, in the eyes of many powerful whites, was one which contained no water, grass, soil, minerals or anything else from which a white man might make a dollar. (One of the satisfying ironies of history lies in the fact that a few of those reservations, once thought worthless by whites, have made some modern Indians oil-rich and uranium-fat. But in the old days, who knew about or cared about oil or uranium?)

The superintendent of Indian affairs for Washington Territory, Governor Isaac Stevens, called a great meeting in the Walla Walla country, and on May 29, 1855, 5000 Indians of the Cayuse, Walla Walla, Nez Perce and Yakima tribes assembled. Garry, who had first met Stevens two years earlier, attended as an invited guest along with several other Spokane chiefs.

Governor Stevens had big plans, all embodied in little pieces of paper called treaties. Under Stevens's proposed treaties, all of the tribes were to be penned on two reservations. The Spokanes, Cayuses, Walla Wallas, Umatillas and Nez Perces were to live on a chunk of what had been Nez Perce land. The Yakimas, Palouses and Klickitats were to move to a reservation in Yakima country.

At first, Stevens's treaties went over like a lead balloon. But the governor knew how to palaver, maneuver, bargain, compromise . . . even lie, if necessary. After all, Stevens's white constituents desperately wanted him to solve the "Indian problem" and solve it quickly; they were not overly fussy about how he did it.

The Indians had two big objections to the treaties as first presented: they required the Indians to give up huge amounts of land and they demanded that some of the tribes move from homelands to unfamiliar territory.

To get the signatures he had to have, Stevens finally set up a third reservation for the Walla Wallas and Cayuses.

Then Stevens, scenting success, had a private meeting with Garry. They agreed to a council at which a Spokane reservation would be discussed. As always, Garry smoothly assured Stevens that the Spokanes wanted to be peaceful, to be friendly with whites in the present and in the future, always and forever friendly.

Garry knew that many of his tribesmen would be livid with anger if he signed a treaty giving up ancestral land. If he signed such a treaty, he would cease to be a chief of the Spokane tribe rather quickly. Many Northwest tribes were governed by a system of democracy that bordered on anarchy. The chiefs didn't have a fixed term of office; they squatted on the throne of power only as long as they pleased the people. The white man, accustomed to a more orderly—but less responsive—form of government, often didn't understand this and trouble escalated as a result.

So Garry talked to Governor Stevens . . . and talked and talked.

The most widely known symbol of the Northwest Coast Indians is a totem pole glowering against the sky.

Surely there was no harm in talking, he figured; he would talk forever if Governor Stevens would go on listening.

It may be that in 1855, not far from the beginning of a long career of negotiation with whites, that Garry had already discovered a golden secret: profess undying friendship, but don't sign anything.

Garry didn't sign anything. Governor Stevens left the Walla Walla parley with a pocketful of treaties but if he left with the thought that his troubles with the horse Indians were over, he was very, very wrong.

The Yakimas no sooner got home from the Walla Walla meeting than they called a solemn council and issued a grim warning to whites: stay off Yakima ground . . . or die on it. (Yakima Chief Kamiakin insisted to his dying day that he hadn't signed a treaty at the Walla Walla conference but had merely made a mark on a piece of paper indicating friendship. Had Stevens led him astray? Perhaps not; poor communication was a continual thorn in both sides.)

Bad trouble soon erupted. Several white miners were killed along the Yakima River. Then an Indian agent was murdered. Now the Yakimas roared down the warpath with a vengeance and proceeded to cut a wide, bloody swath across the sweeping hills of south central Washington.

Stevens quickly called a meeting with Garry and other chiefs of the Coeur d'Alenes and Nez Perces. With the Yakimas running wild, it was crucial for Stevens that he keep other tribes from joining in a general uprising which could produce a blood bath resulting in destruction of the white settlement in the Northwest.

With the pressure on him increasing by the day, Stevens was ready to lay before the Indians a peace offering consisting of everything but the sun, moon and stars.

"We promise you everything which the white men have," Stevens announced at one point during the meeting. "When we talk to an Indian about land, we talk to him about what it is—when we wish to purchase his land, it is for him to say whether he will sell or not. If he does not wish to sell it, he will say so. *We shall never drive him from his lands.* I want you to think of this. I want you to show me your hearts."

Part, at least, of what Stevens said was an outright lie and surely the listening Indians knew it. The Donation Act of 1850, solemnly passed by the U.S. Congress, had given anyone the right to file a homestead claim in the new territory. Indian lands were as open to homesteaders as any. A few claims had already been filed on land the Spokanes considered theirs.

But now Garry, distrustful of Stevens and probably angry, did not lash out as Kamiakin and the Yakimas had done. Garry knew the power of the whites because he had travelled to their land and he had talked to them in their own language. The young hotbloods among the Spokanes were calling Garry a cowardly old woman for not wanting to join the Yakimas but Garry remained unshaken in his belief that the best move for the Spokanes was to buy time with honeyed words, that this was their only chance to survive.

Garry had been appointed to speak at the conference for the Colvilles and Coeur d'Alenes as well as for his own tribe and now he spoke, very sweetly and at great length. As the council ended, he said:

"All these things we have been speaking of had better be tied together as they are, like a bundle of sticks, because you are in a hurry. There is not time to talk of them. But afterwards you can come back, when you find time and see us."

If Governor Stevens wasn't gnashing his teeth then, he surely was a man of steel.

Garry seemed to have won a major victory. At age 44, again he was a hero in the Spokane villages. He had signed no treaty; he had given away no land. While enjoying his new status, Garry worried over the future. He knew that some day Governor Stevens—or someone like him—would come back; some day the Spokanes would have to sign a treaty.

But for the next several years, this worry faded as the Spokanes lived on an island of peace and prosperity. Around them swirled the tides of white-Indian war. Around Puget Sound, in the Yakima country and in Oregon, Indians screamed defiant desperation against white men and fought the bluecoated soldiers in many bloody skirmishes and battles.

Stubborn Stevens invited Garry to yet another council at Walla Walla in 1856. Garry's letter in reply must have infuriated the governor:

"Spokane River, September 12, 1856
"Sir: You had desired our going to meet you at the treaty, but we cannot go on account of the salmon, which is coming up now, and we are laying in our winter's supply . . . As for us, we are for peace; and it does not make any difference about our not going to meet you, for we all want to remain quiet and peaceful . . . When we meet next we can have a good understanding together, for I will keep nothing from you and expect the same from you.

"So I remain, very respectfully yours GARRY"

★

The game Garry was playing with Stevens had to end sometime. In

1857, Stevens went to Washington, D.C., as territorial delegate to the U.S. Congress and immediately began to push for final acceptance of the 1855 Walla Walla treaties, even though Garry had advised him that such action would be a mistake.

Garry had warned Stevens, too, that it would be dangerous for large groups of soldiers to show themselves on Spokane land but on one important day in May, 1858, Stevens was far away . . .

Garry was enjoying a quiet day in camp when some Palouse warriors galloped up to announce that finally the bluecoats had come to steal Indian lands!

Greatly disturbed, Garry soon found out that a large force of soldiers had in fact crossed the Snake River. There were more than 150 of them, plus some Nez Perce scouts. Most alarming of all, they carried two cannon with them!

Garry immediately rode south with the Palouses and sought out Vincent, Coeur d'Alene chief, for a hurried parley.

The soldiers, it developed, were being led by Lieutenant Colonel E. J. Steptoe, commanding officer of Fort Walla Walla. Garry's first thought had been that the soldiers were merely moving along the trail between Fort Walla Walla and Fort Colville, which was not unusual, but this was not so; they were at least six miles off the trail and dangerously close to one of the Spokanes' favorite camas-gathering grounds!

Meanwhile hundreds of Spokane and Coeur d'Alene warriors, painted and primed for action, galloped south for a fight to the death with the hated invaders.

Garry urgently recommended to Vincent that they arrange an immediate meeting with the bluecoat leader; it was done. At the meeting site near the present town of Rosalia, Col. Steptoe insisted that the soldiers were on a peaceful mission, that they were at the camas grounds only because their guide had made a mistake and led them astray.

Garry and Vincent rode out from the meeting and tried feverishly to convince their eager young chiefs that Steptoe's purpose was a peaceful one. When they had done what they could, Garry left the area and camped at a distance.

Then suddenly some Palouse warriors fired on the soldiers!

This is Fort Colville, a famous Hudson's Bay post, as it looked in 1888. At left is the blockhouse and stockade. The long building, center, is quarters for officers and clerks. Fort Colville was established in 1825, abandoned in 1871.

Apparently the troops had already started a retreat toward the Snake but now they had to turn and fight. Although greatly outnumbered, the soldiers were able to make a stand on a knoll and hold off the Indians until darkness fell, whereupon they slipped away to the river. Five men had died, 14 had been wounded and one was missing.

At dawn, it appeared that the Indians had won. They had drawn blood and had driven off the soldiers.

But they had won only a small battle, and in winning the battle, lost the war.

(The Steptoe battle site is now a state park.)

Word of the fight got back to Washington, D.C., quickly. Angrily the Congress approved the 1855 treaties and turned loose the horse soldiers, the cavalry, to march over the Indian lands.

Now the days of sorrow and disgrace were at hand for Spokan Garry, who had neither prevented the Steptoe fight nor joined in it. He lost much influence in his tribe; a few of the wild ones even were crying for his scalp. So Garry stayed away from the villages, spent most of his time at his farm along the Spokane River with his second wife, Nina.

At a Fort Colville meeting, Garry said to a white official, "My heart is undecided. I do not know which way to go. My friends are fighting the whites, but I do not like to join them; but, if I do not, they will kill me."

Garry, his influence withered away, could no longer keep the peace. A large force of soldiers under Colonel George Wright moved in spoiling for a fight and won two battles, one near Medical Lake, the second on Spokane Plains.

Then Wright sent a harsh, shocking message to the Indians through Garry:

"I have met you in two bloody battles; you have been badly whipped; you have lost several chiefs and many warriors killed and wounded. I have not lost a man or animal; I have a large force, and you Spokanes, Coeur d'Alenes, and Pelouses and Pend Oreilles may unite, and I can defeat you as badly as before. I did not come into this country to ask you to make peace; I came here to fight. Now, when you are tired of the war, and ask for peace, I will tell you what you must do: you must come to me with your arms, with your women and children, and everything you have, and lay them at my feet; you must put your faith in me and trust in my mercy. If you do this, I shall then dictate the terms upon which I will grant you peace. If you do not do this, war will be made on you this year and next, *and until your nation shall be exterminated.*"

Now the naked power of the whites was in full view; now the message couldn't be more clear. For emphasis, Wright's army destroyed 900 Indian horses and ruined large supplies of vegetables, camas, dried berries, wheat and oats—all staple Indian foods.

So the tribesmen had three choices: fight and die, surrender unconditionally . . . or starve.

No fools, they surrendered. For the Spokanes, an era of ancient origin had ended; a new era was beginning.

★

In 1870, as he nudged 60 years of age, Garry found himself faced with nagging problems. Personally, he had little to complain about. He still had his rich farm along the river and he lived there with his growing family. But his beloved people seemed to be rotting away before his eyes . . .

The Spokanes, now numbering about 700 persons, still hadn't been forced onto a reservation but Garry knew that the end of their free life was in sight. There was much religious bickering now, as one kind of Christian tried to win theological arguments with another, sometimes with a club. Whiskey flowed like water to the tribe through money-grubbing whites. More and more whites were taking Indian wives in a casual way, then abandoning them much as they might throw away old boots.

The situation visibly worsened almost daily. The pressure which was crunching them as between two moving mountains continued to grow as more land-hungry homesteaders pushed in from the Walla Walla country.

But now the struggle had become a battle for men's minds and Garry could see the point in such a fight. This was his kind of war and he went back to work, opening a second school near what is now the intersection of Euclid and Oak Streets in the growing city of Spokane, and used the dirt floor as a blackboard and a stick for chalk. Again, he preached and taught, with no arguments about prayer in the classroom; Garry's institution was as much church as school.

But Garry, by himself, could not wipe out the rot that was eating away Indian pride and self-respect. The Spokanes were living in an emotional and cultural no-man's land bordered on one side by the old Indian ways, on the other by white manners and morals. By training, Garry was better able to adjust than were most Spokanes, but even Garry felt the terrible tension of a man caught betwixt and between.

★

Finally, in 1881, a Spokane reservation was established as the eastern

part of the area administered by the Colville Agency. Trouble was, the Spokanes and Coeur d'Alenes wanted no part of it. *You can lead a horse to water, but* . . .

So the federal government sent out the Dawes Commission (mentioned in the beginning of this chapter) to show the Spokanes the error of their ways and Spokan Garry experienced one of his last triumphant moments in the spotlight of history. Young Lucius Nash watched and listened, then later described the scene:

"Keyed up to pitch, smarting under the wrongs suffered by him and his people, he (Garry) blazed with righteous indignation at the treatment he had suffered. He knew he was on solid ground, that justice was with him. He arose to transcendent heights of noble oratory to stand beside the famous Indian orators of his or any other time.

"He resorted often to the sign language and pantomime for which the race is singularly gifted. He soared into the refined air of figurative speech, biblical in its simplicity. He spoke of the river, 'their river', as the mother of his people; that she nourished them at her breast, and it did, as the salmon was the principal source of their food; that the white men coveted their ancient mother and intended to rob them of her . . .

"The Boston men, he said, were as numerous as the pebbles in our valley, but he could not make his tribesmen understand that they were too feeble to push the white man back; that they with all their hands could not push the water back over the falls. How could they push the whites back? . . .

"He told of the frightful suffering of the Indians the winter after Wright shot all their horses in the bend of the river near Spokane Bridge; how they had to flee the mountains before the fish finished the run in the river; how they no longer could go to the berry patches or dig the camas or hunt for skins and furs. They were afoot and helpless . . .

"He said at any time of his life if he could have kept the white man out of his land, he would have willingly split open his breast with his own hands and handed over to them his bleeding heart.

"He said that his tribesmen would have to go but . . . as for himself, he would not go, that he would die first; that his bones would be buried in the ground of his ancestors. He removed his magnificent war bonnet, stroked the eagle feathers gently and said, 'I have sworn this on the

Spokan Garry loved the river and his farm lying along it. He had an abiding fondness, too, for white horses. In this exceptional picture, taken late in his life, he and a white horse rest beside the river.

head-dress of my father and my father's father.'

"He straightened himself in the saddle and looked steadily into the eyes of each commissioner, one by one, with withering contempt . . . he turned his back on them and the setting sun and with the dignity of a great chieftain alone, he turned his horse's head towards his home.

"The commissioners shifted uneasily in their chairs and the chairman muttered something about merely obeying orders from superiors . . ."

Spokan Garry had crossed the last peak of his long journey; now only the valley beckoned to Garry, the peace chief, bowlegged on a white horse . . .

★

The 1887 Annual Report of the Bureau of Indian Affairs noted: "Few whites felt that the Indians had any rights. Stock laws were used by the whites to round up the Indians' cattle, which were then sold to the highest bidder as strays. In this way the whites got the Indians' cattle for very little. As most of the Indians could not read the posted notices, nor understand why the whites could take their horses without paying for them, they often took them back—and were promptly arrested for stealing. Life was becoming extremely difficult for the Spokanes, and some went onto the Coeur d'Alene reservation, while others hung around Spokane Falls drinking and gambling away the little money they earned at odd jobs."

Once even Garry got drunk enough to be arrested and to spend a sobering night in the town jail.

★

Old, wrinkled and wizened, Garry had gone to the river with his family to help with the fishing, now more difficult because whites had banned fish traps.

The message came to him at the river that his precious farm had been taken over by white men. Garry rushed home, but was ordered off the land by the whites who had snatched it.

The white men generously let Garry take what he could carry from his cabin, then burned the structure to the ground.

Garry tried in a peaceful, legal way to get back his farm, but on August 3, 1888, the United States Land Office issued to a certain Schyler D. Doak a receipt for a land claim, and Garry's beloved piece of earth had been officially stolen from him.

While he continued to fight in the white man's courts, Garry went to live in a tepee on Hangman Creek, and there, in January, 1892, Garry died.

The funeral was described by Thomas E. Jessett in his book, "Chief Spokan Garry":

"A number of white men and women who had known the old chief in better days, came to pay their last respects, as did all the members of his tribe convenient to the city. After the service, they passed in silent review before the coffin. Poor blind Nina (Garry's second wife) was led slowly up to the coffin, and as she passed her hands over the familiar features she had known and loved so long, tears coursed down her wrinkled cheeks. She moved on, the coffin was sealed, and the body of Spokan Garry passed forever from the sight of man."

★

Garry and the Spokanes had cried out for justice . . . but where was justice?

Garry had been taken as a child to Red River and had been taught the ways of a Christian white man. When he returned to his ancestral tribe, he had enjoyed respect and love. His people expected him, despite his youth, to hold onto the old Indian ways and melt into them the wisdom of the white men.

Wasn't this like asking for a marriage of fire and water? The problem of marrying Indian and white cultures exists to this day and we have the Indian reservations to prove it.

It's not hard in this case to pick heroes and villains, to paint a waxed and curled mustache on Governor Stevens who, on occasion, lied to the Indians, and then hang a halo on the underdog, Spokan Garry.

But Isaac Stevens wasn't acting for himself; he was an agent of white government and white culture. Onrushing white society had to gain possession of Indian lands and Stevens was their tool. The Indians were generally considered a nuisance to be eradicated as soon as possible. There were many more whites than Indians and the whites had most of the weapons; numbers and weapons have always constituted raw power.

Perhaps there should be no heroes or villains, only human beings caught up in a flow of history as unstoppable as ocean tides. Victims of circumstances . . . and victors of circumstances.

★

In Greenwood Cemetery in Spokane rest the remains of Spokan Garry. Part of the cost of his original burial may have been paid out of Spokane

GARRY
CHIEF
OF THE SPOKANES
DIED JAN. 12. 1892

HIS LIFE SPANNED
THE UNFOLDING OF THE
SPOKANE COUNTRY FROM THE
DAYS OF FUR TRADERS AT
SPOKANE HOUSE TO THE
ACTIVITIES OF A MODERN CITY.

NINA GARRY

ERECTED BY SPOKANE CHAPTER
DAUGHTERS OF THE AMERICAN REVOLUTION
1925

County's pauper fund.

But this was only one of the smaller insults. Garry's wife, Nina, got nothing from the government in payment for his land. She was forced with her daughter, Nellie, to move to the Coeur d'Alene reservation. At death, she was buried in the potter's field at Fairfield.

Garry's grave was neglected (only a wooden paddle located it) until 1917, when the Spokane Historical Society supplied a marker. An impressive stone monument was erected over his new grave near the entrance to Greenwood Cemetery in 1962 and Nina's remains were re-buried beside him.

Teacher, preacher and horseman—Garry was all of these and modern Spokane remembers the many sides of this complex man.

A marker at Euclid and Oak streets designates the site of Garry's second school. A stained glass window in the Cathedral of St. John the Evangelist commemorates his missionary work. "Chief Garry Park" was dedicated in 1932.

Garry, the peace chief, once had been rich but when he died, he owned only 10 lean, hungry horses.

Before his daughter could get to the horses, all but two or three had been stolen.

Then little was left but the bowlegged track of a peaceable man trampled under in the stampede toward America's white frontier.

MY KINGDOM FOR A CANOE

Before the white man wandered west, a Northwest Indian boy had just two choices of occupation: (1) he could be a horse Indian; (2) he could be a canoe Indian.

In fact, it was even simpler than that in this era before vocational guidance; his choice was usually made for him by the circumstances of his birth. Born west of the Cascade Mountains, he canoed. Born east of the snowcaps, he galloped.

The canoe Indians lived near the coast and subsisted largely on seafood, which was so easy to come by that these intelligent people had time to develop one of the most sophisticated Indian cultures on the continent. Their main transportation device was the canoe, hence, "canoe Indian."

Spokan Garry and Nina finally lie in honor in Spokane's Greenwood Cemetery. This 1962 group included some of their descendants.

The great Chief Seattle was a canoe Indian.

Horse Indians (or, in Washington, "Plateau" Indians) lived east of the Cascade Mountains, fished for salmon in the Columbia but also rode their gaudy horses east across the Rocky Mountains on annual buffalo hunts. During these trips, the horse Indians encountered the Plains Indians —Sioux, Blackfeet, etc.—and adopted some of their customs and modes of dress, such as the flamboyant feather headdress which quickly came to be *the* thing for a status-conscious brave to wear whenever he chose to appear before the tourists or government negotiators in his homeland.

The main transportation device of the horse Indians, logically enough, was the horse. The more spotted the horse, the better the horse. The Nez Perce bred the Appaloosa, still popular today, and the Spokanes and other tribes soon acquired a fondness for the same breed.

Spokan Garry, Kamiakin, Moses, Joseph—all were great chiefs, all were horse Indians.

The Northwest's canoe Indians made a major contribution to culture and general jollity when they developed the "potlatch," at which a wealthy chief might give away almost everything he owned to his invited guests. The presents were varied—canoes, blankets, guns, goods, cash or even slaves. (Some of the blankets, incidentally, were made from dog's wool. A dog like a Pomeranian was raised for its hair, which grew to ground length.)

In some tribes, the potlatch was merely a status symbol; the more an Indian could afford to give away, the bigger the man he proved himself to be. (Some of our modern status symbols can bankrupt a person just as quickly.)

In other tribes, the potlatch was more of a business investment. Those who received gifts were expected to return them at potlatches of their own, often with interest running as high as 100 per cent. If an Indian threw this sort of potlatch, he would give gifts only to those whose credit had been established. In any event, the potlatch kept the wealth in circulation and provided something to do during a long, wet, winter week.

There is a record of a potlatch to end all potlatches in 1876. Twelve hundred guests attended from 22 tribes. A special potlatch house 300 feet long was built and the bash rattled on for eight days, which is hardly surprising, since preparations had begun several years earlier. The women gave away 10,000 yards of calico and the men passed around $3000 in

An Indian camp in the San Poil Valley, Colville Reservation, shows, at left, what might be salmon drying on racks.

cash, plus more blankets and canoes than anyone could count. It must have been great fun while the loot lasted.

So all in all, it wasn't a bad life, until the white man came along looking for a piece of the action. Fish were so plentiful in the streams that Indians occasionally used dried fish for cooking fuel. Why not? They caught bottom fish at Grays Harbor by wading until they stepped on fish, whereupon they picked them up and dropped them into a basket. There were also clams on the beaches, deer in the forests and berries almost everywhere, plus plenty of wood for houses and logs for canoes. One tribe wore necklaces made of dried clams, thus providing adornment and quick lunch on the same string.

The coastal tribes developed canoeing to a high art. Over the centuries, they had evolved contours for their craft which allowed them to paddle a 70-foot canoe at the brisk speed of 10 knots; it was no accident that the fast clipper ships, marvels of the white man's world, used hull designs very much like the old Indian canoes. (Canoes and other Northwest Indian relics are displayed in highly dramatic settings in what is surely one of the best Indian museums in the country, Burke Memorial on the University of Washington campus in Seattle. The Washington State Historical Society museum in Tacoma, Cheney Cowles Museum in Spokane, Museum of History and Industry in Seattle and Maryhill Museum near Goldendale are excellent, too.)

Canoes were war weapons, too. There is a record of two schooners on their way to Port Townsend being attacked and sunk by Indians in canoes during February, 1859. Having canoes with considerable carrying capacity allowed the coastal Indians to elaborate on the horse Indian custom of taking scalps from enemy dead; the canoe Indians took entire heads for trophies and mounted them on pikes when they returned to their villages.

(Before we condemn the Indians as savages and barbarians, though, we need to remember that after Peu-Peu-Mox-Mox, great Walla Walla chief, was killed by white volunteer troops representing Governor Stevens, the whites snicked off his scalp, sliced off his ears and preserved the parts in a jar full of whiskey so that they might be exhibited later at The Dalles, Oregon. A few volunteers, it was said, even stripped skin from the chief's back and had it tanned for razor strops. The ways of the frontier often seem uncivilized by modern standards but one wonders: which is the more civilized weapon, the scalping knife or the nuclear bomb?)

Coast Indians slice up a whale at Neah Bay. The sea has always been a bountiful provider for Northwest natives.

Another contribution of the canoe Indians was an eminently sensible language called "Chinook jargon." The language developed because few whites could cope with Indian tongues. (The missionary to the Spokanes, Cushing Eells, said that Indians "spoke in such harsh gutturals that it sounded like husking corn.")

The Chinooks who lived around the mouth of the Columbia River were born middlemen and built up a huge trade between upriver tribes and those on the coast, with Hudson's Bay Company and independent white traders throwing guns, tools and trinkets into the pot. The jargon developed out of business necessity. It was said that before Washington became a state, almost everyone in the territory, white and Indian, could speak at least a little of the jargon. (One notable exception was Chief Seattle, who disliked it and would not use it.)

Chinook jargon was composed of Chinook, English, French, plain old phonics and a good deal of common sense. Consider these words from the jargon and their English definitions:

Pusspuss—cat
Tiktik—watch
Tumtum—heart
Toh—spitting
Lum-rum—whiskey
Moosmoos—cattle
Piupiu—stink
Skookum—strong
La peep—tobacco pipe

If in the future English or Esperanto doesn't measure up as the long-sought universal language, the world could do worse than to consider Chinook jargon.

★

Life was good for both canoe Indians and horse Indians until the early 1800s, when the white man came to stay. At first, he was a small minority,

In 1856, Father Pierre DeSmet arranged the surrender of these Upper Columbia chiefs at Fort Vancouver. Seated are Victor, Alexander, Adolphe and Andrew. Standing are Dennis, Bonaventure, Father DeSmet and Francis Xavier.

not much for the Indian to worry about, but without realizing it, he carried the most powerful of weapons: disease.

Beginning about 1829, sickness began to plague the Indians living on the banks of the lower Columbia. Dr. McLoughlin of Fort Vancouver estimated that more than 30,000 Indians died of measles or "fever" or "ague" within a short time after the white man had established himself in the region. Some attributed the epidemics to the plowing of virgin ground but Indian medical practice undoubtedly contributed. The usual treatment for any ailment was a sweat bath, better known as kill-or-cure. Too often, it killed. The Indians blamed the whites, who didn't know enough about germs, bacteria and viruses to help matters. Tragic episodes like the Whitman Massacre resulted.

One can't help but wonder if the Indian wars might not have had a different result if the tribes had not been decimated by disease.

The Indian wars were hideously expensive for the U.S. government, entirely aside from the cost in human life. In 1870, the Commissioner of Indian Affairs estimated that the Indian wars had cost the Great White Father no less than $500,000,000—five hundred millions of dollars. This translates into the appalling figure of approximately one million dollars for each Indian killed! By 1870, the Indian wars had cost the United States more than the combined expense of all our foreign wars up to that time!

Once in a while, however, a clever community managed to recover part of the cost. Frightened citizens in Olympia built a 15-foot stockade around the town when they heard reports of the Indians rising. When the scare faded, they tore down the stockade and used the planks to pave streets.

It wasn't all bloodshed; whites and Indians sometimes gave each other a chuckle. A railroad building through Washington once bought right-of-way from an Indian. Part of the settlement was a lifetime pass on the line. When the first train streamed along the line to Goldendale, the Indian was there, waving his pass like a flag. He rode to Goldendale and back.

Each day thereafter, he appeared and waved his pass. Each day the train stopped to pick him up, then stopped again on the return trip. Finally the train crew grew weary of the performance and one day didn't stop but just slowed down when the Indian appeared on the right-of-way.

On the following day, the Indian stood at his usual spot by the tracks but now he looked battered, very definitely black and blue. When he boarded, he announced, "Me almost go to Jesus yesterday."

From that point on, a limit was placed on the Indian's rail excursions.

★

The clash between the cultures, white and Indian, was often violent and finally tragic. Vastly outnumbered and outgunned, the Indians at last knuckled under to raw white power but the names of brave, wise and eloquent Indian leaders ring across the years and echo through the dusty halls of American history.

Such as Noah Sealth, now better known as Seattle, whose illustrious name was given to the Northwest's largest city . . .

A FEW MORE MOONS

"Whatever I say, the Great Chief at Washington can rely on," announced Chief Seattle. "His people are many, like grass that covers vast prairies. Our people once covered the land as waves of a wind-ruffled sea cover its shell-paved floor, but now my people are few.

"Our great and good Father sends us word that if we do as he desires he will buy our lands . . . allow us to live comfortably . . . protect us with his brave warriors; his wonderful ships of war will fill our harbors. Then our ancient northern enemies will cease to frighten our women, children and old men.

"But day and night can not dwell together. The red man has ever fled the approach of the white man as morning mist flees the rising sun. It matters little where we pass the remnant of our days. They will not be many. The Indian's night promises to be dark . . . a few more moons . . . a few more winters."

Obviously the intelligent, realistic Suquamish chief was willing to read the handwriting on the wall. Chief Seattle was the first signer of the Port Elliott Treaty of 1855 which consigned Washington tribes to reservations.

Eleven years later, at age 80, he was dead. A great city, then only a struggling town, was given his name by grateful whites.

(This is as good a place as any to discuss the sticky matter of spelling of Indian names. The revered Chief Seattle's grave is in a very interesting Indian cemetery at Suquamish 14 miles across Puget Sound from the city of Seattle. The backside of an impressive monument at the grave says: "Baptismal Name Noah Sealth Age Probably 80 Years." The front of the monument bears both names, "Sealth" and "Seattle." Apparently Noah was a favorite Biblical character of Sealth's and when Catholic missionary Father Demers baptized him, the chief asked that Noah be part of his

The panel on the historical marker reads:

CHIEF SEALTH

Born in 1786, his life spanned the period from the exploration of Puget Sound by Europeans to its settlement. He represented the Duwamish & Suquamish tribes in the Treaty of Mukilteo with Governor Stevens in 1855.

Chief Sealth showed his friendship for the new settlement on Puget Sound during the Indian disturbance of 1855. In gratitude for his stand and respect for his leadership, the new city was named Seattle.

He died in 1866 and is buried in the Suquamish Memorial Cemetery near St. Peter's Church.

Erected by the Washington State Parks & Recreation Commission.

The monument inscription reads:

SEATTLE Chief of the Suquamish and Allied tribes, DIED JUNE 7, 1866. The firm friend of the whites, and for him the CITY of SEATTLE was named by its FOUNDERS.

SEALTH

The grave of Chief Seattle across Puget Sound from the city which bears his name.

Christian name. It was done, but no one called him "Noah" thereafter. When he heard that his friend, Dr. David Maynard, first Seattle doctor, had suggested that the town be named for him, Sealth was horrified. The Indians believed that whenever a man's name was mentioned after death, his spirit returned to walk the earth. Envisioning a mighty active hereafter. Sealth was displeased. Before his death, though, he came to like the idea of being thus remembered. Exactly how did "Noah Sealth" become "Seattle" on modern maps? Few historians are willing to speak out bluntly on the matter. Spelling of Indian names was often chaotic. Indians originally had no written language. This caused few problems until whites arrived, took pens and pencils in hand and furiously scribbled letters home and reports to headquarters. For instance, Spokan Garry's rather simple name, originally British, was garbled to "Geiry" and "Geary" and several other variants; you can imagine what happened to "Kamiakin." At any rate, "Sealth" and "Seattle" refer to the same person, a wise and peaceful man who was chief of the allied tribes known as the Duwamish Confederacy. Boy Scouts from the city of Seattle annually conduct a memorial service at his grave and they are well aware of whom they honor, so why argue about the spelling of the name?)

Seattle may have become a friend of whites long before 1855. As a five-year-old in 1792, he seems to have been on hand when Captain George Vancouver's sailing ship *Discovery* entered Puget Sound. The friendliness of the first white man Seattle had ever seen may have made a permanent impression.

Seattle earned his chief's rank the hard way, in battle against horse Indian enemies of the Suquamish. But once he laid down the lance and tomahawk, he never lifted them again.

In 1851 the small band of white settlers who arrived by sea to found a community on the shore of Puget Sound discovered a friend, Chief Seattle, and they gratefully accepted his gifts of seafood and venison. At first the settlement bore the rather ridiculous, foreign-sounding name of "New York," then was renamed "Alki Point" and finally acquired its sturdy, striking, permanent name, "Seattle."

Chief Seattle made his peace with the whites and spared his people much suffering. There are those today who might call him an "Uncle Tom," a non-white who sold his soul for personal gain.

But Chief Seattle was not a man who wanted whites to rest easy while enjoying their conquered lands. When Governor Stevens came in 1854 to talk treaty, Chief Seattle said to him and to the Duwamish and Suquamish people gathered within range of his deep, strong voice:

". . . And when the last red man shall have perished and the memory of my tribe shall have become a myth among the white men, these shores will swarm with the invisible dead of my tribe, and when your children's children think themselves alone in the field, the store, the shop, upon the highway, or in the silence of the pathless woods, they will not be alone. In all the earth there is no place dedicated to solitude. At night when the streets of your cities and villages are silent and you think them deserted, they will throng with the returning hosts that once filled them and still love this beautiful land. The white man will never be alone."

A MAN CALLED JOSEPH

The small cemetery at the north edge of Nespelem, Washington, is dry, rocky and barren. The single, scrubby tree in the cemetery is at the foot of a grave surrounded by a makeshift wooden fence. Plainly, there is something special about this burial place.

The grave is that of Joseph, a strong, wise and gentle man. Young Joseph, chief of the Wallowa band of Nez Perce Indians, does not belong here. The land of his ancestors and the burial ground of his father are near one of the Pacific Northwest's most beautiful places, Wallowa Lake, Oregon.

The cemetery where Young Joseph is buried is on the ground of the Colville reservation; he was not a Colville. Joseph was a Nez Perce and when he was finally settled by the Great White Father on the Colville reservation, he was resented by the Colvilles.

Joseph reached hero status reluctantly and there are still white historians who would deny him the position. The state historical marker at Nespelem calls him "military genius." Too bad; this sort of praise brings on the debunking historians in full cry. The Joseph display in the Cheney Cowles Museum in Spokane proclaims that he "was not a military leader."

The truth, as is so often the case, probably lies somewhere in between.

★

In 1877, Joseph and his people crossed the Snake River into Idaho, reaching out desperately for Montana and a hoped-for haven in Canada. They had refused the reservation offered by the whites; Nez Perce hot-bloods had reacted and killed; now the U.S. Cavalry was on the prowl. Despairing, Joseph and Ollokot and White Bird and Looking Glass led the Nez Perce into the last long march along the Lolo Trail, toward the final battles of the Indian race against the white invader.

The Nez Perce were a proud people. Exile in Canada seemed better to a proud people than servitude in their homeland.

But the United States Cavalry had other ideas. The horse soldiers

"From where the sun now stands, I will fight no more forever."—Chief Joseph, historic hero of the Nez Perce.

pursued the Nez Perce with great determination, even when falling snow heralded the onset of early winter in the mountains. Battles were fought at White Bird Canyon and at the Big Hole River; finally the Nez Perce were beaten, but not until they made the cavalry look foolish a dozen times, not until they had earned the admiration of many whites along their path, not until they had placed their last leader, Joseph, in the pantheon of authentic American heroes and etched an epic of heroism deep into the tablets of American history.

When the Nez Perce finally left their homeland in desperate flight toward Canada, Joseph was the chief placed in charge of the women and children and of the horse herd. It was a key job. Families ranked high in the Nez Perce value system, and without horses, they were nothing.

Finally, though, when Joseph's brother Ollokot and the mighty Looking Glass and the old chief White Bird had been killed, it was Joseph who led the valiant people in the last days of their suffering and it was Joseph who had to surrender them after the final battle in the wintry wilds of northern Montana.

General Howard of the U.S. Cavalry chose a Nez Perce called Captain John to serve as interpreter.

Joseph spoke to Captain John, and through him to General Howard and to the United States of America in the last valedictory of the American Indian:

"Tell General Howard I know his heart . . . I am tired of fighting. Our chiefs are killed. Looking Glass is dead. Toohoolhoolzote is dead. It is the young men who say yes or no. He who led on the young men is dead. It is cold and we have no blankets. The little children are freezing to death. My people, some of them, have run away to the hills and have no blankets, no food; no one knows where they are—perhaps freezing to death. I want to have time to look for my children and see how many of them I can find. Maybe I shall find them among the dead.

"Hear me, my chiefs, I am tired. My heart is sick and sad. From where the sun now stands, I will fight no more forever."

Then Joseph of the Nez Perce shuffled slowly into a tent of the enemy. The last free tribe had been shattered; the last great chief had surrendered.

In the years that followed, the Nez Perce were shipped around the country like cattle, first to the Dakotas, then to Oklahoma. Many sickened and died. But finally magazine and newspaper articles fanned white protests; Joseph and the Nez Perce were returned to the Northwest in 1885 and settled on the Colville reservation.

Joseph did not want to die in this unfriendly place. Many times he asked to return to his beloved Land of the Winding Waters around Wallowa Lake but always the Great White Father refused. In 1904 Joseph died and was buried at Nespelem. After his death, many of his friends, both white and red, fought to return his remains to the Wallowa country; they failed.

THE MAN WITH THE NEEDLE

The great peace chief of the Columbias, Moses, had been given a Christian name at the Spalding mission during his youth but his respect for the white man's religion didn't grow with age.

"If hell is hot," the mature chief is supposed to have asked, "why doesn't the water boil in the white man's well?"

Moses was as strong for peace as Spokan Garry but while Garry was polite about it, Moses sometimes wasn't.

In 1870, the United States decided to take a census of its Indians. Moses's band refused to cooperate. They had a government of their own, they said, and didn't recognize the government of the United States. The only authority they accepted outside of the tribe was that of God, and God, they pointed out tartly, already knew how many Columbias there were.

But Moses, like Garry, was clear-eyed about white power, realized early on that resistance was futile, and was effective in selling his viewpoint to his tribe. Once Moses called his chiefs together for a meeting with representatives of other tribes and lectured them on the importance of maintaining peace.

With a stick he scraped up a pile of sand a foot high, then asked one of his chiefs to count the grains.

The chief shook his head and said, "There are too many . . ."

Moses nodded. "It is the same way with the white man," he said. "There are too many."

Moses finally agreed to live on the Colville reservation and was made chief of all the tribes who lived there. When he died, a great potlatch attended by more than a thousand friends was a highlight of the funeral. Moses's most prized possessions, a buckskin suit and war bonnet which had been given to him by Sitting Bull, were passed on to Joseph, who then succeeded Moses as chief of the Colville tribes.

In 1969, there were three large Indian reservations in Washington: Colville, Spokane and Yakima, all east of the Cascades. Nineteen other small reservations were clustered around Puget Sound. In that same year,

the state's Indian population was about 15,000, of which about 9000 lived on reservations.

One might think that Indian-white troubles were buried in the past, but in recent years the federal government, Oregon, Washington and the Indians have squabbled fitfully over old Indian treaty fishing rights, particularly in the Columbia River. Years and decades and eons pass, but troubles remain. Perhaps this is clinching proof, if any were needed, that Chief Seattle was right: white and red cultures can never coexist; day and night cannot dwell together.

There is little written in the history of white-Indian relations for whites to be proud of, much for whites to feel guilty about. But historical perspective can lift the question above such nagging, niggling matters as guilt or pride.

Chief Seattle, eloquent as usual, also said:

"But why should I mourn the untimely fate of my people? Tribe follows tribe, and nation follows nation, like the waves of the sea. It is the order of nature, and regret is useless. Your time of decay may be distant but it will surely come. Even the white man whose God walked and talked with him—as friend to friend—cannot escape the common destiny. We may be brothers, after all. We shall see!"

SUGGESTED READING

Anderson, Eva Greenslit; CHIEF SEATTLE; Caxton; 1943.

Andrews, Ralph W.; INDIAN PRIMITIVE; Bonanza; 1960.

Farnsworth, Frances J.; WINGED MOCCASINS; Messner; 1954 (Sacajawea).

Miller, Helen Markley; THUNDER ROLLING: THE STORY OF CHIEF JOSEPH; Putnam's; 1959.

Olson, Joan and Gene; OREGON TIMES AND TRAILS; Windyridge; 1965 (Chief Joseph).

Chief Moses posed astride a gaudy horse in 1895.

Chapter Four ★

Westward Migration
THE JUMPING-OFF PLACE

Andy Burge, packer, had a job to do in late September, 1853, and he urged his string of tired pack horses into a brisk clip along the rocky, narrow trail. The men working on the road would be hungry enough to eat tree bark . . . or throw down their tools and head for home.

But there had to be a road, at least a halfway kind of wagon-busting road, if those fool homesteaders were going to make it through to the Sound alive.

He was tired, Andy Burge was, but he didn't realize how tired until his mind conjured up a vision: two women and some children were walking along the trail toward him.

Burge brushed at his eyes and hurried toward the apparitions, expecting them to fade as he neared. But they did not fade . . .

"My God, women, where in the world did you come from?"

They had come, it turned out, from Shawnee Prairie, Indiana. These women and children were the unlikely advance guard of the Longmire party, first to attempt to cross the Cascade Mountains via the difficult and dangerous Naches Pass cutoff branch of the Oregon Trail between Walla Walla and Puget Sound.

The women were Mrs. James Longmire and Mrs. E. A. Light. In the mountains behind them was the wagon train which had left the established Oregon Trail at Fort Walla Walla. When news came to the Sound that a brave party intended to strike out over Naches Pass, a work crew was sent out from Steilacoom to clear a wagon road. Too many settlers had travelled down the Columbia to Fort Vancouver and over the Barlow Road to Oregon City and the Willamette Valley. Some of these had moved north into the lush land around Puget Sound but the overflow wasn't enough; many more were needed and it just might be possible to grab them off the Oregon Trail before the Willamette Valley could snare them with its siren song.

The Longmire party was the first to cut off, to strike out across the fearsome, towering mountains toward the Sound. Had they known what awaited them, they might never have started.

Why did they bother? Why didn't they simply make a few rafts and float down the Columbia to Fort Vancouver, then gather their strength and strike out overland toward the Sound?

Well, for one thing, the Columbia River passage was expensive, and many emigrant parties reached the Cascades and The Dalles a mite short on money. If a party wanted to go downriver, it had to buy or build rafts to float the wagons and stock. It cost a lot of money and it was dangerous.

Or you could swim your cattle across to the Washington side, put your wagons on a boat and follow, then drive the livestock along an Indian trail to Fort Vancouver. There, if you were headed for the Willamette Valley in Oregon, you had to cross that broad, strong river again and almost certainly take more losses.

The size of the problem can be measured when you consider that in 1844, emigrants lost more than half of their livestock trying to whip the Columbia between the Cascades and Fort Vancouver.

There had to be a better way. So Sam Barlow, in 1845, went south of the river and hacked his name into history by carving out the Barlow Road over the shoulder of Mt. Hood to Oregon City, then capital of Oregon Territory. This was a brutal passage but its worst obstacle, Laurel Hill, wasn't a patch on Summit Hill tackled by the Longmire party.

They had begun their journey as far back as Indiana; they had been on the trail for more than six months. They had been stalked by wolves and Indians; poisonous plants had killed some oxen; roaring rivers had swept away both horses and oxen. (One pioneer was fond of saying, with feeling, "Of all variable things in creation, the most uncertain are the action of a jury, the state of a woman's mind, and the condition of a western river.")

Since March, the Longmire party had been half-suffocated in the dust, half-fried by the sun, half-eaten by mosquitoes, half-drowned and half-starved. They had to cross the rivers again and again (the Naches 60 times!) until finally, almost exhausted in body and mind and spirit, they fetched up at Summit Hill on a bluff overlooking the Greenwater River.

A member of the party was George Himes, then a barefoot lad of nine. One of his letters written in 1905 (and preserved in the files of the

Oregon Historical Society) describes the scene which assaulted the weary, battered emigrants as they stared bleakly down from Summit Hill:

"In due time the summit of the Cascades was reached. Here there was a small prairie—really it was an old burn that had not grown up to timber of any size. Now it was October and bitter cold to the youth with bare feet and fringed pants extending half way down from knees to feet. My father and the teams had left camp and gone across the little burn, where most of the company were assembled, apparently debating about the next movement to make. And no wonder, for as we neared we saw the cause of the delay. For a sheer thirty feet or more there was an almost perpendicular bluff, and for more than a thousand feet further down the mountain it was so steep that a team could not stand up.

"It was at this point my mother exclaimed, after looking over the precipice, 'Well, George, I guess we have got to the jumping-off place at last.'

"Heavy timber at all other points precluded the possibility of getting on by any other route. So the longest rope in the company was stretched down the cliff, leaving just enough to be used twice around a small tree which stood on the brink of the precipice, but it was found to be altogether too short.

"Then James Biles said, 'Kill one of the poorest of my steers and make his hide into a rope, and attach it to the one you have.'

"Three animals were slaughtered before a rope could be secured long enough to let the wagons down to a point where they would stand up. There one yoke of oxen were hitched to a wagon, and by locking the wheels and hitching on a small log with projecting limbs, it was taken down to a stream then known as Greenwater.

"It took the best part of two days to make the descent. There were thirty-six wagons belonging to the company, but two of them, with a small quantity of provisions, were wrecked on this hill. The wagons could have been dispensed without much loss. Not so the provisions . . . as the company came to be in sore straits for food before the White River Prairie was reached."

★

Andy Burge eased the food problem. The roadbuilders he had come to supply had already fled to avoid starvation, so Burge gave most of the load

This wagon train is a relatively modern re-creation but the originals must have looked much the same as they wound across the sage flats.

on his horses to the Longmire party.

Then Burge tried to convince the emigrants that the way ahead was impossible. He urged them to go back to where there were grass and water for their animals and food for themselves.

The Longmire party met in council and decided to move on west, toward Puget Sound.

Andy Burge shook his head sadly and started out ahead of them, blazing trees and leaving notes tacked to them reporting on the condition of the road ahead.

Wrote James Longmire: "We crossed the Greenwater sixteen times and followed it until we came to White River, which we crossed six times. Then we left it for a dreaded pull over Wind Mountain, which was covered with heavy fir and cedar trees but destitute of grass, with a few vine maples, on whose long leaves our poor oxen and horses had to live for seven long days, not having a blade of grass during that time."

They crossed White River for the seventh time and slogged along to the Puyallup River, which was running full with salmon. Excitedly taking clubs, axes or any other weapon in hand, members of the party splashed into the river. Almost with every blow, they took a fat salmon. According to James Longmire: "Some of the party stayed up all night cooking and eating fish. All relished them but my wife, who was indisposed, but she was fortunate enough in finding an Indian who had just killed a pheasant, which she bought—her first purchase on Puget Sound, and which caused merriment in our party, as the Indian was a perfect nude.

"We moved on to Nisqually Plains and camped on Clover Creek, some three hundred yards away from the home of Mrs. Mahan. On the 9th of October, the day after we camped at Clover Creek, the men all went to Stilacoom Fort to see Puget Sound, leaving the women to keep camp. During their absence Mrs. Mahan took the ladies to her house, where she had prepared dinner which to these tired sisters, after their toilsome journey, was like a royal banquet. After months of camp life to sit once more at a table, presided over by a friend in this faraway land where we thought to meet only strangers, was truly an event never to be forgotten.

". . . I will mention the fact of my arrival in this country with torn and ragged pants and coat, my cap tattered and torn, and with one boot on, the other foot covered with an improvised moccasin made from a piece of cowhide from one of the animals we had killed a few days previous.

"In this garb I was to meet a party of well-dressed gentlemen from Olympia, who had heard of us from Andy Burge and who came out to welcome the first party of emigrants direct from the east over the Cascade

Mountains north of The Dalles. My dress was a fair sample of that of the rest of the party. When together we felt pretty well, all being in the same fashion, but when brought face to face with well dressed men I must confess I felt somewhat embarrassed. But our new friends were equal to the emergency. Our embarrassment was soon dispelled, while answering questions amid handshaking, hearty and genial."

★

An old mountain man said that a pioneer could choose among four ways of dying: "To get sculped, squozed by a grizzly bear, tromped by a buffler herd, or froze to death in the mountains."

Even allowing for the habitual exaggeration of a mountain man, the Oregon Trail didn't sound much like an air-conditioned freeway. Why, then did swelling numbers of emigrants follow the hard road to Washington?

Well, for one thing, advertising paid off in those days, too. A newspaper in Jefferson City, Missouri, published the following on July 21, 1846, after an interview with Joel Palmer, member of the historic Sam Barlow party:

"A party among which was one of our informants had explored the country north of the Columbia River as far as Puget Sound. The silly tales about its sterility are grossly false, and have with many others of a similar character been manufactured by the Hudson's Bay Company. It is a fertile country, admirably well suited to the production of wheat and other small grain. Its general features are rolling and mountainous, but interspersed with the most fertile valleys, covered with heavy and valuable timber, with occasional plains and prairies, well watered and the streams abounding in fish. A belt of country from 40 to 60 miles in width, extending around the southern portion of the Sound, is of a level character. It is believed that there will be a large settlement of Americans on the north side of the Columbia the present season."

There was more than one reason for coming west. The women and children came, most of the time, because the head of the family hankered to go. Many of the farming men were attracted by the lure of free land, perhaps better land than the prairie acres they were working in Missouri or Indiana or Ohio. Some went west to escape the "ague" and "fever" plagues of the Midwest's river bottoms and the bitter winters which could freeze a man in his tracks. In the West, it was said, the air and water were clear and pure and a man could hardly hold himself in for healthiness. And winter, they said, was little more than a wet spell. Anyway, wasn't it

worth a look?

One pioneer wrote of the Midwest: "There was still plenty of room there, but all our lives we had been hearing tales of the far west, beyond the Rockies. I think many of us were tired of the flat country and the short grass of the prairies and plains."

There, perhaps, was the kernel of truth. Americans have always been a restless, rambling breed; even today they own a lion's share of the world's automobiles and wear them out almost as fast as they are manufactured.

More evidence is in a letter from the Oregon Country to a friend east of the Rockies in 1844:

"Notwithstanding the ease with which the necessaries of life are acquired, I never saw a more discontented community, owing principally to natural disposition. Nearly all, like myself, having been of a roving, discontented character before leaving their eastern homes. The long, tiresome trip from the States has taught them what they are capable of performing and enduring. They talk of removing to the Islands (Hawaii), California, Chile, and other parts of South America with as much composure as you in Wisconsin talk of removing to Indiana or Michigan."

After 1849, when John Sutter made his strike in California, there was a simpler reason for picking up and facing west—the natural human greed for gold.

After Sutter's discovery, the Oregon Trail developed a fork. One emigrant wrote: "Oldtimers told how in gold rush days, immigrants arriving at Pacific Springs had to choose between the road to California, marked by a heap of glittering quartz, and the northwesterly road indicated by a sign bearing the words 'To Oregon.' Those who could read went to Oregon."

But it would be wrong to assume that travellers on the Oregon Trail were mere drifters, losers where they were, so wanting desperately to be somewhere else. By and large, emigrants weren't fleeing bill collectors. Proper equipment for wagon travel cost from $800 to $1200, not a huge amount by modern standards, but in those days wages were less than $1.50 a day and good land in Illinois sold for $3–6 per acre. No sir; pioneering wasn't for losers, unless they wanted to walk for 2000 miles or hire out to a wagon train.

Chamber of commerce puffery goes way back. This dreamy maiden pillowed on a sheaf of grain in a bed of potatoes, fish and roses surely attracted thousands of frostbitten easterners to the fertile shores of Puget Sound. Who could resist her?

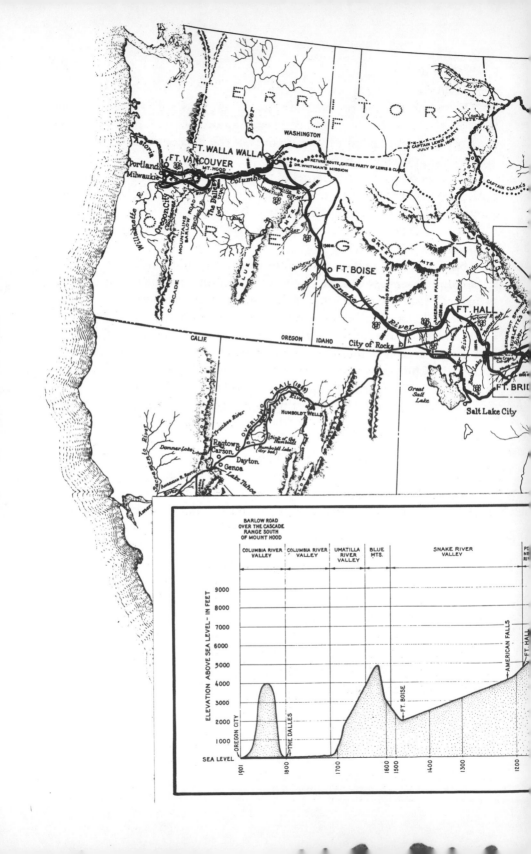

OREGON TRAIL
AS OF 1846
COMPILED FROM AUTHENTIC DATA

United States Department of Agriculture
Bureau of Public Roads
WASHINGTON, D.C.

MAY 15, 1938   DRAWN BY L.E.KNIGHT

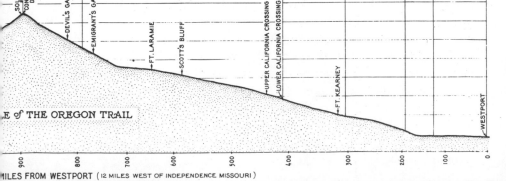

E of THE OREGON TRAIL

MILES FROM WESTPORT (12 MILES WEST OF INDEPENDENCE MISSOURI)

Generally, pioneering males were solid family men who felt a strong yen to see what lay beyond the western horizon. Proof is easy to come by; just pick apart the first big wagon train to the West, the train of 1843 guided by none other than Dr. Marcus Whitman.

That first big train carried nearly 900 persons. About 600 of those were children. These were *families* pushing toward the sunset, not lone wanderers.

And how was it along the trail? Here's how . . .

★

From the Shively Guide to emigrants: "Let each man be provided with 5 or 6 hickory shirts, 1 or 2 pair of buckskin pantaloons, a buckskin coat or hunting shirt, 2 very wide brimmed hats, wide enough to keep the mouth from the sun. For the want of such hat thousands suffer nearly all the way to Oregon, with their lips ulcerated, caused by sunburn."

About those buckskins, from an observer at Fort Hall: "There were a few soldiers and other white men, also some Indian squaws, about this fort. Some of those white men were wearing buck-skin breeches, and they looked as if they were sitting down while standing up. It was owing to their having been out in damp weather, and then allowing their breeches to dry while in sitting position."

When the fur trade faded, some of the mountain men decided to mend their wild ways and become solid citizens: homesteaders, sodbusters, dirt farmers. Among these were Robert Newell, Joe Meek and Caleb Wilkins, who wrestled the first wagon through to Fort Walla Walla in 1840, thus officially opening the glory trail.

Glory there was, but trouble, too, in all its many shapes and sizes. In 1843, the emigrants had great difficulty with almost constant rain and raging rivers to cross. In 1852, there was so much dust that a driver could hardly see the wagon in front. There was cholera, as well, in 1852.

Cholera. The word struck terror into the hearts of emigrants at the jumping-off places. In the bad years, the disease struck swiftly and took a heavy toll. An emigrant wrote of his journey through the Platte Valley in 1852: "I have counted from 25 to 50 new graves daily."

Burial of the dead was a harsh ritual. It seemed that if wolves didn't dig up the bodies, Indians would. One man was buried in the middle of the road and wagons driven over the grave but Indians dug him up just the same and scalped him. A young man in a following train found feet sticking out of the grave. He wrote: "Every company that came along had to rebury him as the Indians kept digging him up."

Another emigrant wrote of how sad it was to bury relatives "without even a stick or rock to mark the resting place. Even if it could be marked, there was no assurance that they would be there 24 hours later. I have seen the remains of bodies that had been scratched out by the wolves and all of the flesh eaten off of the bones, which didn't seem, by the looks of them, to have been buried over 24 hours."

The popular conception of a wagon train on the Oregon Trail has it stretching from horizon to horizon. True, some were long enough to fill the trail for miles but the average train had only about 60 wagons.

Trail routine soon hardened into a pattern. Oxen were most favored as motive power. They were strong and hardy and were less attractive to Indian marauders than horses. Also, when hunger rode the trail, ox tasted better than horse.

Their major fault was that oxen don't walk; they *plod.* An emigrant grumbled: "All our teams are oxen, and our travel of consequence is vexatiously slow, not averaging more than 16 or 17 miles a day."

He was lucky; other reports indicate that the average daily trek was only 12 miles.

The party along the trail was usually awakened at daylight, because most wagonmasters liked to make a start by 7 A.M. An hour's rest at noon was customary. The afternoon's march usually ended by 5 P.M.

The day's work, however, was by no means over. Wheels had to be greased, metal tires re-set and brake blocks tightened. Some wheels had to be soaked in water overnight to tighten spokes. Whips had to be spliced out. Somebody had to herd the livestock all night long. There was plenty of livestock; most trains trailed sizeable cattle herds, as well as oxen and saddle horses.

As they ground along across the endless miles, emigrants grew wise in the ways of the trail. They learned, for instance, that animals are less likely to stray if regularly salted. They learned that articles worth less than a dollar a pound weren't worth hauling. They learned that the broad leaves of the thimbleberry bush served wonderfully well as toilet tissue.

There were no supermarkets along the trail, so supplies called for a good deal of thought. The lower section of the wagon, one emigrant recommended, should be packed with "flour, corn meal, sugar, dried fruit, sorghum molasses, butter, lard and other things in jugs and jars, well wrapped bacon and hams, some vegetables, home-made soap, stock salt,

➡

A welcome rest beside the trail provided an opportunity for a photographer to take this exceptional picture of a family moving west.

rosin and tar, medicine for both man and beast, extra bedding and clothing and other equipment. All had to be carefully levelled up, then a strong canvas cover formed a sort of second floor on which all sorts of things more commonly in use must be stored."

Often the grub box was kept at the front of the wagon; it contained a Dutch oven, coffee pot and kettle. An outside box was provided for halters, ropes, axe, shovel and hammer. In front was a rack for a gun. On one side was a small keg with a lid for drinking water, with a gourd dipper. At the rear hung a frying pan, water bucket and 10-gallon brass kettle. Beneath the wagon was suspended a tar bucket; tar served as lubricant for the wheels.

Watching a family prepare its wagon, one amused observer was moved to comment, "It reminded me of birds building a nest."

They learned little tricks along the trail, such as hanging milk in a covered bucket under the wagon in the morning. By evening, a small pat of butter floated on top.

Their trail diet ranged from succulent to nothing. A girl reported, "When Mother and I found some sourdock and other harmless weeds and made some greens, they were greatly relished. Our usual bill of fare continued to be bacon, gravy, bread and molasses. However, about every Sunday we had a mess of dried fruit; also we had dried corn now and then. Blackie still gave us a little milk, for which we were grateful. We occasionally were able to get some fresh meat, but we pined for vegetables and fruit."

But it wasn't all trouble and tribulation, disease and hunger. There are accounts left by some who made the long journey as children which indicate that the months on the trail were some of the most enjoyable times of their lives. (These were the lucky ones, of course.)

A covered wagon worked just fine for a game of Anty Over. Crossing Nebraska in the springtime, girls in the train liked to gather wildflowers. Soon wagons and baby sisters were decorated with garlands and bouquets. While walking along, they gathered sticks and twigs, too, looking ahead to the night's campfire.

The family pets came along, naturally. One dog's paws got so tender that its mistress contrived canvas shoes for it. The dog's paws were bathed and powdered before the shoes were put on. At first the dog tried every trick he knew to get them off, but failed. From that point on, his paws hurt less but his pride hurt more. The embarrassed dog wearing shoes became a joke along the trail.

The same dog was placed occasionally on horseback with a member of the party. Neither the horse nor the dog were exactly delighted about the arrangement, but the dog finally became resigned. Said an observer, "Rover did look comical sitting up there in John's lap, especially when barking at the squirrels along the way."

But Rover didn't always ride. A girl in the family said: "While we were moving along I could step out onto the brake block, then jump down onto the ground, and then Rover and I could have great times playing; even if the wagon should get ahead, we could soon overtake it by running a little. Consequently, I often walked for miles with Rover at my heels . . . After we were through, 'twas said that I had walked over half the way to Oregon."

Another account tells of a sick little girl whose life may have been saved by her cat along the trail when food was short. Each night the cat would bring a rabbit back to camp. The rabbit was made into stew and fed to the girl, who eventually recovered. So a cat, too, earned its passage over the trail . . .

There was time for courting, of course. A too-large train split up, with the Oregon group containing several attractive young women going ahead of the California segment. The trailing train included several single men, who almost daily rode out ahead "to hunt." Hunting was good and several weddings took place before the trails divided.

Across the treeless prairies, cooking fuel was hard to come by, so emigrants learned to burn a staple of the plains—buffalo chips, which, according to a pioneer, "made good hot fires and did not need any chopping up." The chips burned like peat. An amused emigrant wrote, "For two days past we have been cooking with buffalo chips. I think with Col. Russell that it is rather a hard matter that the buffalo should furnish the meat and then the fuel to cook it with but nature seems to have so ordered."

Most of the emigrants worried about Indians; much of their worry was wasted. There is a standard scene in the Western movie in which Indians encircle a wagon train and shoot it out with desperate pioneers, just before the U.S. Cavalry arrives. It makes dandy film footage but it never happened.

At least, there is no record of it ever happening along the Oregon Trail. Indians ran off a few head of stock once in a while and stole a rifle or two but that seems to have been the extent of their depredations. Some pioneers suspected that Indians burned grass along the trail to starve stock, but the deed might just as well have been done by white traders, who then could hope to buy hungry cattle for a low price.

There are recorded instances in which Indians actually helped the emigrants. When the Longmire party was traversing Washington, an Indian band followed closely for days, scaring some members of the party half to death. But when the Indians discovered that the party was in doubt as to which road to take, instead of attacking with bloodcurdling whoops, they tried to show them the right way!

For some unlucky ones, the trail was a brutal experience which they wished only to blot from memory. Others, like Ezra Meeker, remained fascinated by the adventure to the end of their days.

Meeker came west behind a team of oxen in 1852. In 1906, trying to stir up interest in preservation of the historic route, Meeker made the oxcart journey again, painting inscriptions on landmarks along the way. He repeated the trip in 1910. In 1916, he covered most of the trail by automobile. In 1924, at age 94, he did it again, this time by airplane.

Ezra Meeker died in Seattle in 1928. His wagon and giant oxen—the latter thoroughly stuffed—are in the basement of the fascinating Washington Historical Society Museum, Tacoma.

Meeker left another mark. The town of Puyallup was platted by him. He wanted to give his town a name unlike any other in the world. He succeeded. (The state has many other odd place names, though, with origins just as odd. The town of Pe Ell, for instance, was supposed to be named "Pierre" but Indian pronunciation changed "r"s to "l"s. Anacortes by rights should have been "Annacurtis," since the town was named in honor of Anna Curtis, wife of an early settler. Pasco got its name because of the town's resemblance to a Peruvian mining center, Cerro de Pasco.)

Meeker's great effort to sanctify the Oregon Trail may have increased the stature of a neglected artifact of the frontier heritage: the ox. Generally the mighty feats of oxen have been overlooked by historians and poets of the westward movement. (A notable exception, of course, is Babe, Paul Bunyan's blue monster.) The Oregon Trail would have been much more difficult without ox power.

The working ox of those days was no bony, puny male cow. He was a huge, muscular beast who looked strong enough to pull anything that wasn't cemented down . . . and a few things that were. The size of Meeker's oxen in the Tacoma museum is startling to modern eyes; one suspects that they don't make draft animals like that any more.

Or men like Ezra Meeker, either.

Ezra Meeker, with his oxen Dave and Dandy and his dog, retraced the trail from Washington to Missouri.

Meeker's wagon has been in the museum since 1915, but it wasn't until 1963 that a batch of his private papers was discovered under the wagon's floorboards. The papers are now in the museum's reference library.

(Speaking of historic wagons, one of the finest collections in the country was put on display during 1975 at the Yakima Valley Museum, Yakima; it was the Gannon collection of Mabton.)

THE STRANGE STORY OF WILLIE KEIL

All kinds came over the trail, the old and the young, the rich and the poor, the sick and the healthy. Many died along the way. There was even one who was dead before he started.

His name was Willie Keil. His trek west in a tin-lined coffin filled with 100-proof whiskey is one of the most bizarre tales of frontier history.

The macabre yarn was told well by Lee Ryland in a 1968 issue of "Northwest Magazine."

Dr. William Keil, leader of a religious sect called the Bethelites, was preparing to shepherd his group west from Bethel, Missouri, in 1855. His 19-year-old son, Willie, had been training his three-yoke ox team for two years and his stern father had given him permission to drive the lead wagon.

But with the departure date approaching, Willie fell ill; doctors called his ailment malaria. From his sickbed, Willie extracted from his father the promise that, malaria or no, the boy would go west with the Bethelites. Dr. Keil immediately ordered the lead wagon converted to an ambulance.

Willie's condition grew worse. Four days before scheduled jump-off, Willie died.

His strong-willed father rallied swiftly from the blow. He had promised his faithful followers that he would take them to a "cool, green and beautiful land beside a rushing river." He had promised Willie that the boy would accompany the group to the distant paradise.

Now he resolved to keep both promises. He ordered the elders to build a coffin and line it with tin. The elders muttered and shook their heads, but complied.

Then Dr. Keil ordered a load of Golden Rule whiskey, poured it into the coffin, put Willie in, ordered the lid nailed down and the coffin loaded into the lead wagon.

The train left Bethel, Missouri, on the appointed day in May, 1855, with the corpse of Willie Keil sloshing around in alcohol in the lead wagon.

Many in the group were fearful that no good could come of such a sacrilegious act; they felt cold hands on the napes of their necks.

Their fears were unfounded. Willie's coffin and Willie went to the Oregon Country unmolested. Once, though, west of Fort Laramie, there may have been a close thing, if accounts of the episode are to be believed.

An Indian war party suddenly appeared to threaten the wagon train. The doom-criers among the Bethelites expected the worst as a painted brave rode slowly toward the lead wagon and gestured at the black coffin.

Dr. Keil opened the box. The brave took one look and drew back; his horse reared. At a signal from the brave, each member of the war party rode by and gazed into the coffin.

Then the Indians turned away and rode slowly out of sight.

It was on a wet, chilly November day that the Keil party arrived at Paradise—Willapa, near the Washington coast. There Willie Keil was finally buried.

Paradise proved to be less than perfect for the Bethelites. The wet climate defeated them before long, so Dr. Keil sought out a new haven in Oregon's Willamette Valley and named it "Aurora," after his daughter. It is Aurora today.

But Willie Keil, who crossed the plains in a coffin, was left at Willapa. What remains of Willie Keil is there today, near the present towns of Raymond and Menlo. Some modern highway maps make note of the gravesite. Only a few of those who read "Willie Keil's Grave" on the maps know of his weird journey along the Oregon Trail.

★

The Oregon Trail served as the main road to the Northwest for most emigrants until 1869. In that year, the Union Pacific railroad reached San Francisco and the iron horse quickly superseded the ox. Pioneers headed west rode the U.P. to San Francisco, then took boat passage to Washington. The trickle became a flood.

What happened in the way of human migration and progress and development in the American West from the second quarter of the 19th century to the first quarter of the 20th is without precedent or parallel in the history of man's march across the earth. The speed of the westward movement was nothing less than fantastic.

Think of it: a single individual could and did live through the whole empire-building, nation-changing process.

In 1835, a young Indian left the Rocky Mountains with a Flathead delegation and walked and rode and boated to St. Louis in search of priests who would bring the white man's religion to the Indians of the West.

That same Indian became a respected Montana cattleman, watched the Northern Pacific railroad thunder past his house for 40 years and finally died in 1919, after World War I, when the American West had become just another vacation destination.

The pace of change stuns the imagination. If only there had been more time, could white men and red men have learned to adapt to each other? Could the different cultures have peacefully merged, given a few more years?

The question without an answer continues to haunt modern America.

THEY CAME TO STAY

After they reached trail's end, it was like this:

Nathaniel Hill, who settled on a donation claim on Whidbey Island in 1852, wrote to his brother in Sonoma, California: "Send down Will's rifle and fixings belonging to it. We must shoot our living and we want arms to protect us from the Indians. We believe our prospects good . . . we want you to come up immediately . . . bring the rifle . . . two pairs of thick shoes for me . . . fish hooks . . . a lot of seeds and plants . . . a jug of ink . . . two dozen pairs of woolen socks for Humph and myself . . . if flour is down to $20 per barrel, bring two barrels . . . a butcher knife or two . . . one of those porcelain pots . . . needles and thread and beeswax . . . a ball of twine . . . castor oil and salts and a little quinine . . . a box of tea . . . Dutch oven . . . bag of salt . . . ginger, pepper, mustard, cloves and cinnamon . . . scythe and snead . . . about 50 lbs. common tobacco to trade with the Indians, two dozen or three of looking glasses with sliding lids . . . a few pocket combs . . . my razor and shaving cup and brush."

★

A census in 1849 found only 304 persons north of the Columbia River. The 1850 census showed 1049.

Willie Keil came west in a coffin filled with whiskey and was buried near Willapa.

★

The John R. Jackson house near Chehalis is one of Washington's oldest standing residences. The Covington house in a Vancouver park is another.

★

For a time after the arrival of railroads, more than twice as many emigrants came to Washington as to California. During the first year after statehood, Washington surpassed Oregon in population and hasn't been headed since.

★

Port Angeles was the first town site after Washington, D.C., to be planned by the federal government; population at the time was 10.

★

Francis Pettygrove founded two cities: Portland, Oregon, and Port Townsend, Washington. His weapon against the Indians was an ivory flute; they considered him a medicine man.

★

The country around Puget Sound attracted many persons of Scandinavian descent. Finns formed a colony at Hoquiam, the Dutch in Nooksack Valley. Swedes and Norwegians descended like locusts, attracted by the familiar water and woods; their sturdy descendants remain in large numbers all over the state.

★

For nearly 20 years, men had to back-pack supplies from Hoh River to Forks on the Olympic Peninsula, a distance of 42 miles. A man carrying 80 pounds in to the lumber camps got regular pay but if he could carry 160 pounds, he got two men's pay.

★

John Huelsdonk homesteaded 24 miles from Forks along the Hoh River. He carried a stove in from Forks on his back and to make a load,

A homestead in Washington might look like this one near Wilbur. Note young orchard beyond house. They don't build swings the way they used to, either.

assorted groceries were stuffed in, including a 50-pound sack of flour. The only problem, John said, was that the sack kept shifting around.

★

The Inland Empire was closed to settlement during the Indian wars. When the territory was opened up again, settlers flowed from west to east; no other part of the U.S. was populated in this direction.

★

Slow transportation made government especially difficult. Hiram "Okanogan" Smith, delegate to an early territorial legislature, lived in the Okanogan Valley only 200 miles from Olympia as the crow flies. No crow, Smith needed two weeks for the trip and small wonder. He had to tramp through British Columbia, catch a boat on the Fraser River and transfer at Vancouver, B.C., to a steamer which then carried him to Olympia. On his return trip home, his baggage included small apple trees and peach seeds which became the first orchard in the Okanogan Valley.

★

The first Seattle settlers landed from a ship on an unknown shore and were met by friendly Indians (including Chief Sealth), just like the Pilgrims at Plymouth Rock.

★

Settlers had difficulty finding places to hide valuables, since houses and hollow trees could easily burn. They finally used tree stumps. Many years later, valuable caches were found in stumps and some may still await discovery.

★

Mail for Washington settlers in the early days was addressed to "Puget Sound Country" or "Fort Vancouver" if they lived west of the Cascade Mountains, to "Walla Walla Country" or "Fort Colville" if they lived east of the mountains. They tell a barely believable tale of one Wesley Smith, who carried mail on foot along the beach from Neah Bay to La Push. For amusement on his route, he played an ocarina; seals, attracted by the music, followed Smith to get more of it. Once the mail carrier met a bear and some letters delivered that day had marks of bear's teeth.

★

The lining of a deer's belly, settlers quickly discovered, made a fine window, keeping out the weather and letting in some light. They chinked their chimneys with clay from the riverbanks, then had to keep fires going all the time to keep the masonry dry in the wet climate.

★

A grandmother liked to tell the story of her first garden in Cowlitz County. She had only a precious cupful of seed corn which she had carefully carried overland; no more could be had. While she was digging to plant the corn, her rooster sneaked up and gobbled down the kernels. Without hesitation, Grandma butchered the rooster, snatched the corn from its crop and planted her garden.

★

A homesteader in Hoh Valley on the Olympic Peninsula had cattle to take to market in Port Townsend, a two-week drive through the forest. During his first afternoon at home after the trip, he shot four cougars and netted more money from cougar hides and bounty than he received from sale of his cattle.

★

The winter of 1861–62 was terribly cold. Ice rarely forms at Cathlamet on the Columbia, but that winter the little steamer *Multnomah* was frozen in along the great river's shore. But homesteaders didn't despair. Six weeks of bitterly cold weather were filled with sleigh riding, games and dancing. From the hills of Cathlamet to the river, men, women, boys, girls, white and Indian, coasted continually on sleds. When food grew scarce, a horse was butchered and served as roast beef. In the log houses and in the lodges, great fires blazed and "there was nothing of sorrow or fear."

PROVING UP PARADISE

Said one homesteader: "The government bet us 160 acres against five years of our lives that we could not stick it out." Anyone who took up a

➤

Many early settlers in Washington carved homesteads out of the woods, thus creating "stump ranches."

homestead had to live on it for five years before it was "proved up," as the saying went, and became the homesteader's property.

For most it was a hard life. Some, of course, didn't make it, but others found they had little choice but to stay and "tough it out." Rhymed one of these:

"I tried to get out of the country
"But poverty forced me to stay;
"Until I became an old settler —
"Now nothing could drive me away."

Some early settlers in Washington actually lived in stumps. This one, of course, is an improved, upper class, solid cedar stump with double-hung window.

Living conditions were usually primitive. There is more than one recorded instance of families living in hollowed-out tree stumps! Like the McAllisters in Nisqually County: "During father's trips he had seen two stumps standing only a few feet apart and he laughingly told mother that she might live in them. Thus the idea came to mother and she so insisted that father clean them out, put on a roof, that he did, and we moved in, a family of eight persons. Mother said they found them to be very comfortable, indeed. She used the burned out roots for cupboards and closets and so we lived in them until fall; during this time father had built a log house . . ."

Even when a permanent house was built, it was often crude. Sawed boards were expensive, so floors in the cabins often were dirt, sometimes spread with wall-to-wall gravel. Said a Chelan County pioneer: "The women wore moccasins and their sweeping was done with a rake. They would ask each other, 'Have you done your house raking today?' When they prospered and could afford a floor . . . the women put on shoes again. They stepped high and had to become accustomed to walking in them . . . I picked snakes out of my dresser drawers . . . I carried water from the lake . . . Only the strong and sturdy toughed out the early days . . . I pause to wonder at the cultivated, educated people who lived in little log cabins and later what cheap people lived in the big houses."

A Kittitas County pioneer remembers: "The home of the early settler was of necessity a workshop. My father brought from The Dalles, Oregon, once a year, a side of sole leather and one of upper leather. He made wooden lasts for our shoes. Pegs were made from chokecherry wood. Mother sewed the uppers and father put the shoes together. It took two days to make one pair. I can say this for the shoes, they wore. Mother made our hats out of wheat straw. I can see her now, braiding and sewing the wheat into big wide-brimmed hats. The coffee mill was used to grind the wheat and corn when flour supplies were exhausted. It was truly whole wheat flour, for nothing could be taken out, and everything but the stalks was in the bread."

★

As is so often the case when humans find themselves in a deprived, difficult situation for an extended period, there was good feeling among them and humor was often the saving grace.

A salty oldtimer put it this way: "Nobody had nothing and we all used it."

One way of earning a few dollars was to cut cordwood for the steamboats which churned up and down the rivers until the railroads came. Settlers cut wood and stacked it along the banks; steamboat captains swung in and bought it as they needed it.

The latch string was always out. From a Lewis County pioneer: "Hungry travelers were welcomed into every home they passed, and it was customary to feed them. It was not unusual for settlers, returning to their homes, to find that visitors had come and gone, helped themselves to food and lodging perhaps, but custom decreed that the dishes be washed and the unused food replaced as found."

Another wrote: "In those days, newcomers found themselves welcome almost anywhere they stopped. An extra pair of willing hands could always be used, and new people brought fresh topics for conversation. There was also the chance that they might become neighbors and help the community to get started. Growth of the settlement depended on newcomers who might be tempted to stay."

A sense of humor might not have been absolutely necessary for survival, but it was a great help. Said one tart tongue: "If you congregate a hundred Americans anywhere in this Northwest, they immediately lay out a city, frame a state constitution and apply for admission to the Union, while 25 of them become candidates for the United States Senate."

Humor even intruded on the solemn business of court proceedings. In a region where men were scarce (and where women, of course, weren't considered fit for jury service), it was necessary to take some of the prisoners out of jail and put them on the jury in order to conduct the trial of others!

James Nesmith (later Senator Nesmith) said, "The pioneer men are courageous; they endure much hardship. The pioneer women are even more courageous; they endure the hardships and they also endure the men."

A political remark, if ever there was one . . .

Even in moments of danger, humor cropped up. One small group of pioneers had been having trouble with Indians stealing cattle. (It was the custom in those days to blame most unexplained catastrophes on Indians.) So the men made a fortification of rocks near the corral, armed themselves and settled down watchfully for the night. One recorded the adventure: "Having arranged the cattle guard, our resolves were of little use when tired nature resolutely claimed her own. We awoke in the morning to find

The University of Washington student body, 1884–1885, aprons and all. The only beard-wearer is the University president.

our heads and bodies in communicating distance of each other, and ourselves very much refreshed by an unbroken night's sleep."

The country changed rapidly and the units of government adjusted their neat little lines to fit. A Lincoln County pioneer said with a grin: "It wasn't necessary for me to move to different states, territories, or counties, as they came to me. I lived in Washington Territory, Washington State, Spokane, Stevens and Lincoln Counties without moving from the house in which I first lived here."

It's a safe bet, though, that the confusion didn't prevent his tax bills from arriving on time.

SCHOOL DAYS, CRUEL DAYS

Unlike today, girls in pioneer times usually got more formal education than boys. The reason was simple: boys left school early to help support their families by working in harvest fields, logging camps and sawmills. Money was scarce; the need for education ran a poor second.

Children usually walked or rode horses to school. Where modern schools might have a gymnasium, pioneer schools usually had a barn. (In some districts, transportation is anything but easy even now. Tonasket school busses must collect children from an area larger than the state of Rhode Island.) The school year was giddily short—sometimes no longer than three months. Winter was favored for the school "year" because there was less work at home for the children in that season.

Physical education and athletic programs consisted mainly of recess games like Drop the Handkerchief, Anty Over and Pom-Pom-Pullaway. To say nothing of Prisoner's Base. (There is no record of state tournaments in any of these thrilling sports.)

The girls wore calico dresses to school, often with big aprons to protect them; gingham was saved for Sunday wear.

In those days, school boards found their teachers here, there and everywhere. Usually teachers were those who had more education, if only a year or two more, than the oldest student. Often the teacher was a teen-ager; sometimes she was a young mother.

Wrote one child: "In 1854 my mother taught the first school in Pierce

School busses aren't new, either, as demonstrated by this 1883 photo taken at Newport. Find the nervous bus driver, complete with twitching mustache.

County . . . Mother at this time had a small baby, so she would assign the children, in turn, to care for the baby while she taught the rest of the pupils . . ."

The school buildings were quaint, to say the least. From San Juan County comes this account: "I remember that the first school was built of hewed logs with shake roof. It had gun holes all around. This log school was built during the boundary dispute. Thinking that because it was being put up by American settlers . . . it was being built for use as a blockhouse, the English commander ordered it to be torn down, but was overruled and embarrassed when, upon its completion, a full-blooded Englishman from Victoria was imported to teach their children . . ."

In those days, as now, experience was an excellent teacher. From a Lewis County boy: "My first lesson in school was when I went in and sat down at the end of a split cedar log. When another boy came in and wanted to sit down, instead of getting up and moving over, I just slid over for him. I never forgot to be polite after that, and not to try sliding about on a rough bench."

Hubbart Stowell earned his teaching spurs in King County. He wrote: "Those of us who graduated from the high school were given third grade certificates, good for a year. In October of 1887 (I was 16 years old in June of that year), I went to teach a four-month term of school at Bellevue. I had eight pupils, five in one family . . . while the three Rs and geography and history comprised the curriculum, I was able to teach algebra.

"I received thirty dollars a month and paid ten dollars a month for my board. I was rich. The school opened at 9 o'clock, closed at noon, opened at 1 o'clock and closed at 4 o'clock, with recesses both morning and afternoon.

"My next school was at Fidalgo, near LaConnor. There was an 8 by 10 school house with a 4 by 6 blackboard and an excellent eraser made of sheepskin with fur outside. I had 20 pupils here. The boys chewed tobacco, used rough language, and in deportment were sadly lacking. They sat lounging in their seats. The teacher preceding me had sometimes gone to sleep at noon and remained so until the middle of the afternoon . . ."

But not all the teachers snored on the job. Some of the one-room schools were surprisingly good. One pioneer student in Klickitat discovered that "an industrious student could review last year's lessons, study his present ones, and learn next year's by listening to the recitals in front of the room."

Old Rosedale school in Pierce County had an excellent pupil-teacher ratio.

THE PROHIBITED PIONEER

The 80-wagon party led by Michael Simmons came west in 1844, pointing toward the Willamette Valley, but it was not to be. When these hopeful pioneers reached Oregon, they discovered to their great surprise that they were not welcome.

One member of the party was not only unwelcome, but a law of the Oregon Territory actually excluded him. Because of that law, the Puget Sound area acquired some of its most distinguished pioneer families. Oregon's loss, through a quirk of history, was Washington's everlasting gain.

Simmons, a swashbuckling Irishman, was angry. George Bush, the prohibited pioneer, had been a leader on the trail; his quiet strength had helped the group over many hard bumps. In addition, Bush was a prosperous man and he had loaned money to those in need. It was expected that Bush would be a bulwark on which others could lean in the new land, just as he had been along the trail. Way back in Missouri, members of the train had voted to include the Bush family. They had been given no cause to regret their action and some of them, at least, weren't about to desert George Bush now.

So the friends of George Bush moved across the Columbia and squatted for a time near Washougal, while Simmons made several forays into the Puget Sound area looking for a likely spot.

Dr. McLoughlin of Fort Vancouver took pains to point out to Simmons that the company did not consider the land north of the Columbia, particularly the Puget Sound area, open to settlement by Americans.

Simmons and Bush decided to go north anyway. At their departure, McLoughlin gave Simmons a letter to the Hudson's Bay post at Fort Nisqually ordering that the Americans be supplied grain and potatoes from company stores, which were to be charged to Fort Vancouver. McLoughlin was like that.

★

In time, George Bush developed a farm that was the envy of his neighbors. In 1852, he further proved his mettle. A large number of emigrants came off the Oregon Trail that year in desperate shape. Unusually bad conditions along the trail caused most of the parties to arrive hungry; many had even eaten the seed they had intended to plant to make their first crop in the West.

In that year, Bush had a bumper crop of wheat, corn, beans and pumpkins. By selling it to the starving newcomers for what the traffic would bear, he could have made himself rich, but instead he gave it away. All he asked was that the recipients repay him in kind some day, if and when they had crops of their own.

As the Tumwater area attracted more settlers, some of them tried to force George Bush off his claim for the same reason that he had been driven out of the Willamette Valley; people like George Bush weren't eligible to take land under the homestead law.

But his friends rose up in righteous wrath and stirred such an uproar that it was heard in the U.S. Congress and a special act was hurried through insuring that George Bush and his heirs could keep their good land forever.

Why did George Bush have to leave the Willamette Valley? Why did he have trouble holding onto his Tumwater homestead?

One reason only: George Bush was a Negro.

★

Any thoughtful reader of history must grow weary of reading about the exploits of "white" persons in the West. The impression swells and festers that nothing happened on the frontier unless it happened to a "white" person.

"The first white woman to cross the Rockies . . ."

"The first white child born in the Oregon Country . . ."

"The first white man to explore the lower Columbia . . ."

Et cetera, ad nauseum. Most history books are shot through with this kind of smug nonsense.

Thus it is with wry satisfaction that a writer of Washington history can set down: "The first white child born to a homesteader family in the Puget Sound area was a Negro."

The child was born to George Bush and his wife not long after their arrival.

Bush Prairie in Thurston County was named after George Bush. There is feeling in the state that more honor is due the Bush name. Each state is allowed two statues in Statuary Hall in the Capitol in Washington, D.C. The state of Washington has had only one, that of Dr. Marcus Whitman. A strong nominee for the second statue has been George Bush.

Over the years, throughout the United States, one of the surest ways to stay out of history books was to be born with black skin. Washington's George Bush is a rare, ironic exception. Without doubt George Bush was an important pioneer, a truly good man, but so were a fair number of

124

whites whom history has forgotten. Somehow the name of George Bush survived in the annals of the state not in spite of his blackness, but because of it. One can't be sure whether this fact indicates something about Washington, or about George Bush.

The Northwest's first census in 1850 turned up 13,294 persons, including 110 called "colored."

It may come as a surprise to many modern Washingtonians, but the thriving town of Centralia in the southwestern part of the state was founded by a Negro. In 1850, a donation land claim was filed on the site of Centralia by a man from Missouri who had a slave named George Washington.

Later George Washington was set free and adopted as a son by his former master. In 1852, the former slave bought the former master's claim for $6000. He built a home, platted a town, sold lots and donated land for a city park—"George Washington Park," of course.

Within 15 years, 2000 lots had been sold and the town Washington had first called "Centerville" was thriving. But in 1893, when a panic threw the nation into an economic skid, George Washington had to fight again for the life of his town.

Hauling rice, sugar and flour from Portland by the ton, he eased the hunger of many of his neighbors. He loaned money with the understanding that it would be paid back with no interest if and when the borrower got on his feet again. He gave work to many Centralia citizens.

The town was saved and George Washington is usually given credit for saving it.

His end came suddenly in 1905 when he was thrown from a buggy and killed. He died at age 88, a wealthy and respected businessman. The town recognized his worth with the largest funeral in Centralia's history to that point. The mayor proclaimed a day of mourning. Services were conducted in a church built on land Washington had donated; burial was in a cemetery he had provided for the city.

Early in 1968, the State Capitol Museum in Olympia presented a special display of "relics and reminders" of two pioneer Negro families— the Bush family of Bush Prairie and the Washington family of Centralia. As a supplement, an extensive bibliography of Negro history in the Northwest was prepared by Mrs. Randall Mills of the Washington State Library.

George Washington was most instrumental in the founding of Centralia. History does not record the name of his dog.

(Incidentally, there are pixies among us who think that George Washington of Centralia passed up a sensational opportunity. If he had named the town "George," then he could have been known as George Washington from George, Washington. Chances like this don't flutter by every day.)

Another prominent Washingtonian who happened to be a Negro was Horace R. Cayton, who published a Seattle newspaper devoted to political events. As the city's Negro population grew, more and more space was devoted to Negro-oriented news. In 1917, as the country frothed with war hysteria and fear of radicalism, Cayton published a front page story dealing in detail with the lynching of a Negro in Mississippi.

Immediately cancellations of subscriptions and advertising began to flood in. Three months later, the newspaper died.

A pioneer hotel owner of Seattle was William Gross, a Negro. William Owen Bush, a son of George Bush, was a member of the first state legislature.

A pioneer in Wahkiakum County near Cathlamet remembered: "At first there were no schools here. Then a school was held at the Birnie house, with six pupils. Mr. Powell, who was part Negro, taught."

★

Negroes finally are beginning to emerge from the dustbins of the past. Those who write Washington history a century from now may be able to point to a landmark, the elections of 1968.

On the ballots were a candidate for lieutenant governor, Arthur Fletcher of Pasco, and a candidate for governor, Jack Tanner of Tacoma. Both are Negroes. Early in 1969, President Nixon appointed Fletcher to one of the highest posts ever held by a Negro in the U.S., assistant secretary of labor.

SUGGESTED READING

Andrews, Ralph W.; PHOTOGRAPHERS OF THE FRONTIER WEST; Superior; 1965.

Andrews; Ralph W.; PICTURE GALLERY PIONEERS; Superior; 1964.

Florin, Lambert; (any and all of the ghost town series); Superior.

Holbrook, Stewart H.; FAR CORNER; Macmillan; 1952.

Johnson, Jalmar; BUILDERS OF THE NORTHWEST; Dodd, Mead; 1963 (George Bush).

Judson, Phoebe Goodell; A PIONEER'S SEARCH FOR AN IDEAL HOME; Washington State Historical Society; 1966.

McDonald, Lucile; COAST COUNTRY: A HISTORY OF SOUTHWEST WASHINGTON; Binfords & Mort; 1966.

Salisbury, Albert and Jane; HERE ROLLED THE COVERED WAGONS; Superior; 1948.

WESTWARD ON THE OREGON TRAIL; American Heritage; 1962.

This drawing of Narcissa Whitman was made after her death from descriptions offered by friends and family. She is usually portrayed as a blonde goddess.

Chapter Five ★

The Women
BLOOD ON THE RYE GRASS

A cold, damp shroud of fog hung over Waiilatpu at dawn and an ominous quiet lay heavily on the awakening land. Cayuse Indian lodges lurked like crouching ghosts in the trees by the river, first dimly visible, then fading into empty grayness as the dismal vapor loosened its clammy grip for a lingering moment, then tightened down again.

To the 70 white persons at the Whitman mission, the dawning day offered only bleak prospects and depressingly few of those. It promised to be a day good only for the contemplation of suicide . . . or murder.

The fateful dice were thrown and came up murder.

On this day, November 29, 1847, the Cayuse chose to kill and forever ringed the date with blood on the calendar of Washington history and scrawled in funereal black beneath it: "Whitman Massacre."

★

There was a belief among the Cayuse that a medicine man, or *tewat*, should make only one mistake. If a patient died after treatment, the offending *tewat* soon died, too, usually at the hands of a vengeful father or brother or son. It followed then that a Cayuse *tewat* was a hesitant healer; he took on only those patients he thought he could cure.

Dr. Marcus Whitman, medical missionary, had learned in a different school, from other teachers, in a society far removed from the wild environment in which he found himself in 1847. Whitman had been taught that a doctor existed only to heal the sick. No matter how difficult the disease or terrible the injury, he responded when called and did his best. A doctor learned to live with death. He had no magic in his satchel, only a smattering of science, skill and sympathy. Dr. Whitman was no *tewat,* no witch doctor, and he did not care to be. The Cayuse simply didn't understand . . .

On November 29, 1847, the blood-ringed date, Chief Tilaukait lost another son to an epidemic of measles which had been sweeping the territory in the wake of heavy immigration along the Oregon Trail. Dr. Whitman had treated the boy, as he had treated many others, Indian and white.

Most of the white children lived; most of the Indians died. Perhaps the Indians died because it was their habit to follow Dr. Whitman's treatment with a sweat bath and a plunge into the cold river; perhaps they had less natural immunity than the whites. No matter. The dark-skinned children died and the light-skinned lived and the contrast did not escape the Cayuse chiefs.

The Indians had other grievances. They had been promised payment for the land which they had given up for the mission site; the promise had not been kept, unless one considers frequent lectures on their lazy, sinful ways a sort of partial payment. Also, Dr. Whitman had been too free in allowing the use of poison to kill predatory animals. Indians became deathly sick when they ate the poisoned meat. A severe cathartic was used to discourage theft of melons; Indians suffered as a result.

Apparently Dr. Whitman's wife, Narcissa, was anything but a favorite with the Indians at the mission. They felt that she was aloof and not really interested in their welfare. The Cayuse were known as a proud, even haughty people who had never asked for white teachers. Whitman failed to gain and hold their confidence. In disputes, they felt that Whitman usually took the side of whites. The doctor, they became convinced, was giving Oregon away to white settlers.

With the seeds of trouble thus planted, it was inevitable that trouble-makers would appear to cultivate and harvest. In this case, the busiest were Joe Lewis and Nicholas Finley, half-breeds who lived near the mission. They passed snarling among the Cayuse and warned of the great stream of white immigration flowing in canvas-covered wagons through the passes in the Shining Mountains. Hadn't Dr. Whitman himself, they hissed, led

This peaceful vista once echoed to the horrified cries of massacre victims at the Whitman Mission. Pond at left was built by Dr. Whitman; original buildings were among trees to the right of pond. The rail fence running diagonally through the picture borders a restored section of the Oregon Trail. The building at the far right is the visitors' center. The hill on which the photographer stood to take this picture is the one where Narcissa Whitman often watched for the return of her husband. During the massacre, Indian scouts used the vantage point to watch for advancing soldiers who didn't come.

the first great train of wagons only a few years before? And now the white *tewat* was poisoning their children, their precious sons, to prepare the way for his kind, to wipe out the Cayuse and the Nez Perce and the Walla Walla and the Umatilla in order to steal the Indian hunting grounds. They had seen it happen in the mountains, muttered Lewis and Finley, and on the great prairies east of the mountains and now it was going to happen here, in The Place of the Rye Grass. Hissing and snarling, hissing and snarling . . .

On the morning of November 29, Dr. Whitman was called to the burial ground, where he shivered in the cold fog and read from the Bible over the grave of Chief Tilaukait's son. They didn't kill the doctor then, but perhaps they had already decided to kill him.

Early on the afternoon of November 29, Narcissa Whitman came from the pantry with a glass of milk for one of the children, then stopped short.

In the kitchen stood Tilaukait and Tomahas, another chief. Her first glance told her that a long-feared moment had arrived. Doom was in their eyes.

Harshly they asked to see Dr. Whitman. Narcissa hurried into the sitting room where the doctor was preparing medicine.

"They're here!" she whispered tightly. "Tilaukait and Tomahas! They want to talk to you! Don't go, husband! Don't go!"

He rose slowly and wiped his hands, then touched her. "I must. Bolt the door, Narcissa."

Dr. Whitman stepped into the kitchen to face his enemies. Behind him, his wife dutifully bolted the door.

Young John Sager, an orphan adopted with his six brothers and sisters by the Whitmans, was in the kitchen winding twine on a spool. As Tilaukait talked angrily to the doctor, Tomahas edged into position and brought his tomahawk down twice in murderous blows on the doctor's skull.

Frantically John Sager clambered toward a pistol on the wall. Tilaukait snatched a rifle from under his blanket and killed the boy.

Bleeding terribly from his head wounds, Dr. Whitman struggled against Tomahas and stumbled through a doorway to the outside. Tomahas struck him again; Tilaukait shot him in the throat. Leaving the doctor for dead, the chiefs ran into the yard, where scattered whites were working. Indian blankets fell to expose guns which quickly found white targets. Shouts of the frightened and screams of the wounded and dying sent panic flashing like a storm wind through the settlement.

Narcissa Whitman ran through the blood-smeared kitchen and lifted her dying husband out of the mud. With the help of others, she dragged him into the sitting room and put him on a couch as life ebbed quickly from him.

On this memorable day, the mission was crowded, but then, it usually was. Twenty-three persons were living in the main mission house, eight more in the blacksmith shop, 29 in the "emigrant house," 12 in a cabin at the mission sawmill 20 miles away. There were two more—Lewis and Finley, the half-breeds, who occupied lodges on the mission grounds.

Despite the depressing weather, the day's work was bustling along when the first blow was struck. Several children were in the classroom where L. W. Saunders was teaching again after a vacation caused by the measles epidemic. Isaac Gilliland, tailor, was sewing on a suit of clothes for Dr. Whitman in the emigrant house. In the east wing of the mission house, Peter Hall was laying a floor. In the yard, Walter Marsh was operating a grist mill while four other men dressed a beef. There were more Indians than usual about the yard but everyone assumed that they had been attracted by the butchering of the beef. Not quite true; they had another kind of butchery in mind . . .

The school teacher, Saunders, was shot dead while trying to reach his wife in the emigrant house. One of the butchers fought fiercely with an axe but he died, too. Gilliland, the tailor, was killed at his work. Walter Marsh met his end in the grist mill.

Francis Sager, whose brother had been shot in the kitchen, was in the schoolroom when the attack began. With the other children, he hid in the rafters but Joe Lewis found him and soon young Francis was dead, too.

Then the horror flashed again into the mission house. A man named Kimball, who had been working on the beef in the yard, and Andrew Rodgers, who had been down by the river, ran to the mission house and were quickly admitted by Narcissa Whitman.

Then Narcissa found the courage to look through a window and was shot by an Indian standing on the schoolhouse steps. Screaming, she fell to the floor but soon regained her feet and staggered upstairs with Kimball, Rodgers and several children just as Indians burst into the living room.

An old musket was found in the attic; it served to hold off their attackers for a time. Catherine Sager wrote of the moment many years later: "For the space of an hour all was still as death except the low voice of Mr. R. engaged in prayer for the safety of all." Then, from the lips of old Tamsucky, a trusted Indian, they heard an ominous warning of still another threat—fire! Tamsucky said the rampaging Indians in the yard intended to burn down the mission house. They must go to the emigrant house where they would be safe.

Feverishly they discussed Tamsucky's proposal. The noises of the terror rolling around the mission buildings rose and fell, then leaped up again in wild outbursts. Was there a safe place left? It seemed unlikely and yet they must not give up; perhaps the first wave of horror would pass and sanity would return or help would arrive. No, they must not give up . . .

Narcissa and Rodgers decided to go down to the living room. There Mrs. Whitman had to look on the horribly mutilated face of her husband, now dead. Feeling weak from her own wound, she lay down on a settee. Rodgers and Joe Lewis, who seemed to be having second thoughts, carried her into the yard . . . to her death.

Firing broke out almost as soon as they left the house. Rodgers dropped his end of the settee and fell. Narcissa, shot at least twice more, slipped off into the mud.

An Indian ran up to her as she lay dying, lifted her by her golden hair and struck her in the face with his riding whip.

In horror's aftermath, quiet oozed in. As the day wore on, there was reason to hope that rage was spent and the terror ended. The hope lived only until Tuesday's dawn . . .

Kimball had stayed upstairs in the mission house with the children throughout the night. Just before dawn on Tuesday, he slipped out and went toward the river to get them water, but he was discovered and killed. Later on Tuesday, James Young drove unsuspectingly toward the mission with a load of lumber from the sawmill. He was the second to perish on Tuesday.

And still the horror would not end. Two sick boys, Crocket Bewley and Amos Sales, foolishly criticized the Cayuse for the massacre several days later. They became the 12th and the 13th to die.

Peter Hall, who had been working in the mission house when the massacre began, managed to escape to Fort Walla Walla. After reporting the uprising, he set out along the north bank of the Columbia for Fort Vancouver. He did not arrive. Perhaps he drowned; perhaps the Cayuse caught up with him.

But some did escape. The most harrowing tale was told by Josiah Osborn, his wife and three children. During the attack, Osborn pried up floor boards in a room in the mission house. Crouched under the floor throughout the afternoon and evening, hardly daring to breathe, they listened to the moans of the dying and the stomping and yelling of looting

Indians only inches over their heads.

Reported Josiah Osborn in a letter about five months later: "When it had become dark, and all was quiet, we concluded to leave everything, take our children and start for the Fort, which was twenty-five miles distant, knowing that if we remained until morning death would be our portion. Taking John Law on my back and A. Rogers in my arms, we started. The first step we made outside was in the blood of an orphan boy. Some of the murdered had their heads split open—some were lying in the mud, disemboweled. This night we traveled only two miles. We hid in the brush, and then spent another mournful day in the Indian country. When night came, finding that Margaret was unable to travel, I took John Law on my back and started for Walla Walla, yet twenty miles distant. When I had arrived within six miles of the Fort, I laid down in the wet grass till morning. About 9 o'clock I reached the Fort where Mr. McBean met me, and told me that he had reported me among the dead. He gave me about a half pint of tea, and two small biscuit . . ."

Eventually the Osborn family was reunited and brought to Fort Walla Walla. The Cayuse held 47 captives for a month. On December 29, the captives were exchanged for 62 blankets, 63 shirts, 12 guns, 600 loads of ammunition, 37 pounds of tobacco and 12 flints.

The Cayuse were jubilant but they soon discovered they had nothing to celebrate. Over the next two years, they were hounded nearly to extinction. Finally they gave up five of their braves in a last-ditch effort to make peace with the whites.

The five were tried at Oregon City and hanged there in 1850. The hangman was Joe Meek, who may have taken some pleasure in the work because his daughter, Helen Mar Meek, had been taken captive after the massacre and had died before she could be released.

The Whitman Massacre had far-reaching effects. For one thing, it made historic martyrs out of Marcus and Narcissa Whitman. (The site of the massacre is now a National Historic Site. Whitman College, Whitman County and Whitman National Forest all honor the name in Washington. The cool, green, well-watered grounds of the historic site seven miles west of Walla Walla are as welcome as an oasis in the desert to hot-weather travellers along Highway 12. Once the mission was a watering-place for tourists along the Oregon Trail, so actually nothing has changed very much.) The massacre virtually ended Protestant mission activity to the Indians of the Northwest, thus closing a vivid chapter of history but opening another; suddenly the East was truly concerned about civilizing the West; the floodgates leading to the frontier were flung open.

The groans of the dying at Waiilatpu had carried for 3000 miles to echo through the halls of national government. The Cayuse braves who raged through the rye grass killed not only 13 whites but hastened the death of a way of life as well—the American Indian way of life. The Cayuse helped to kill it and left it to be ground into the soil of the ancient hunting grounds by the iron-clad wheels of a thousand westering wagons, then another thousand, and a thousand more, until the flood became endless and unstoppable.

So it is that everyone has heard of Narcissa Whitman—but how many have heard of Mary Richardson Walker?

Unlike Narcissa, she was not beautiful and her death was natural, late in coming and utterly unspectacular. She did the same work as Narcissa and suffered the same privations and accepted the same hazards, but there is no Walker College, no Walker County, no Walker National Forest. There should be. Sometimes history plays tricks in the names it sends ringing down the years . . .

★

Word of the Whitman Massacre came to the mission at Tshimakain, near the present city of Spokane, 10 days after the horror had struck. An Indian named Solomon brought a letter with the stunning news to be read by Mary Walker and her husband, Elkanah, who shared the mission duties with Cushing Eells and his wife, Myra.

Let Eells's diary paint the scene:

"We were in the height of our fun when this Indian arrived. There was nothing unusual for an Indian to come, but this one brought a letter. We all stopped playing and gathered around Mr. Walker to hear the news. When he broke the seal and glanced at the page before taking in the full import of its contents, his face blanched and he turned so pale that we all became frightened. He then read in trembling accents, how Dr. and Mrs. Whitman, Mr. Rodgers, another member of the mission, the two Sager boys, their adopted sons, and many other men had been killed by Cayuse Indians, and that the women and children had been taken prisoners. It seemed as though a black cloud of horrors settled down upon us . . ."

The "Great Grave" at the Whitman Mission held the bodies of many massacre victims when this photo was taken about 1865. Ranch buildings in the background are those of Rev. Cushing Eells, who lived at the site after Indian trouble had subsided.

And well it might have. Not only had they lost friends in the blood bath at Waiilatpu, but it was entirely possible that Tshimakain would be the next target of the rampaging Indians.

Despite the looming threat, Mary Walker was anything but eager to leave Tshimakain. On January 23, she wrote in her diary: "A lonely anxious day. Our way is so dark and I feel so uncertain what duty is. It seems almost as bad as death to think of leaving here."

Her feeling was understandable. The Walkers had lived in the eastern Washington valley for nine years. Five of their six children had been born there. The lonely outpost had become home.

The diary note makes clear how far Mary Richardson Walker had come from her birthplace in West Baldwin, Maine. She had left her native state on March 5, 1838, the day after her marriage to Elkanah, whom she had known for a year. One might say that their marriage was not made in heaven but in the Boston offices of the American Board of Commissioners for Foreign Missions. Elkanah had offered his services as a missionary but needed a wife to accompany him. Mary had volunteered, too, but the board frowned on sending unmarried females into the field. It was suggested that they get together. They did and their marriage worked as well as most. Elkanah was moody and irritable and very, very straight-laced; Mary's mind was quicker than her husband's and her spirit more independent. Elkanah was often halting in speech and couldn't deliver a stirring sermon to save his soul; Mary, on the other hand, spoke her mind readily, bluntly and at some length. At first, they had little more in common than their religion and their intense desire to be useful as missionaries. Apparently it was enough.

When informed that Mary Richardson was going to marry and travel overland to the frontier, a neighbor who knew her well is supposed to have said, "Well, if that isn't just like Mary Richardson to go dashing off across the plains on a wild buffalo!"

Actually it was not a wild buffalo but a tame horse that Mary rode sidesaddle from Independence, Missouri, over the Oregon Trail in the company of her husband and three more newly-married missionary couples—the Eellses, the Grays and the Smiths, plus a bachelor, Cornelius Rogers, who joined in St. Louis. Wild buffalo or no, the neighbor's remark tells something about Mary.

The group was being sent across the plains to reinforce the Whitman mission at Waiilatpu and expand the work of turning heathen Indians into

The Walker-Eells mission at Tshimakain looked like this to an early artist.

psalm-singing Christians. The overland journey was every bit as difficult as they had been warned it would be and signs of strain soon appeared. Mary's diary for May 27 commented: "Mr. W. and Gray appear pretty well now. Mr. S. and Walker apart. We have a strange company of missionaries. Scarcely one who is not intolerable on some account."

The honeymoons were over but the group managed to hold together through the harrowing summer and reached Waiilatpu on August 29, where they were greeted with great joy by the Whitmans and Henry and Eliza Spalding, who had established the mission two years earlier. Unfortunately Dr. Whitman had not expected so large a reinforcement. There was food enough but the Whitmans were still living in the small hut they had built soon after establishing the mission. Housing for the new arrivals was going to be crude and crowded for a while. The missionaries who had been snapping at each other on the trail soon would have an opportunity to growl in earnest.

Mary wrote in November:

"Sun. 11 Oh, that I had a little chamber where I might secrete myself and not see so many people all the time.

"Wed. Dr. W. sick with toothache. Mrs. W. stays with him. Mr. W's favorite mule kicked him. Mr. E's mule threw him and made him lame. Maria is sick, I found her husband sitting on her bed weeping.

"Fri. 16 Mrs. W. seems in a worry about something; cross with everyone; went out and blustered around and succeeded in melting over her tallow."

In December, Mary gave birth to a son, Cyrus Hamlin. During the year just past, Mary Walker had married, left her home and family, undertaken a gruelling trip which had been accomplished by only two other white women before her and settled into a strange new life of great difficulty and danger in a vacant wilderness where now she would have to bring up a son. A lesser woman might have cursed her lot, but Mary Walker could write on the last day of the year:

"Mon. 31 I have now reached the close of another year. It has been a year of mercies. A year ago to-night, I sat by the fireside of my father, and watched to see the old year go out. Now I find myself on the other side of the mountains, a wife and mother. Surely this is a changing world. With no one has God dealt in more mercy than with me . . . Affection drops a tear at the thought of friends and home, I have left, but it is not a tear of regret. I rejoice to find myself where I am with a prospect of entering ere long on the labors I have so long sought. Farewell departing year: I number thee among my happiest . . ."

Mary Richardson Walker, missionary woman of the West.

On March 20, 1839, the three Walkers (with a cow to provide milk for little Cyrus) and the Eellses reached Tshimakain and settled into a log cabin and a tent.

Indians helped chink and roof two log cabins 14 feet square, twenty feet apart. Cotton cloth and deerskin were used at first for windows. Cooking was done over an open fireplace. The reminiscences of Cushing Eells as reported in his son Myron's book, "Father Eells," tell the story well enough. Speaking of the Eells home at Tshimakain, Myron said:

"They had one chair during the ten years. For a table three boards, each three feet long, were packed a hundred and fifty miles, and a center table made by driving four stakes into the ground and placed the boards on them. Timber split and hewn was used for other articles."

During her first months at Waiilatpu, Mary Walker had refused to eat horse meat. She did, finally, and must have eaten a good deal more at Tshimakain. Myron Eells wrote:

"The beef neither chewed the cud nor parted the hoof. It was made out of the Indian pony. Cattle were very scarce. The Hudson's Bay Company owned all in the country, except what the missionaries had brought. Neither love nor money could procure one from the company. About half a dozen horses were killed for beef at Dr. Whitman's during the winter of 1838–39, and for several years Mr. Eells was accustomed to salt one down every winter. They were fattened on the rich bunch grass and with few exceptions were eaten with a relish, even by the fastidious."

But at least they had departed from the bickering and snapping and backbiting at Waiilatpu. The work began, although much of the time it was not the work Mary had intended to do when she left Maine. Housekeeping and farming and baby-sitting used up huge amounts of their time. It seemed to Mary that all of the energy which she had hoped to pour into saving Spokane souls had to be expended instead in keeping the Walkers' bodies and souls together. The American Board gave each missionary couple $300 a year for living expenses and the Walkers seldom used all of it! But they paid with their time and energy and Mary must have wondered if it was a good bargain. They needed to learn the Spokane language before they could bring the Indians the message of the Bible but there was too little time for study. They tried to learn from a Spokane chief named Big Head but he had lost most of his teeth and his pronounciation was rather mushy as a result. There was nothing in the training of missionaries which equipped them to cope with toothless Indian chiefs. There was no written language; Elkanah Walker labored for years before he finally produced the first little book in the Spokane tongue.

Mary's diary reported on May 16: "Washed. Have had to work hard since I returned home. I rise before sunrise most of the time: find my health very good which is a blessing for which I ought to be thankful. Regret that I am able to devote so little attention to the language. Live very comfortably in my little house without floor, door or window."

In nine years at Tshimakain, not one Indian was converted to Christianity. The Whitmans had better success at Waiilatpu and the Spaldings did best of all at Lapwai, in what is now western Idaho. (Among the Lapwai conversions, if only a temporary one, was Old Chief Joseph, father of the famed Nez Perce warrior-statesman.)

Father Pierre Jean DeSmet, one of three early Catholic missionaries who spent many years working among the tribes of Old Oregon (Father Modeste Demers and Father Francois Blanchet were the others) happened to camp for the night near Tshimakain in April of 1842. His written observations indicate his doubt about the effectiveness of the mission:

"Here, on a gay and smiling little plain, two ministers have settled themselves, with their wives . . . During the four years they have spent here, they have baptized several of their own children. They cultivate a small farm, large enough, however, for their own maintenance and the support of their animals and fowls. It appears that they are fearful that, should they cultivate more, they might have too frequent visits from the savages. They even try to prevent their encampment in the immediate neighborhood, and therefore they see and converse but seldom with the heathens, whom they have come so far to seek. A band of Spokanes received me with every demonstration of friendship, and were enchanted to hear that the right kind of Black-gowns intended soon to form an establishment in the vicinity. I baptized one of their little children who was dying."

On the evidence, one would have to call the mission at Tshimakain a failure. Yet, in 1842, when the American Board decided to cut down its work among the Indians, it ordered Waiilatpu and Lapwai closed and left Tshimakain open.

It was to save these threatened missions that Dr. Whitman endured great hardship to make his historic trip to the East during the winter of 1842–43. Returning along the Oregon Trail in 1843, out of the goodness of his heart he offered to guide the first big wagon train. It is ironic that in so doing, he may unwittingly have signed his own death warrant, and Narcissa's, too.

Does history make small mention of Mary Walker because she failed at what she came West to do? If Mary failed, so did the Whitmans, but the name "Whitman" rings loud and clear in the annals of the frontier. History has a way of misplacing persons.

Mary Walker deserved to succeed. She was intelligent, strong-minded, energetic and dedicated. Then why did she fail? Well, in the first place, the missionaries set impossible goals for themselves. They weren't satisfied with merely converting Indians to Christianity; they insisted that the Indians shuck off centuries of habit and tradition and live like white men. Indian males, for instance, had grown accustomed to taking wives when they felt like it and dropping them as casually. The missionaries, of course, frowned on such a practice and in so doing, struck at the roots of the Indian male's power and comfort. How was a man to live without several strong women to gather food and firewood and prepare a lodging?

In similar fashion, Dr. Whitman rattled the underpinnings of Indian culture when he tried to turn Indians into settled farmers. Nomads for centuries, they were quite content to settle around the missions during the winter for food, warmth and hymn-singing, but when the spring grasses sprouted under a warm sun that loosened a man's muscles, they wanted to follow the old game trails. It was normal; it was natural; it was what they had always done and what their revered fathers had done before them; the pull of a way of life centuries old was too strong to be resisted. (Modern males, hemmed in by traffic and smog and clock-punching and time payments, might well understand the Indians' reluctance to adopt the white man's ways; still more centuries of human existence will be needed to breed out the call of the wild.) When they returned to the missions with the first cold winds of autumn, they had backslid; much of the work of civilizing and Christianizing had to be done all over again.

Small wonder that this was discouraging duty undertaken by Mary Walker, Father DeSmet and all the others. Note that today, more than a century later, we still agonize over the difficulty of bringing modern reservation Indians into the mainstream of American life.

It is likely that missions served best in a role for which they were not originally intended, as comforting oases of a familiar, "civilized" culture in a strange, wild land for the thousands of Easterners who were bound and determined to become Westerners. (There were times when the American Board which supported Dr. Whitman's mission wondered if the good doctor wasn't more interested in running an inn for weary travellers off the Oregon Trail than he was in converting heathen. There is evidence that Dr. Whitman may have been a little confused, too.)

There had to be a turning point. It came on November 29, 1847. It rose out of the fog at The Place of the Rye Grass.

Mary Walker and her family, the Eellses and the other survivors—those who had come to convert—suddenly found themselves converted, from missionaries to pioneers in the Willamette Valley.

Mary lived in Forest Grove, Oregon, until her death in 1897. Her longevity at last gained her a clear distinction: she was the last survivor of the original Whitman missionary band.

In 1888, Mary Walker had made her last long journey, to Whitman College, for the commencement season which celebrated the 50th anniversary of the coming of the Eells-Walker party to nearby Waiilatpu. Forty years had passed since she had last walked the historic ground at The Place of the Rye Grass; forty years earlier she had paused briefly on her way to the Willamette Valley and had taken a few strands of Narcissa Whitman's hair from a shrub, then hurried on to close her mind to the place and to the horror of what had happened there.

There is a monument at Tshimakain near Spokane. The Longview unit of the Daughters of the American Revolution is called the "Mary Richardson Walker Chapter." The Oregon Historical Society Museum in Portland has on display her old sidesaddle, the same one she rode overland in 1838. Her trunk and writing case can be seen in the Washington State University museum in Pullman.

At death, Mary Walker was very old: 86. She never had been one to give up easily. It was said that in her last years she would take her weathered saddle, put it on a chair and sit upon it with her old cape drawn over her shoulders.

One wonders if she didn't smile a little then, remembering:

"Well, if that isn't just like Mary Richardson to go dashing off across the plains on a wild buffalo!"

HELP WANTED: WOMEN

The Protestant women of the Whitman group were not the only members of their sex who worked on the frontier. One of the most famous was Mother Joseph, superior of a group of Catholic Sisters of Charity who arrived at Fort Vancouver from Montreal, Canada. For almost 50 years thereafter, Mother Joseph was a strong force in the development of the Vancouver area.

It seemed that almost everyone in the Oregon country knew of Mother Joseph. In 1874, her group had completed construction of a huge, three-story brick building called Providence Academy and there was a large debt to settle. Mother Joseph decided to hold the first of many bazaars to provide money. Hearing about the plan, a farmer near The Dalles on the Columbia decided to donate a cow but wasn't sure how to get it to Vancouver.

A freight handler on a river boat couldn't see that it was much of a problem.

"Just put a tag on her horn," he said, "and mark it 'For Mother Joseph.' Everybody knows the old Mother. She'll get it."

She did, too, and the cow brought $250 when it was sold at the bazaar.

When Providence Academy closed in 1966, it was the oldest school of any kind in Washington and the oldest permanent Catholic school in the Northwest. Before opening the school, Mother Joseph's group had operated a hospital at Fort Vancouver. Members of all faiths were treated for $1 per day. Anything was accepted in payment, from chickens to whiskey.

In late 1966, a drive was started in Vancouver for funds to build a new hospital to replace the old St. Joseph's, in hope of continuing a tradition that had begun 108 years earlier. Highlight of the fund drive was the transporting of a cow down the Columbia on an amphibious vehicle, from which the animal was lifted to the dock by a helicopter.

This wasn't quite the way it was done in Mother Joseph's day, but the sentiment was pure, at any rate.

★

The first president of the University of Washington, Asa Mercer, was a man of action. When he wanted students for his new college in Seattle, he paddled his own canoe around Puget Sound and sought out strong men in the woods who were willing to work their way through college—Asa Mercer's college—by chopping wood.

Most of these young men were unmarried, for an obvious reason: there were nine men for every woman in Washington Territory in the early 1860s. It was a deplorable situation and most certainly one that could not be allowed to exist for long.

Asa Mercer couldn't solve this problem by paddling his canoe but he thought there might be another way. The shortage of women was really nothing more than a matter of geography. There were plenty of husband-hungry women in the East but the men who desperately wanted to marry them were pioneering in the West. The men weren't about to go back East so there was nothing to do but bring the women West. Thus developed one of the most charming chapters of Washington history, the sentimental journeys of the so-called Mercer Girls.

Mercer set out to speak in churches from Kansas to Maine, offering

Mother Joseph was a prominent figure around Fort Vancouver for almost half a century. She founded Providence Academy and St. Joseph's Hospital.

Civil War widows and their daughters work as teachers, seamstresses and milliners if they would emigrate to Washington. (He also took pains to mention all those young and handsome bachelors, pining away in the woods.)

In 1864, 11 carefully selected girls came west by boat, via Panama. They were quickly snatched up on arrival in Washington.

Three hundred came on the second trip and received a delirious welcome from the bachelors assembled on the Seattle waterfront.

Soon all but one of the Mercer Girls had married. Miss Lizzie Ordway decided that she would rather teach school, which she did for 30 years on Whidbey Island and at Port Madison. Finally she became superintendent of schools in Kitsap County.

The Mercer Girls established a proud record, despite snide predictions to the contrary. Not one of them "went wrong," to use the term of the day. In spite of much ridicule and misrepresentation, Mercer's plan worked wonderfully well and resulted in the establishment of many of Washington's oldest, finest families.

And what of Asa Mercer himself? He married a Mercer Girl, of course. He was a man of action, not a man who would be caught behind a door when something interesting was going on.

★

After the raw edges of pioneer life had been smoothed off, Washington women were freed from the grubby details of survival which had necessarily occupied them in the early stages of settlement. Given a little time to think, they soon began to think of woman's suffrage—the right to vote. Men across the nation turned pale and groaned as organized womanhood began to march in the streets and vocally assault the male animal in their meeting halls and harangue the legislators, both regional and federal.

During the first session of the Washington territorial legislature in 1854, an amendment to an elections bill was proposed which would have allowed white women to vote. The amendment was beaten by one vote cast by a delegate who had a strong reason for his stand: his wife was an Indian.

In 1871, the territorial legislature of Washington invited two of the nation's outstanding suffragettes, Susan B. Anthony and Abigail Scott

Members of the Washington Equal Suffrage Association post propaganda in 1910.

Duniway, to address a joint session. A bill for woman's suffrage was introduced in that same year, but failed. In 1883 another bill was introduced and carried—by a majority of one!

As a result, women voted in Washington Territory in 1884 and 1886. It was a short-lived victory. The supreme court overturned the suffrage law and a new law wasn't passed until 1910. By this time, suffrage had become almost fashionable around the country as male citizens bravely faced up to a future fraught with equality at the polls.

Modern women take voting for granted, but the fight to gain the right was long and hard, with considerable bitterness on both sides. Much hard work for the cause was done in Washington by May Arkwright Hutton of Spokane. Also very active throughout the Northwest was Abigail Scott Duniway of Portland, Oregon. (Scott's Prairie near Shelton was named after John Tucker Scott, who settled there in 1854; Scott was Abigail Scott Duniway's father.) She operated a suffrage newspaper there, "The New Northwest," and throughout her career was the target of much male abuse. But Abigail needed no one's sympathy; her quick mind and sharp tongue usually gave as good as she got, or better.

Once Mrs. Duniway was travelling by stagecoach between Goldendale and Yakima. The day was cold, with wind-driven snow lancing out of a gray sky. She was the only woman in the coach. One of the male passengers, growing bored and bold, said, "Madam, you ought to be at home, enjoying yourself, like my wife is doing. I want to bear all the hardship of life myself, and let her sit by the fire, toasting her footsies."

Mrs. Duniway let the remark pass. It was almost dark when the stage reached Yakima. The driver went out of his way to leave the man who had spoken to Mrs. Duniway at his own doorstep.

In the yard was a woman, obviously the man's wife, huddled against the wind as she chopped wearily at a pile of snow-covered firewood.

As the man stepped down from the coach, Mrs. Duniway politely cleared her throat and said, "I see, my friend, that your wife is toasting her footsies . . ."

Later Mrs. Duniway heard that the man had become known around Yakima as "Old Footsie Toaster." Naturally, she tried to remember to mention the man at least once whenever she spoke in Washington.

Another woman of note lived and worked for a time in Washington —Bethenia Owens-Adair, the first graduate woman doctor on the Pacific

The imposing figure of May Arkwright Hutton of Spokane was prominent in Washington women's suffrage circles.

Coast. She had a medical practice in Yakima from 1884–1905.

The women who dared to thrust the toes of their button shoes into male territory in the frontier West had to be smart, unafraid and above all —stubborn. Dr. Owens-Adair was all of these. After she had won her personal battle, a woman who had once condemned her appeared in her office for treatment. The woman, expecting rejection—or worse—was startled when Dr. Owens-Adair clasped her hand and thanked her for putting obstacles in the path of the presumptuous Bethenia Owens, the foolish girl who wanted to be a doctor.

Then Dr. Owens-Adair explained, "A friend once said to me, 'If I wished to increase your height two and a half inches, Bethenia, I would attempt to press you down, and you would grow upward from sheer resentment.' "

To women like these, obstacles became challenges, as surely as pumpkin seeds become pumpkins.

★

A modern woman of Washington parlayed a few years of chicken ranching on the Olympic Peninsula into a best-selling book in 1945 and a literary career which ended with her death in 1958. The woman was Betty MacDonald and the book was "The Egg and I," a free-swinging account of her chicken-rearing days in Washington which provoked giggles and guffaws around the United States. (And a lawsuit, as well, when former neighbors thought they recognized themselves as Ma and Pa Kettle in the book.) The book was the basis for a popular movie and the Kettle characters were spun off into more movies of their own.

(Incidentally, "The Town" referred to in "The Egg and I" sounds like Port Townsend, although Mrs. MacDonald didn't name it. "Docktown" could be Port Ludlow.)

Another popular MacDonald book was "Onions in the Stew," an account of her life on a Puget Sound island (Vashon) during World War II.

Educated at Roosevelt High School in Seattle and the University of Washington (where she apparently learned little or nothing about chickens), she earned with her candor and humor and flowing style a deserved role as Washington's most widely-read author.

Ella Higginson, who died in 1940, just as Betty MacDonald was about to burst upon the literary scene, came west as a baby, then moved from Oregon to Bellingham in 1888. Here she settled down and proceeded to write poetry, short stories, travel articles and a novel, "Mariella of Out

West," published in 1904. She won national short story awards and for a time was poet laureate of Washington. Her most famous poem was "Four Leaf Clover," published in 1890.

★

The pioneer woman of the West has often been glamorized in books and in movies and on television but in truth, her lot was brutally hard. Usually she died young but took an old face to her grave. Life in the Wild West when the West was truly wild was hard for strong men; it is remarkable that women accustomed to the refinements of the East were willing to attempt it, much less survive it, and in the case of some, carve their record of accomplishment deeply into the monuments of history.

SUGGESTED READING

Johnson, Jalmar; BUILDERS OF THE NORTHWEST; Dodd, Mead; 1963 (Abigail Scott Duniway and Narcissa Whitman).

McKee, Ruth Karr; MARY RICHARDSON WALKER: HER BOOK; Caxton; 1945.

Miller, Helen Markley; WESTERING WOMEN; Doubleday; 1961.

Miller, Helen Markley; WOMAN DOCTOR OF THE WEST: BETHENIA OWENS-ADAIR; Messner; 1960.

Olson, Joan and Gene; OREGON TIMES AND TRAILS; Windyridge; 1965 (Abigail Scott Duniway).

Ross, Nancy Wilson; HEROINES OF THE EARLY WEST; Random House; 1960.

Ross, Nancy Wilson; WESTWARD THE WOMEN; Random House; 1958.

Chapter Six ★

Lumbering
DAY OF THE DRAGON

The big wagon vibrated with the happy sounds of children headed for a picnic as it rolled upward toward Trout Lake on the western slope of Mount St. Helens, Washington.

The time was September, 1902. The day was hot but the air was crackling dry and not uncomfortable; the sun's glare was blunted by a blue-gray haze. Smoke . . .

The curtain which dimmed the distant view and blurred the scenic edges of the rugged land was plainly smoke but no one in the picnic party considered it worth mentioning. After all, land clearing fires were common at summer's end.

The wagon rattled along the rough road, climbing ever closer to the softly-rounded snowcap of St. Helens, a cool, comforting ice cream cone in the sky.

They had left the homestead on the north fork of the Lewis River in southwest Washington. In the party were Mr. and Mrs. Ira Reid, Mr. and Mrs. C. A. McKeen and six children. The picnic was in honor of Uncle George Smith, only recently arrived from distant Kansas.

Uncle George was fated never to see Trout Lake. Disaster struck with shocking suddenness about two miles above Yale postoffice.

Like a tornado the gout of flame stormed down the gully, erupting in ear-splitting sound and fury as it raced toward the wagon, throwing exploding balls of fire in all directions.

The horses reared, the men bellowed at them, the women and children screamed, and then quickly it was over and the angry dragon moved on, reaching out again with its fiery tongue, destroying with its flaming breath the land and the creatures who lived upon the land.

Helicopters are being used to seed steep slopes in burned-over forest.

The Yacolt Burn, worst of the incredible forest fires of 1902, was scorching its way into history.

★

Relatives of the families which perished near Yale, Charley Hartsuck and Charley Smith, reached Speelyai Creek a month later after chopping their way through down timber still smouldering in places.

They examined the dismal spot with heavy hearts.

Only blackened iron hoops marked the wagon location. Eleven persons had died within 150 feet of the wagon. The horses, unhitched before the fire struck, had done only a little better. The goal of all the victims, human and animal, was Speelyai Creek. The water was less than 100 yards away, but even that is too far when the enemy is a fire dragon galloping down a mountain draw.

Not far away, the Newton Graves family watched the flames crash through the woods and ran for the safety of Speelyai Creek and the open ground of Speelyai Prairie. Mrs. Graves delayed, said she would be along presently.

She died for her Singer sewing machine and several jars of fruit. They found her in the yard not far from the house, surrounded by the blackened remains of her prized possessions.

A star route mailman, W. E. Newhouse, should have had a better chance. He owned two strong, fast horses and a sturdy buggy. When he saw the fire storming toward his home, he quickly hitched up the animals to the mail buggy and whipped them down the road at a wild clip.

One horse had made a last, mighty jump onto a log felled beside the trail but the fire had leaped after. This, at least, was the diagnosis of those who came on the scene a long time later. Newhouse had left the buggy and sought refuge in a small gully. There they found him, skin and clothes burned away, leaning against a log clutching a short piece of steel—the unburned core of his rattan whip.

In the Dole district, a woman named Schmidt and her three children tried to hang onto life by clambering into a cellar beneath their house. It was a fatal mistake. The house burned and fell in on the cellar, making of it a furnace hot enough to melt metal.

Some along the Lewis River were luckier than others. A fair number were able to reach Speelyai Prairie, a quarter mile wide and a half mile long, with "clover more'n two foot high," according to a resident of the area.

To this once-peaceful meadow, ahead of the rampaging flames, came the creatures of the deep forest—men and women and children, cats and dogs, horses and cows. Wild things, too. All came running to this haven and waited there breathlessly with ancient animosities forgotten as the dragon stalked the hills around them.

There was one farm on the prairie; it was owned by S. F. Murray. By the morning of the next day, September 13, more than 40 refugees were at the Murray farm. When there was no more room in the house, they slept in the barn and in the fields as the fire raged around them.

At noon on the 13th, it was dark on Speelyai Prairie, dark as night. The great rolling pall of smoke had stolen the light of day and fear pressed in through the gathering gloom.

They stood in little groups and muttered and watched the animals come out of the woods—six bears, eight deer and a lynx.

The humans stayed at Speelyai Prairie for four days. The wild animals left after the second night. The creatures lucky enough to reach the meadow in the woods had thwarted the dragon . . .

So, too, had those who happened to be near Trout Lake when the enemy struck. Farmers, prospectors, hunters and fishermen—60 or more —built rafts from fallen trees on the lakeshore and then literally began to paddle for their lives. For two days and two nights they paddled to avoid the burning shores and survived.

Unless one has experienced it, the effect of a great forest fire's smoke pall is hard to believe. Sophus Jacobson, writing of a Mason County fire in September, 1902, said: "We fought it day and night, and during the day the smoke was so heavy that we had to use lanterns to light our way. There was really no difference in lighting between the day and the night, and it became confusing as to which was which."

Describing the effect of the Yacolt Burn, Frank E. Barnes wrote: "The smoke darkened the sun, so that, although we were fully one hundred miles distant, we had to use lights to run our mill and the chickens went to roost in daytime. All day, leaves would come floating through the air and light on the lake. When touched they dissolved into ashes. Many people believed the world was coming to an end . . . ."

Allen Carter of Cowlitz County said: "The smoke was so bad one couldn't tell a man at arm's length at 10 o'clock in the morning. The headlight on the engine looked like the head of a match. For three days the section hands couldn't take out the hand car. Trains crawled in with mail only, hours behind time. Lights burned all day and that day is known as 'dark day.' "

Throughout Washington minds became unhinged. A confused woman

ran down the smoky streets of Olympia and cried out, "Mount Tacoma is erupting!"

Near Woodland, some religious fanatics were in the throes of a camp meeting. When the smoke blotted out the midday sun, they bellowed, "Glory be to God! The Last Days are at hand!"

Then they ran for their lives.

A pioneer living at Stevenson wrote: "In 1902, we had a terrible forest fire along here. Many people were burned to death. Many trees fell across the road and blocked the way out. We were hemmed in here and couldn't get out. We sat in our yard with our grips packed from Monday night until Saturday morning, expecting every day to be burned to death. We lay on the ground most of the time and we kept the babies there all the time, because the only air one could breathe was next the ground. The fire went in a semi-circle around this town (Stevenson) or we would all have died."

The Yacolt Burn was not the only forest fire of the period, by any means, but it climaxed a terrible series of conflagrations which had begun in August. During the week prior to the Yacolt fire, blazes were touched off from up near Bellingham south to Eugene, Oregon. Cinders floated down to coat Portland to a depth of half an inch. Twenty towns were erased by onrushing flames. Hundreds of farmers and ranchers lost everything but considered themselves lucky to have survived. The night sky bore the weird smears of firelight produced by 700,000 acres of giant trees which were eaten away from the bottom up as flames raced through the thick jungle which had been allowed to grow on the forest floor.

No doubt there were Indians on reservations during that terrible week who shook their heads sadly at the white man's stupidity. When the Indians owned the woods, they burned the underbrush every autumn. The fires scorched the big trees, but didn't hurt them since there wasn't enough fuel on the ground to develop great heat. When the Indians still owned the forest land, it was said, one could ride a horse through the woods almost anywhere and really destructive forest fires were unknown.

But the white man took over and in his wisdom, let the jungle develop on the forest floor. Then at the end of the dry season, a spark from a locomotive and a hot wind out of the east could send fire of enormous heat blasting through the underbrush, igniting the great trees, leaving charred catastrophe in its wake.

Mount Adams dominates the view from a fire lookout tower in a Washington forest.

They called it the Yacolt Burn because Yacolt, with its 15 buildings, was then the metropolis of the region. The residents of the town, on that fateful day in early September, saw the fires approaching over the hills to the south.

Then the fire dragon galloped down the hill, heading straight for the town. Paint began to blister on some of the buildings nearest the fire; the flames were still half a mile away but the heat was great enough to cause paint to run.

Some of the old folks moaned that the end of the world was at hand, sure enough. Then the entire population of Yacolt went to a nearby creek and stayed there all night . . . and survived.

In the morning they returned to their town and saw with wondering eyes that the fire had stopped short of the buildings.

Near Yacolt at the foot of Tum-Tum Mountain, a homesteader heard a sound in the night and left his house to investigate.

He later described a wild scene: "The whole range of hills back of Tum-Tum lighted up. It was just like pressing a button and seeing the lights go on."

The man was not a victim of a feverish imagination. There had been another bad fire on those slopes in 1868; now the old, dry snags left by the earlier blaze had burst into flame even before the visible fire had reached them.

Unless one has had the experience, it is not easy to imagine the awesome power, headlong speed and fantastic impact of a fire like the Yacolt Burn. A graphic account of such a firestorm appeared in "Everybody's Magazine" in 1910:

"The stillness of desolation rested above camps and towns where men by hundreds lived. There was no carrying power in the air; sounds were muffled as if by a vacuum. Bewildered birds fluttered through the smoky chaos, panting, lost. Horses strained at their halters, looking upon their masters with questioning eyes, uncomforted by caresses, unassured by words. If a beast, by a terrified lunge, broke its restraining tether, it dashed away into the wilderness. Even dooryard fowls here and there deserted their coops, seeking a refuge at the margin of some stream. Dwellers in the woods and travellers on the dim trails saw forest creatures flying in one general direction, as if pursued by a force that struck a deeper terror than man. The fear of man, indeed, seemed lost in them. Scarcely would bear,

Ox teams did yeoman work in the woods pulling huge logs over log skids. This photo was taken about 1900.

mountain lion or deer lift their heads at sight of a man or move out of his path to let him pass.

"A great tragedy was imminent in nature . . . there came at length a timid wind, sighing through the tree-walled canyons. It struck hot upon the forehead, it burned dry upon the lips, ruffling the smoke mantle for a moment, soon to die away . . . It freshened steadily, rolling away the smoke, showing the sun red as iron under the smith's hammer, far down near the edge of the world.

"That was all the warning the tempest of fire gave. It was as if it indulged the oft-voiced desire of dying men to look once more upon the sun. Out of the Northwest, over the mountains, it came. Howling, roaring, the fires, but a few minutes before miles away, were upon the hamlets and camps, upon the lone cabins of settlers, leaping up the green mountain sides, streaming across canyons their long banners of obliterating flames . . .

"It swept uphill and downhill with unabated speed, although a fire in a mountain country usually rushes up hillsides much faster than it burns down. When the vanguard of the fire reached a canyon, it merely leaped across, no matter how wide the chasm. In one known instance it leaped a mile . . . The flames caught the resinous foliage and long streamers of . . . moss with the hissing roar of great skyrockets. In a breath, the proudest, oldest knights in this ancient guard of the mountains were stripped . . . their blackened trunks hurled to the ground by the tempest which drove the wild ocean of fire before it.

"Living man has not witnessed a more appalling sight. Days afterward men who went through it were struck dumb in their struggle for words to measure its horrors. 'The world was afire,' they said, 'the earth, the air, everything.' Lightning flashed out of the great clouds of smoke; incandescent flames, burning like carbon gas, sprang up, whistling their sharp notes above the roar of tempest and fire and the crash of falling trees, sprang up with nothing to feed on but air. In the superheated atmosphere it appeared that all nature had become outlawed . . ."

★

Almost everyone in the Pacific Northwest knew even before newspapers printed the ghastly stories that the Yacolt Burn was no ordinary fire.

A former president of the University of Washington, Henry Schmitz, commented: "One of the most vivid memories of my childhood is the utter

Once many logs raced through flumes like this to mills or loading yards.

ASAHEL CURTIS
64480

darkness that fell on Seattle one late summer day in 1902 caused by the smoke of the Yacolt Burn. There was darkness so complete that it necessitated lighting the city's gas street lights by early afternoon."

As soon as the news of the disaster penetrated the Northwest, help began to flow into the stricken areas. The Portland *Oregonian* of September 28, 1902, reported cash receipts of $9150; this amount, plus huge quantities of food and clothing, streamed across the Columbia from Portland and south from Seattle to Camas, Battleground, Lewis River and other burned-out communities.

When the grim fire season of 1902 finally sputtered to a close, 110 fires in Oregon and Washington had burned over 700,000 acres, 239,000 in the Yacolt Burn itself. As many as 45 persons may have died; the exact figures will never be known. The property loss in the two states was 13 millions of dollars. A much greater loss was the destruction of timber which some day would have reached market. The Yacolt Burn alone destroyed over 12 billion feet of timber and that timber was worth perhaps 20 million dollars to the owner of the stumpage; it is impossible to calculate how much more it would have been worth to the mill owners and the merchandisers of the finished wood products and to their employees in the form of payrolls.

Four years after the Yacolt Burn, the Washington state legislature provided for a state board of forest commissioners with power to appoint a fire warden and deputies.

Uncowed, the fire dragon wasn't through with his wild rambles through the Yacolt Burn. In 1929, much of the same area burned again. As a result, there are parts of the area which are still without substantial regrowth. Each successive fire left more of the dead, dry snags which are little more than tinder. In 1929, 187,000 acres burned over in two days; 80,000 acres were second growth.

Still, nothing of importance was done to prevent future holocausts until the Tillamook Burn flared in northwest Oregon in 1933, eating up as much lumber as had been used throughout the U.S. during the previous year!

Public sentiment crystallized as aroused citizens finally realized that the great forests—cool, majestic retreats for man and animal and one of the richest sources of payrolls in the Northwest—were doomed unless drastic action could be taken soon enough.

A drive to educate the public was needed. In 1940, the Keep Washington Green movement was kicked off; Oregon soon started a similar organization. Fire losses began to drop.

Fire fighting practices were studied and improved. Modern technology was put to work. Helicopters, radio, smoke jumpers, retardant chemicals dropped in great colored clouds from low-flying bombers—all were tried and given a part to play in the fight against the fires of the future.

But in the far reaches of the dark forest, the ancient dragon still lurked, waiting for summer, 1967 . . .

★

It was a terrible season, 1967, one that will be long remembered. A deadly combination of unusually hot, dry weather and lightning storms and the usual careless humans caused 1800 forest fires in the Inland Empire of Washington and Idaho. At the worst moment, 123 planes and helicopters flew over the Northwest in the battle against stubborn blazes. Some of the big bombers which dropped retardant chemicals had flown from home bases as far away as Houston, Texas.

The 1967 fire season was the worst in many years, but without the new techniques and equipment, 1967 might have brought not only disaster, but complete catastrophe for Washington's forest products industry.

And how important is that industry? Washington's forest products business tops that of any other state. Until 1956, when booming Boeing took over first place, forest products produced more payroll dollars than any other of the state's industries.

Large corporations like Weyerhaeuser, Simpson and Rayonier now do most of the lumbering in the Pacific Northwest. A new concept called "tree farming" is one reason; great resources were needed to handle the new idea. Clemons Tree Farm in Grays Harbor County, started by Weyerhaeuser in 1941, marked the dawn of a new day in timber management. In the old days loggers stripped the land, then moved west for more of the same. Only the Pacific Ocean stopped them. Now trees are considered a crop; the goal is to hold the annual cut to a point no higher than the annual growth. They call it "sustained yield." In other words: trees enough forever.

Now there are tree farms in almost every state in the union, 70 million acres of tree farms. And it all started in Grays Harbor County.

In 1966, they ran off a little ceremony in Grays Harbor County at the first tree farm, which was enjoying its silver anniversary. A Weyerhaeuser official said, "They say the old timers moved westward, cutting as they came. Starting here at Clemons in 1941, we at Weyerhaeuser have been moving eastward, planting as we go."

The future for Washington's forest products industries is bright and is

sustained by one simple fact: one-sixth of all the standing timber in the United States grows within the borders of Washington. Only Oregon has more. Washington's trees grow in two distinct regions: the Douglas fir area west of the Cascade Mountains and the western pine area east of the mountains. Washington leads all states in manufacture of wood pulp.

Logging has changed radically over the years. Where brawny men with axes and handsaws once sweated and strained, now giant machines handle much of the work. Experiments have been conducted with helicopters and giant balloons for snaking logs out of inaccessible locations. Despite the changes, however, logging remains a noisy, boisterous and romantic industry. Taking the measure of Washington's big trees has always demanded big men; it's likely that it always will.

Men like Henry Yesler. He built the first steam sawmill around Puget Sound in 1853 and went on to become a wealthy, important man and key figure in early Seattle history. The term "skid road," according to Stewart Holbrook, the Northwest's best-known logging historian, was first applied to the road down which Yesler skidded logs to his mill. The skid road later was given the name of Yesler Way; it is Yesler Way today.

It's hardly surprising in a state dotted with outstanding historical museums that there should be a topnotch outdoor logging show in Point Defiance Park, Tacoma. Bearing the full-flavored name of "Camp Six," the museum is designed to recreate the look of an old logging camp in the Cascade foothills at the turn of the century or thereabouts.

They couldn't recreate the big trees, of course, not the real monsters of the old days. A tree grows in nature's own good time. Now that forests are to be treated as a farm crop, they won't make trees like that any more; they will be harvested much younger, when ripe for the market.

But modern Washingtonians, deep in the shadowed splendor of a majestic Cascade forest, may still taste much of the goodness of the green woods. If humans with their suicidal carelessness (90 per cent of forest fires are man-caused) can somehow keep from burning over the country and wiping out this golden heritage, many future generations of Washingtonians can share the awesome experience of standing in a great forest in Washington, and can still be envied by the bleak, cut-over world beyond.

Lumber schooners crowded Port Blakely in 1890 or thereabouts.

BULL OF THE WOODS

Paul Bunyan was his name and logging was his game. To hear Paul tell it, he invented logging, but then, to hear Paul tell it, he invented practically everything worth inventing.

Whenever two loggers get together in the Washington woods, one talking and one listening, the history of Paul Bunyan is likely to gain another thrilling chapter. The true life experiences are fanciful, sometimes even wild, and if it weren't for the fact that one logger has never been known to lie to another, a dedicated historian would have to cast a veil of doubt over some of the narratives.

Take Babe, the Blue Ox, Paul Bunyan's most important piece of logging machinery. They say that Babe measured 42 ax handles (and a plug of chewing tobacco) between the horns. They say that when Paul stood by Babe's front legs and tried to watch the action of Babe's back legs, he had to use a telescope. Babe was BIG, no question about it.

Paul Bunyan was born deep in the mists of antiquity, so long ago that the time is known as the Good Old Days. The state of Maine claims to be his birthplace. Along the Maine seacoast they say that when Paul was a baby, his cradle was so large that it had to be anchored offshore. Once Baby Paul ate too much salt pork and turnips and began to roll fitfully in the night, sending a 75-foot tidal wave up the Bay of Fundy, driving ships onto the land and pushing salt water through the villages.

To awaken Baby Paul, the British Navy fired all its guns for seven hours. Baby Paul then waded ashore, stirring up waves enough to sink seven ships. Angrily the King of England ordered that Paul's cradle be broken up and the timbers used to build seven more ships.

It's hard to believe . . . but it was done.

Canadians claim Paul Bunyan and to this day insist that his name should be spelled "Bunyon." Everyone seems agreed that Paul Bunyan, or "Bunyon," spent his youth in Canada, rescued a blue calf from drowning during the Winter of the Blue Snow (This calf, of course, grew into Babe, the Blue Ox. And grew. And grew.) and then crossed over into what he chose to call "Real America."

"What greater work could be done in Real America than to make logs from trees?" cried Paul Bunyan. "Logging! I shall invent this industry and make it the greatest one of all time! I shall become a figure as admired in

For sale: Used Mack log truck, chain drive, air conditioning, driven only seven days a week by youthful madman.

history as any of the great ones I have read about."

It's hard to believe . . . but he did just that.

Paul Bunyan's life was full of adventures and with each passing year, more of the adventures come to light. You may have wondered, for instance, why surveyors' township maps never show a section 37; they always stop at 36. This is how it happened:

They were in the Twin Rivers Valley, Paul Bunyan and Babe, and they had trees to cut and move to the river. (At this stage of his barely believable career, Paul didn't have the super-efficient crew he developed later; he had only Babe.)

So what Paul did was hook up Babe to a square mile of timber land. Babe pulled the land, trees and all, to the river, where Paul logged off the 640 acres in practically no time at all. (You have to believe Babe could perform an enormous feat like this, because before Babe and Paul left Canada, when Babe was little more than a calf, Paul occasionally loaned him out to the Canadians, who hooked him up to twisting roads, which he pulled out straight. Babe was STRONG.)

After Paul had logged the square mile, it was Babe's job to pull the land back to its original place.

"I handled a township a week in this fashion," Paul said. "But I always left section 37 in the river on Saturday night and the stream would wash it away."

It's hard to believe but . . . in no township today is there a section 37.

Paul built a permanent camp on the Smiling River and soon hired the best logging crew ever to set cork boots on American soil. For instance, there was Johnny Inkslinger, bookkeeper and doctor, who slept three hours a week and kept books so fast that his fountain pen needed a hose connected to 12 barrels of ink.

But one of Paul's first camp cooks, Pea Soup Shorty, was on the lazy side. Once Shagline Bill's freight sleds broke through the lake ice and the season's supply of split peas sank underwater.

Did Shorty despair? Not a bit; he merely boiled the lake water and served it for pea soup. The next cook, hired soon after, was Sourdough Sam, who turned logging camp cookery into an art. Sunday dinners during the cookhouse reign of Sourdough Sam were enough to make a logger dream feverishly through Tuesday night and drool in his sleep for several nights more.

Hot Biscuit Slim, Sourdough Sam's son, wasn't bad, either. They said that Hot Biscuit Slim's kitchen was as large as 10 Ford factories and as noisy as the Battle of Gettysburg.

The dining hall was so big that four-horse teams pulled wagon loads of salt, pepper and sugar down the aisles. Conveyor belts carried clean dishes to the tables and hauled dirty ones away. Flunkies on roller skates performed table service and it was said that the fastest of them could circumnavigate the dining hall in 47 minutes.

The kitchen, Hot Biscuit Slim's pride and joy, boasted of steam-driven potato mashers and air-cooled, sleeve-valve egg beaters. (To say nothing of gigantic stew kettles in which beef carcasses floated "like chips in a mill pond.")

One of Paul Bunyan's most curious adventures was the Round River Drive. Paul and the crew had spent most of the summer logging in the Leaning Pine Forest, where all of the trees leaned in the same direction, making logging almost as easy as it was in the Pine Orchard. But that's another story.

They put a record number of logs from Leaning Pine Forest in the Round River and started the drive to the mill.

For nine days they drove the logs and never reached the mill, but passed their old camp three times! Finally Johnny Inkslinger was asked to survey the river.

It was perfectly round! They had driven the logs three times over the same route!

Paul Bunyan knew there was nothing to do but to saw up the logs and transport them overland, so he built a sawmill 19 stories high. The smokestacks were so tall that Paul had to install hinges in them so they could be lowered to let the clouds go by.

It's hard to believe . . . but this is what Paul Bunyan had to do.

Paul Bunyan had a farm. The products of the farm were hauled by Shagline Bill to the logging camp. On Paul Bunyan's farm, he had some cows. Boss was the butter cow; you had only to put salt in her milk and stir it a little, let it stand for a bit and you had the finest butter in the world. Baldy's milk never turned sour; it was wonderful in cream gravy. S'manthy's milk wasn't the best but she liked to eat balsam boughs. As a result, her milk in winter was about the best cough medicine a man could get.

He had chickens, too, Paul Bunyan did. Snow hens, for instance, which made nests in the snow and laid nothing but hard-boiled eggs. On Paul Bunyan's farm, carrots grew so deep that stump-pullers had to be used to snatch them out of the ground; it took two men an hour and a half to cut the average cabbage from its stalk. Chewing tobacco grew on Paul Bunyan's farm in plugs, shreds and twists, and it was well-flavored by the

natural licorice in the soil.

It's hard to believe . . . but so it was.

The history books don't tell about it, but it was Babe, the Blue Ox, who made Kansas the flat state it is today. After Paul's crew had logged off a section of rolling ground, Babe was hitched to the land. Babe grunted and strained and got the earth to moving, then with a twitch of his shoulders turned it over. And so they discovered that although the land was rolling on top, it was *flat* underneath. Kansas remains flat to this day.

Babe was strong, all right, and he ate hay bales by the hundreds, wire and all, but there came a time when his stomach acted up on him. Soon Babe was very sick and the situation grew desperate. Without Babe, Paul Bunyan's logging operation was finished. Johnny Inkslinger, camp doctor, thought deep thoughts and decided that the old fashioned medicines, alcohol and Epsom salts, weren't good enough for a blue ox; the only medicine which would cure Babe was the milk of the Western Whale. Exactly; the milk of the Western Whale . . .

Immediately Paul Bunyan ordered the camp moved west. At a rest stop along the trail, Paul and his foreman, the Big Swede, passed the time by building a landmark. They heaped dirt around a pike pole and when the pile was finished, Paul liked it so much that he gave it the name it bears today, "Pike's Peak."

Finally they reached the seacoast and Paul quickly set the crew to building a whale corral with dirt walls. Babe was still very sick but he did manage to muster the strength to kick a hole in the seaward side of the corral so the sea could enter. The whales weren't far behind. The corral then was closed off, trapping a fair number of the great beasts.

However, it is one thing to corral a whale; it is quite another to milk it. But the Big Swede (who in his youth was considered the greatest milker in Sweden) managed to extract a pail of milk after a day of bruising work. (The little whales kept thumping him with their tails.)

Babe drank the milk but it didn't seem to help.

Johnny Inkslinger's reputation was at stake, so he raced around until he found a soapbox, mounted it and cried; "It is a nature cure! It cures slowly because nature cures slowly, but it cures surely and divinely! It is a great cure because it is a great idea, a marvelous idea, a heaven-sent idea, an original idea, my own idea, and it is the idea which will save us all!"

Once the Spokane River was choked with logs on their way to the McGoldrick Lumber Company. In modern Spokane, the Olive Street bridge crosses at approximately this point.

Against his better judgment, Paul let the treatment proceed. Always before, Dr. Inkslinger's treatment for almost any ailment had been Epsom salts and medicinal alcohol. Now that he had switched to whale milk, Paul suspected, his medical career might be nearing its close.

For a week Babe drank whale milk. By the fourth day, he refused to open his eyes while he drank. Then he refused to drink at all. Except that his eyelids twitched once in a while, Babe, the Blue Ox, might have been dead.

"He is dying," Paul Bunyan finally said with a mighty sigh.

Johnny Inkslinger leaped onto his soap box and cried, "Listen! This miraculous idea—"

"Quiet!" roared Paul Bunyan.

Then not even the wind dared to whisper in the trees.

For 69 hours, Paul Bunyan proceeded to deliver Babe's funeral oration and at the end of it, he announced that the last job they would all undertake together would be to go north and dig Babe's grave. He did not blame Johnny Inkslinger, he said. Inkslinger had been a good doctor; now, as a doctor, he was still a good bookkeeper.

Tears streamed from the eyes of most of the loggers and the tears fell to the ground and puddled there until most of them were standing knee-deep in mud.

Disgraced, Johnny Inkslinger slunk into his office and closed the door. The loggers cleaned the mud off their boots and set out for the north with heavy hearts, leaving the Big Swede with the dying ox.

Johnny Inkslinger sulked in his office, then fought his way out of his funk. An idea burrowed into his brain. He rushed out to the Big Swede, who sat in sorrow by the blue ox, and ordered, "Listen now! You are to sit here and repeat continuously in a soothing voice, 'You are well. You are well. You are well.' Do you understand? Do as I have told you and Babe's life will be saved. Do not fail, for all depends on your faithfulness! When I have returned with Mr. Bunyan, I will finish the cure myself."

The timekeeper then hurried off to tell Paul Bunyan that he could stop his dismal digging because Babe was going to get well after all.

Following his orders, the Big Swede said into Babe's ear, "You ban well. You ban well. You ban well."

Carefully-constructed rafts like this one photographed on the lower Columbia in 1910 were first used by Simon Benson, pioneer Northwest lumberman, to transport logs as far as San Diego. Benson led the way in the use of rail locomotives and steam donkey engines in the woods, too.

For 31 hours, without interruption, he said into Babe's ear, "You ban well." At this point his mouth dried up completely and his voice grew hoarse. At last he had to whisper and finally he couldn't even do that.

Then he remembered that once Johnny Inkslinger's medicinal alcohol had aided his own recovery from serious injuries; perhaps it would help him now! Fired by the knowledge that Babe's life was at stake, he ran to Inkslinger's office, took three barrels of the doctor's medicinal alcohol under his arm and returned to Babe's side, whereupon he slurped a great drink from one of the barrels.

His voice promptly returned. He was able to go on with the treatment, taking only one drink every few hours, but then the hoarseness got worse and he had to drink oftener. When it came time to tap the third barrel, his brain was getting fuzzy and instead of saying "You ban well," he sighed and lolled on Babe's neck murmuring, "You poor ol' sick feller . . you poor ol' sick feller."

And then the Big Swede fell over in a snoring sleep and as he did so, he knocked over the last barrel of medicinal alcohol and it began to spill onto the ground! History often hangs on little accidents and so it was at that time and place.

Some of the alcohol oozed into Babe's nostrils, then into his mouth. The ox opened his eyes, shook his head and quivered from horns to tail. He sat up, looking around for more of the healing potion.

Finding none, he rose clumsily and swung his head. His eyes fastened on the barrels visible through the open door of Inkslinger's office.

With his tongue hanging out, Babe lurched toward the open door, kicked a wall in, knocked the ends out of the barrels with a few flicks of his tail, and then, in exactly 19 minutes, drained all of the barrels dry.

In seven gulps, he cleaned up the store of Epsom salts; a few more gulps took care of the remaining stock of Dr. Inkslinger's oldtime medicines.

Whereupon Babe raced outside and pranced around looking for his master and playmate, Paul Bunyan. Not finding him, he set out in search, but his brain soon fogged. He began to wander aimlessly (staggered, really) and he lost his way. The way grew hard; he sank knee-deep into the desert with every step; sweat rolled down his back and formed a crooked river in his crooked path.

The fever left his blood but he grew weak. When his strength was

Shades of Paul Bunyan! A mechanized Babe the Blue Ox, the world's largest log stacker, works at Chelatchie.

nearly gone, he clambered onto a plateau and lay down and closed his bloodshot eyes.

It was here, on this lonely plateau, that Babe was found by Paul Bunyan and his loggers three weeks later; they had been searching that long.

At first it appeared that Babe was dead but Johnny Inkslinger would not give up hope. He had finally shaken off his radical notions about doctoring and carried with him the case containing the last of his oldtime medicines. Working with the speed of a desperate man, he poured all of the medicinal alcohol and Epsom salts down Babe's throat, whereupon Babe lifted his head and let out a healthy bellow which knocked down everybody for miles around.

"He is cured!" hollered the loggers as they picked themselves up.

"Yah," said the Big Swede, with a Big Smile.

And so it was, back in the Good Old Days.

The stream which flowed down the crooked trail left by the blue ox came to be called Snake River. (You may check this in any geography book.) The whale corral became Coos Bay, Oregon. The unfinished grave for Babe is now known as Puget Sound. Washington's Cascade Mountains are composed of the dirt thrown up by Paul Bunyan and his crew when they dug the grave and the biggest pile is called "Mt. Bunyan" by loggers, "Mt. Tacoma" by Indians and residents of Tacoma, "Mt. Rainier" by tourists, who for some soggy reason consider the weather of this region rainier than that of almost any other.

So says James Stevens, whose scholarly book of 1925, "Paul Bunyan," cast new biographical light on the inventor of logging. Stevens had been a Washington logger himself, so one hardly dares to doubt him. He picked up most of his historical accounts in the bunkhouses of logging camps, which surely makes them as authentic as a Paul Bunyan chronicle can be.

Said Stevens about his bunkhouse days: "A Paul Bunyan bunkhouse service is a glory to hear when it is spontaneous and in a proper setting; preferably around a big heater in winter, when the wind is howling through crackling boughs outside, and the pungent smell of steaming wool drifts down from the drying lines above the stove . . ."

You have to believe it. Would a logger lie?

SUGGESTED READING

Andrews, Ralph W.; GLORY DAYS OF LOGGING; Superior; 1956.

Andrews, Ralph W.; HEROES OF THE WESTERN WOODS; Dutton; 1960.

Hurst, Randle M.; THE SMOKEJUMPERS; Caxton; 1967.

Johnson, Jalmar; BUILDERS OF THE NORTHWEST; Dodd, Mead; 1963 (Henry Yesler).

Rounds, Glen; OL' PAUL, THE MIGHTY LOGGER; Holiday; 1949.

Stoutenburg, Adrien, and Laura Nelson Baker; WILD TREASURE: THE STORY OF DAVID DOUGLAS; Scribner's; 1958.

A workboat from Pasco nudges a barge into the lock at The Dalles Dam on the Columbia.

Chapter Seven ★

Water Commerce
A SEA, A SOUND, A RIVER

The area entered history with the world's greatest ocean lapping its western shore and bouncing on the billows of its storms the impudent little sailing ships of brave and greedy explorers. There was the swift river, too, majestically flowing south and west and providing a heart-racing highway for bold spirits who meant to reach the great ocean or die.

There was the saltwater sound, a wide and winding gash in the northwest corner, with its countless intriguing bays, inlets, coves, islands and peninsulas. And there was a large freshwater lake close to a splendid bay in the sound, a most logical site for a city of size, a city that would gladly face the sound and encircle the lake and draw its lifeblood from the water. Washington . . .

Washington and water, then and now, are as inseparable as trees and wood. And where man exists near water, there will be boats. A century of human life on the land called Washington separate the Duwamish canoe and the glistening ferry *Hyak;* they are utterly unlike in size, speed and capacity. But they sprang from the same basic urge and need: man must transport himself, his belongings and his trade goods across water.

It's hardly surprising, then, that the state of Washington now operates the largest ferryboat system in the world. Or that boat ownership in the Puget Sound area, per capita, is the highest in the United States and powerboat ownership highest in the world. Washington's 16 deepwater ports attract ships from 69 ocean shipping lines which connect the state with most of the world's harbors. More than a tenth of Washington's families depend upon international trade for a livelihood. Watch the clock for five minutes; during that five minutes in 1968, the state of Washington exported $15,000 worth of goods and imported $9000 worth. The end is by no means in sight because during the decade beginning in 1959,

Washington's imports doubled and Washington's exports tripled!

Where there is water, there will be ships. Ships and water equal wages and profits; boats and water equal fun. Washington has a full measure of both. The lure of the sea for man is legendary. Man has always huddled around the water for the riches in it and upon it. Washington is a colorful, lively, romantic place to live and it always has been; water is mainly responsible. Much of its folklore has to do with water.

When a Washingtonian brags, it is likely to be a wet brag, if not quite a fish story.

Like sea storms, for instance. Even outsiders help with the bragging about these. David Douglas, pioneer botanist after whom the fir tree is named, was an awestruck witness to a storm off the Columbia River bar in 1825. As a passenger on the good ship *William and Ann,* Douglas described the gale as "a thousand times worse than those of the noted Cape Horn."

In pioneer days around Puget Sound, Tacoma grabbed an early edge over Seattle. Tacoma's main boast was Commencement Bay, so deep, the first settlers insisted, that any ship could be moored simply by tying it to trees along the bank. It might have been true, once upon a time, but a long search today through Tacoma's busy, elaborate waterfront wouldn't turn up a single ship tied to a tree.

Seattle got a slow start but in time it dredged up a resounding boast that holds good today. "Bring your ship here," said the Seattleite, "and you may choose between saltwater moorage or freshwater. If you choose freshwater, the barnacles will be cleaned off your hull automatically."

And it was true. Saltwater moorage was available in Elliott Bay. With the completion of the Lake Washington ship canal in 1916, an ocean-going vessel could leave the bay, pass through the locks and Lake Union, then moor in the fresh water of long, wide Lake Washington. The saltwater creatures called barnacles, glued to the hulls and growing, could not survive a prolonged stay in Lake Washington. (Lake Union, once fresh water, is gradually getting salty.)

The aforementioned locks, incidentally, shouldn't be passed over too lightly, so long as we're boasting. Only the Panama Canal locks have a greater capacity on this continent.

One good boast deserves another. In Washington, even small towns can get into the act. Charming little Port Townsend, for instance, which overlooks Admiralty Inlet on one side and the Strait of Juan de Fuca on the other, once was second only to New York City in ship traffic. Multi-storied stone and brick buildings, mostly empty, remain to remind of the glory that was . . . but wasn't quite. At one time rich and powerful men had grand plans for Port Townsend but the bubbles burst; today Port Townsend peacefully watches as ship traffic glides down the inlet toward Seattle, Tacoma, Olympia or other ports on the Sound. One gets the pleasant feeling that modern Port Townsend couldn't care less. Once only New York City surpassed it; it seems enough for any town to say.

When Washingtonians tire of bragging big, they brag small. Native Olympia oysters are the smallest in the world; it takes the meat of 500 to fill a quart jar.

Bridges are always good for a brag or two. A proud citizen of Seattle can point out that the floating bridges across Lake Washington are some of the largest concrete pontoon bridges in the world. The Longview Bridge across the Columbia once was the longest-spanned cantilever bridge in the country and also the highest bridge over a navigable stream.

With some bridges, though, one must get one's boasting done quickly. Tacoma Narrows Bridge, when dedicated on July 4, 1940, was the fourth largest suspension bridge in the world. Four months later, Tacoma Narrows set a new world's record by falling down.

Soon after its opening, the bridge earned a sour nickname: "Galloping Gertie." On a still day, the bridge was firm and sturdy. But let a light breeze filter down the Narrows and Gertie began to gallop, pitch, roll, twist and turn.

Now even the engineers became concerned and tried to calm the jittery center span of the bridge with long, heavy wires attached to the main suspension cables.

On November 7, 1940, the wind through the Narrows had reached a velocity of 42 m.p.h. by 10:30 A.M. Two Tacoma news photographers, Leonard Coatsworth and James Bashford, took many remarkable pictures of the span in its mounting frenzy.

Coatsworth was the last to cross the bridge; the trip cost him his car and his dog because the bridge twisted itself to pieces and plunged to the bottom of the Narrows.

Back to the drawing board. Ten years later, a new Narrows bridge was opened to traffic. This time the designers had been careful to put plenty of holes in the structure, reasoning that it was better to let wind pass through

➡

Galloping, going, gone! Tacoma Narrows Bridge writhes, then falls. In first picture, note car on center span. Steel recovered from the wreckage was used to build bridges on the Alaska Highway.

than to force it to bat the bridge out of the way. The new bridge galloped only during earthquakes and everyone who uses it agrees that this is a worthwhile improvement.

Having solved the pressing problem of getting cars and people across Tacoma Narrows, shall we for a moment brag about the river? The Columbia, of course.

Over the centuries, this aggressive river has carried sand and silt from an area larger than France. This greedy habit causes a serious problem only when the river reaches the end of the line, at which point the sand and silt get off.

At its mouth, the Columbia smacks head-on into the Pacific Ocean in a classic example of the irresistible force meeting the immovable object. (Or perhaps the irresistible force meeting the irresistible force, which is exciting, too.)

The river's current vs. the ocean's tides—a mighty match, with the winner still in doubt.

At first, the ocean seems to have an edge as the Columbia yields and allows the rise and fall of ocean tides to be felt as far upstream as the base of Bonneville Dam, 140 miles from the river's mouth!

But the river strikes back with a snarl and dumps its load of sand in treacherous bars and islands where it meets the sea. Columbia River sand, dragged laboriously downstream over many centuries and flung in the face of the ocean, covers a hundred miles of Oregon and Washington coastline.

The resulting beaches delight bathers and clamdiggers but the sandbars drive ship captains and marine insurance people out of their minds. A modern ocean-going ship represents an investment of several millions of dollars. Poke that ship into a sneaky sandbar at the Columbia's mouth and craft and cargo can be battered to bits in a matter of hours by a northwest gale.

If the sand would only stay put, it might be coped with. But how can it stay put with ocean tides pushing and pulling from one side and river current slamming at it from the other?

There is a record of a certain Captain Menes who followed his charts faithfully in shepherding his French bark, *Morning Star,* through the pitfalls of the Columbia's gaping maw. When his ship scraped sickeningly to a stop on an unannounced sandbar, Captain Menes muttered a few

The Columbia meets the sea at the bar dreaded by seamen for more than a century. At the center of the picture is the north jetty; at middle left, the surf marks Peacock Spit, with North Head beyond.

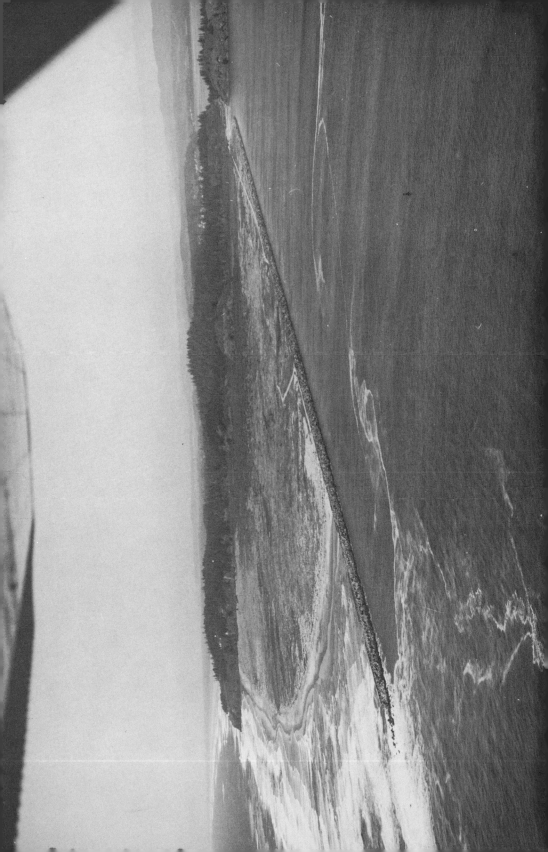

fervent words through his mustache, then stepped to the rail of his trapped and tilted ship and pitched all of his charts overboard.

The U.S. Navy sent *U.S.S. Peacock* to survey the Columbia River in 1841. The ship promptly stuck itself on the north spit of the river entrance. "Peacock Spit" has since taken a fearful toll. Mariners continued to complain that the channel across the bar was seldom in the same place from one crossing to the next. In time, dredging and construction of two jetties helped to stabilize the ship route through the shifting sand. The life of a sailor became a little easier; at least the days were gone when sailing vessels might have to wait offshore for as long as six weeks before their captains dared to send them across the bar.

Marine insurance companies had special reason to hate Peacock Spit. The Columbia Bar didn't really earn its grim nickname "Pacific Grave-yard" until the turn of the century, when ships under sail were going out of fashion and steam propulsion was coming in. Most of the ships wrecked on the spit carried sails and the loss of life was suspiciously low. If a captain rammed his sailing ship aground on Peacock Spit at high tide, there was almost no chance to get it free, but come the next low tide, the crew could walk safely ashore. The insurance payoff provided a handsome down payment on a modern steamship.

Along about 1948, a man and idea met and threw a challenge into the teeth of the Columbia Bar. Fred Devine of Portland developed a giant tugboat called *Salvage Chief* and announced to insurance companies that he was ready to pull ships off the sands and would work on a "no cure, no pay" contract. In 1952, the *Salvage Chief* pulled *S.S. Yorkmar* off the sand north of Grays Harbor and as soon as the news flashed along the water-fronts of the world, the entrance to the Columbia lost some of its terror.

But there was, and is, more to the Columbia than a mouth. There was a freeway of water reaching far into the interior of a rich, developing land. Captain John C. Ainsworth saw the need and the opportunity and sent his sidewheelers and sternwheelers churning up and down the river with wood smoke pouring from their funnels and a glorious chapter of history trailing in their foaming wakes.

In the half century following 1850, during those gruelling but excit-ing days when the American West was conquered, transportation was a horse or ox-drawn wagon on land or some sort of boat on water. Ains-worth's Oregon Steam Navigation Company ruled the Columbia from 1860 until the railroads sank the glamorous steamboats no more than two decades later.

As transportation, railroads undoubtedly made more sense but from the standpoint of romance and excitement, they were poor substitutes for an Ainsworth steamboat charging down the Columbia with pitch-pine smoke spewing from its funnel and the froth behind it a banner of defiance waved in the face of lesser mortals and machines bringing up the rear. Proud vessels they were, with proud men aboard.

One of the proudest was the *Bailey Gatzert,* named for a Seattle mayor. Often two steamers would race; the winner tied a broom to the jackmast to proclaim that she had swept the field.

Trickery sometimes carried the day. A steamboat named *The Old Settler* ran through Puget Sound in 1878 between Shelton and Olympia. Its whistle was very loud and proud, due to the fact that it drew a ridiculous amount of steam. This was known by a certain Captain Chapman, who had put an engine on a grubby scow, then dared to name it *The Capitol* and run it through the same waters coursed by respectable steamers.

Encountering *The Old Settler* off Olympia, the cunning Captain Chapman blew his whistle. *The Old Settler,* bound by rigid rules of seagoing courtesy, had to answer with a thundering blast and then slowed as its steam pressure fell off sharply.

As *The Old Settler* gasped for power, Captain Chapman's sluggish scow passed her and beat her into port. Moral: hares can win races against tortoises but not if the hares insist on whistling.

Big money was made quickly in steamboating on the river. It wasn't unusual for a boat to earn $3000–5000 from a single trip. The record may be held by the *Tenino,* which is said to have cleared $18,000 from just one rich cruise above Celilo Falls to the gold rush areas.

But the railroads wouldn't be denied. The steamboats foundered before the turn of the century. Captain Ainsworth sold his Oregon Steam Navigation Company to a railroader, Henry Villard. The iron horse, whipped across the prairies and through the mountains by such titans as Jim Hill, E. H. Harriman and Henry Villard, was too fast and dependable; steamboats couldn't compete. Thus a colorful chapter of Northwest history ended but some of the aftertaste, if not all of the tang, lingers on in Washington's ferry system.

★

The many thousands of square miles of salt waterways which make up Washington's inland passages have borne upon their usually quiet surfaces some startling craft, beginning with clipper-hulled Indian canoes which paddled about their business for centuries before the white man decided to take over the real estate and subdivide.

There was the *Beaver,* for instance, first steamship to operate in the Pacific. Then there was *U.S.S. Decatur,* perhaps the only federal warship ever to play a major role in defending a frontier settlement under attack by Indians.

The *Beaver* was 100 feet, 9 inches long. The current queen of Washington's inland sea, the super battleship *U.S.S. Missouri,* is almost eight feet wider than *Beaver* was long!

The name *Beaver* was doubly suited to this sturdy little craft with copper-sheathed wooden hull. Beavers in the wild, according to rumor, are busy, and their namesake chugged energetically around the Northwest coast carrying dairy products to Russians in Alaska, livestock to Vancouver Island, furs (including many beaver pelts) to Fort Vancouver, mail and supplies from Fort Vancouver to all the outlying Hudson's Bay coastal stations.

Built in England, *Beaver* voyaged into the Pacific under sail, with her paddle wheels stowed on deck. It seemed that her greedy little firebox demanded as much as 40 cords of wood per day. Forests in the Atlantic Ocean are notably sparse, so she sailed before the wind. At Fort Vancouver, *Beaver* lost its sails, regained its paddles and was put into service despite an apparent lack of enthusiasm on the part of Dr. John McLoughlin, who was running the region for Hudson's Bay Company. McLoughlin was thinking, no doubt, about those 40 daily cords of wood.

But sailing ships had to depend upon nature's erratic breezes. Sometimes *Beaver* moved when sailing ships lay in the water becalmed. So what if *Beaver* did have to stop every other day to allow the crew to go ashore and cut those 40 cords? It was a steamship, the only one around, and it worked . . . after a fashion.

Writing in "Northwest Magazine," Art Chipman recreated a *Beaver* voyage in this manner:

"Each spring the *Beaver* would make a trip to the Russian settlement at Sitka for trading and then work back down the coast, stopping at the various Indian villages and company stations along the way, trading knives, beads, guns, hatchets, cloth, etc., for furs and other items. As an indication of the busy trading activity of the time and area, following is a list of the furs and items traded for at Fort Simpson during August 1837: 7 large black bear, 9 small black bear, 2 small brown bear, 581 large

This unusual picture of Beaver *on the skids for maintenance shows many details not visible in other pictures.*

beaver, 234 small beaver, 23 pup and cutting beaver, 6 fishers, 1 cross-fox, 16 lynx, 1 lynx robe (8 skins), 736 martens, 9 marten robes, 96 mink, 70 musquash (muskrat), 39 large land-otter, 5 small land-otter, 1 small sea-otter, 1 pup sea-otter, 2 wolverines, 2 meat of beaver, 85 pounds of deer's tallow, 28½ bushels of potatoes (one wonders where these came from), 154 halibut, 58 deer, 10 geese, 1,033 fresh and half dry salmon and 23 seal skins. This is over 1800 furs, along with a number of other items of value, so one can readily see why the fur trade could be a very profitable venture."

The *Beaver* finished its service with Hudson's Bay, carried passengers to Alaska during the gold rush, then served the British charting the north Pacific coast and finally did duty as a tugboat.

In 1888, working out of Vancouver, B.C., *Beaver* died a grinding death on the rocks off Burrard Inlet.

She was a pioneering machine, the *Beaver,* and few of the craft which came after deserve more acclaim. Today an ancient boiler of the historic sidewheeler lies in state behind the museum of the Washington State Historical Society in Tacoma.

★

The war sloop called *U.S.S. Decatur* sailed into Elliott Bay off the tiny settlement of Seattle on the afternoon of October 4, 1855. The three-masted ship dropped anchor and fired a gun through one of many ports high in her hull. It was a heartwarming sound to pioneers on the beach. At any moment, they feared, angry Indians would attack and overwhelm their struggling community. Then there would be American skulls displayed on pike poles in the Indian villages.

Decatur had been lying off tropical Honolulu, in what was then called the Sandwich Islands, when its Captain Sterrett received orders "to cruise the coast of Oregon and California for the protection of settlers." Sterrett chose to operate in Puget Sound, where there was Indian trouble and threats of more to come. Governor Stevens was in the Rocky Mountains, desperately negotiating with the Blackfeet. Stevens had worked hard but ". . . the first of his treaties had blown up before the last was signed."

The stage was set for the Siege of Seattle; the spotlight was on *Decatur,* uneasily at anchor in Elliott Bay. Fear oozed out of the thick forest behind the town but the developing drama wasn't entirely tragic after all; it was partly comic opera.

Her hull encrusted, Beaver *died this ignominious death in Canadian waters.*

According to the rumors flickering among the citizens of the few log and split cedar cabins called Seattle, thousands of angry Indians from across the mountains, as well as the surly locals, were about to descend and destroy. There had been isolated attacks on homesteads near the town. There had also been strange noises, both real and imagined, arising out of the forest almost every night. (There is nothing quite like a dark forest when it comes to producing fearsome noises.)

There were Indians, all right, only two hundred or so, and they did have designs on Seattle; what they mainly wanted was not skulls but food and powder.

Then it was found necessary to beach *Decatur* and settlers felt even more vulnerable with the warship on the sand. Morale hit bottom when inspection indicated that *Decatur* was a rotten hulk, little more than dry rot glued together loosely by an inch of outside wood.

And so it became possible that a bored young sailor from *Decatur,* John Drew, could attempt to crawl through a window of a house near the edge of town. A young lady was awakened as Drew was halfway in. The young lady slammed down the sash, pinning the sailor at a point where her brother, aroused by her screams, could trot into position with his fowling piece and pepper the skull of John Drew.

It was characteristic of the Siege of Seattle that the first man killed was one who was being paid to defend the town. It also figured that a *Decatur* gun crew, trying to cut a trail for one of the ship's mortars in order to gain a better field of fire for the impending attack, should have been stopped by a mere woman. Maybe not "mere"; the woman was Mary Ann Conklin, an early Seattle character better known as "Madam Damnable,"· and besides, she was supported by several irritable dogs.

To shorten a long comic opera, Seattle was saved. The rotting *Decatur* helped considerably by firing shells which, according to startled Indians, *"mox poohed";* that is, fired twice, once when they left the barrels of the *Decatur,* again after they landed ashore. A Lieutenant Phelps of the *Decatur* described a band of Indians which danced around one of the shells after it landed, then when the shell *"mox poohed,"* was blown to smithereens.

The U.S.S. Decatur *was photographed at anchor in Elliott Bay off Seattle in 1856.*

196

From *Beaver* to *Decatur* to *Missouri*—a natural progression in the waters of Washington. *Missouri* was the last super battleship to be built by the United States and Washington has her.

Missouri has been tied to a pier at Bremerton since 1955, when she was taken out of active service and consigned to the Navy's "mothball fleet" in which ships not needed at the moment are preserved for possible future use. Now aircraft carriers and nuclear submarines rule the seas. But *Missouri* still lifts her long, graceful snout in pride before the nearly 200,000 persons who visit her every year, for *Missouri,* all 888 feet of her, is not merely the last of the big battlewagons; she is a historic site. The world's most widespread war officially ended on her deck.

A plaque on *Missouri* reads: "USS MISSOURI . . . OVER THIS SPOT ON 2 SEPTEMBER 1945 THE INSTRUMENT OF FORMAL SURRENDER OF JAPAN TO THE ALLIED POWERS WAS SIGNED THUS BRINGING TO A CLOSE THE SECOND WORLD WAR . . . THE SHIP AT THAT TIME WAS AT ANCHOR IN TOKYO BAY."

Before her quiet role as surrender site, "Mighty Mo" had earned three battle stars for supporting the climactic invasions of Iwo Jima and Okinawa and for Third Fleet operations against the home islands of Japan.

Tourists visiting the great ship at Bremerton receive a pamphlet which sets down some of her vital statistics. It has four main engines, for instance, each of 53,000 horsepower! (This explains, at least in part, why *Missouri* could outrun some swift destroyers in any kind of weather.) Its wartime crew consisted of 2700 sailors; it was nothing less than a floating town.

A battleship is only as good as its armament. *Missouri* carried nine 16-inch guns and 20 five-inchers. A single shell for its big cannons weighed one and one-half tons. (Talk about *mox pooh!*)

U.S.S. Missouri is the showpiece of Puget Sound Naval Shipyard, which is far and away the largest installation of its kind in the Pacific Northwest. Established way back in 1891, the yard has become Bremerton's largest single employer as it goes about its daily business of building, repairing and storing ships. In the process, it not only injects important vitamins into Washington's economy but supplies as well a strong dash of color in the maritime landscape.

Where there are ships, one expects to find shipbuilders. So it was and is in Washington. In 1875, there were 14 shipyards around Puget Sound.

Mighty Mo, the super battleship Missouri, *was photographed at its Bremerton berth in 1968.*

But shipbuilding remained a minor industry in the Northwest until 1915, when World War I hypoed the demand. Some ships still were built out of wood in those days and Washington had plenty of raw material. One of the major scandals of the day had to do with ships hurriedly built from green lumber out of Washington's woods. As the new ships steamed south toward the Panama Canal, sometimes the green wood shrank and the ships sank.

Shipbuilding slipped into doldrums when the war ended and didn't revive again until 1941, when a new war created a huge demand for ocean-going cargo carriers. This time a bald, fat and determined man by the name of Henry Kaiser leaped into the breach.

Soon Kaiser had 200,000 workers building ships in seven yards along the Pacific Coast, including Vancouver in Washington. He started out building a Liberty ship in an average of 253 days. Then the average was dropped to only 26 days. Finally a Kaiser yard laid the keel of a ship and splashed it into the water only four days, 15 hours and 26 minutes later! When the war ended, one Liberty ship per day was coming out of Kaiser yards and one aircraft carrier per week. At the peak in 1944, the payroll at Kaiser's Vancouver yard exceeded a million dollars per week. When housing ran short, Kaiser built two temporary cities, Vanport across the Columbia in Oregon and McLoughlin Heights near Vancouver. Vanport, destroyed in a 1948 flood, was once the second largest city in Oregon. McLoughlin Heights is now a part of Vancouver.

Todd-Pacific Shipbuilding Corporation, with yards at Tacoma and Seattle, also contributed mightily to the war effort.

★

The state of Washington and particularly its queen city, Seattle, owe a lot to Alaska. Life and breath, for instance, plus a dominant role in the economic life of the Pacific Northwest.

Along about 1873, the men who were running the Northern Pacific railroad decided that Tacoma was to be their terminus on the Pacific Coast.

Those hardy souls who were struggling to bring little Seattle out of the doldrums groaned. Tacomans gloated: "Seattle, Seattle. Death rattle, death rattle."

Portland, prosperous metropolis of Oregon, joined in throwing stones at the anemic settlement on Elliott Bay.

But the citizens of Seattle were stubborn. If the Northern Pacific

Seattle's great fire in 1889 left dramatic ruins like these.

wouldn't build them a railroad east across the mountains, they would build their own. They failed, in a way, but did manage to stretch their rails into nearby coalfields. Hauling coal, their little line prospered quickly while the Northern Pacific, with its big ideas, went broke again and again, thus gaining time for Seattle as Tacoma was held back.

Both towns made a big pitch for new residents as they disembarked by the hundreds from steamers inbound from San Francisco. One cynical newcomer was moved to remark that "this was a fishy country. Salmon in the sea, sharks on the shore and suckers on the ships."

But at times Seattle and Tacoma were friendly enemies. In 1889, a terrible fire destroyed Seattle's entire business district, 50 blocks of it. Seattle proved capable of lifting itself out of the smoking ruins but its suffering would have been much greater without help from Tacoma. Seattle businessmen resumed operation quickly out of tents hastily erected on ground still "almost too hot to stand on." In one hour, Tacomans raised $10,000 for relief to fire victims and later doubled the amount. By dawn of the next day, Tacoma had sent a boatload of provisions. In addition, residents of Tacoma set up a relief tent which prepared more than 41,000 meals during the first month after the fire. Tacoma sent firefighting equipment, too, as did Olympia, Portland and Victoria, B.C.

The depression of 1893 clutched the throat of the country and wounded Seattle again, but in 1897, a wild shout rose out of the Klondike: GOLD! Seattle had nothing to do with making the strike but Seattle was there to take advantage of it, both coming and going.

Soon after the big strike, the first steamer from the gold fields docked in Seattle carrying $35,000 worth of gold. It was only the first few drops of a cloudburst.

Gold fever erupted like influenza. Writing in "One Man's Gold Rush," Murray Morgan reported: "Nils Anderson of Seattle, who had been unable to find work in the lumber camps in the summer of 1895, had borrowed three hundred dollars and gone north with nothing in his favor except desperation. His wife, whom he had left with several small children and no income, had heard he was on his way out and was waiting on the dock, hopeful that their luck had changed. Indeed it had. Anderson debarked with so much gold a friend had to help him carry it—112,500 dollars' worth.

"Another Scandinavian rushed to the express office with a canvas sack

Tacoma fought Seattle for supremacy on the Sound but after Seattle's terrible fire of 1889, Tacoma quickly set up a relief tent and fed thousands.

TACOMA RELIEF BUREAU

he wanted to forward to the mint at San Francisco, Seattle having no assay office at the time. 'I tank I have twenty tousand five huner dollar,' he told the clerk, who put the gold on the scales and corrected him. It weighed out at approximately forty-two thousand dollars.

"William Stanley of Anacortes had left his wife with only twenty dollars when he went north. She had been supporting herself by taking in washing and picking blackberries. She hadn't heard that he was coming Outside. He wired her from Seattle to stop washing and start buying, they were worth ninety thousand dollars."

A reporter from the *Seattle Post-Intelligencer* boarded the steamer *Portland* as she entered the Strait of Juan de Fuca. He telegraphed to his newspaper that the ship carried "more than a ton in gold." Actually, the *Portland* carried almost two tons and was booked full for her return trip even before she reached Seattle.

The Alaska trade soon reached astounding proportions as miners and supplies went north and miners and gold came south. The jumping-off place for the Klondike quickly became Seattle and the town promptly adopted Alaska. To this day, Alaska trade is a staple of Seattle commerce and the city burghers hope it shall always be.

So many gold-hungry prospectors flocked to Seattle that citizens near the business district rented rocking chairs on their porches for 25 cents an hour to those who needed to catch their breath before boarding a ship outward bound to destiny.

Klondikers bought up Seattle sled dogs (real and fanciful) so eagerly that the supply soon was exhausted and for a time the bustling town, in the words of a reporter, "became a cat's paradise."

Spurred by the Alaska trade, Seattle not only survived but prospered wildly. Even after the gold cargoes petered out, wealth continued to pour out of Alaska toward Seattle in the form of fish. Fishermen began to make fabulous catches in Alaskan waters and Seattle accepted eagerly the countless tons of salmon, halibut and cod which weighed down the homecoming boats. The city became home port for many Alaska fishermen and fish processing quickly developed into a major industry.

Seattle was on its way to becoming the undisputed queen of Puget Sound and the largest city in the Northwest. It is hardly surprising that today Seattle (and all of western Washington, for that matter) looks with considerable fondness on Alaska and Alaskans.

The Alaska gold ship Roanoke *discharged and took on hundreds of stampeding Klondikers at a Seattle wharf.*

If the truth were known, Puget Sound is a whole lot deeper than it needs to be. After all, who needs 900 feet of salt water under his ship?

But the depth of the sound and its major harbors has attracted shipmasters and town planners for more than a century. A ship stuck on a sandbar is useless, merely flotsam and jetsam in the making. The entrance to Puget Sound is the wide Strait of Juan de Fuca which feeds into Admiralty Inlet, the latter not so wide as the strait but still carrying enough water to give a sober ship captain considerable margin for error. A captain doesn't even have to take on a pilot to enter the Sound in clear weather but on frequent foggy days and nights he might well ask for such assistance.

The ports of Seattle, Bellingham, Everett, Tacoma and Olympia are far inland but the world's shipping lines gladly enter the friendly waterways leading to them.

Canada is the most important international trader in the Washington Customs District. (Washington's Columbia River ports of Longview, Vancouver and Kalama are included in the Oregon Customs District, an indignity which they must suffer because international trade is regulated largely at the federal, not the state, level.) In the late 1960s, trade with Canada accounted for as much as 43 per cent of total Washington international commerce. Automobiles and trucks are the most important exports to Canada through Washington.

After Canada, Japan is Washington's most valuable trading partner. The crowded islands of Nippon show a ravenous appetite for logs; almost half of Washington's exports to Japan consist of this commodity, with wheat in second place.

The state's trade with Japan has one important advantage over that with Canada: the Oriental country buys more than it sells. With Canada, the reverse is true.

Those in the United States who worry about Japan swamping this country with cameras, radios and little automobiles might do well to study the figures; it is more likely that the U.S. will flood Japan with logs and wheat. All countries, of course, prefer a trade surplus; that is, they would like to sell more to others than they buy. But international trade has always been a two-way street. Because America buys Japanese cameras, radios and automobiles, Japan can afford to buy American logs and wheat.

Bellingham, with a bay four times the size of Seattle's Elliott Bay, is a major Puget Sound port. Freeway at top is Interstate 5—north to Canada, south to Seattle.

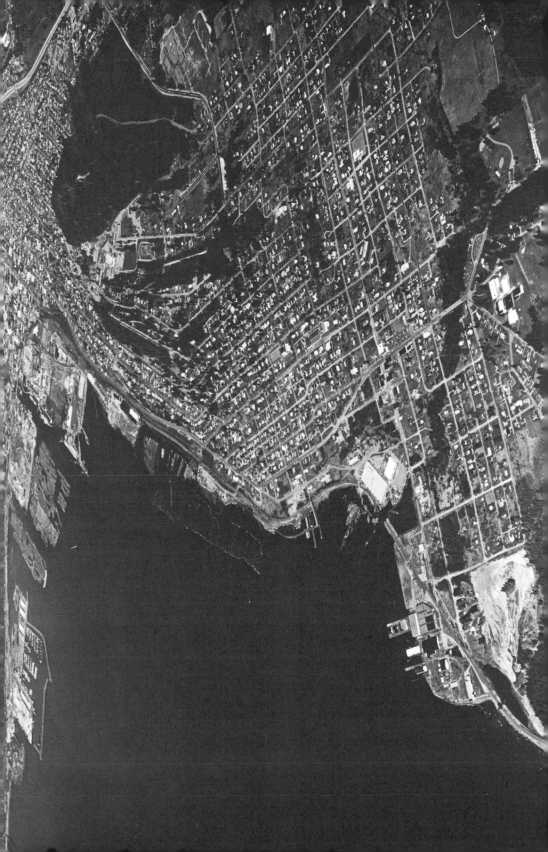

World trade operates on a simple principle: you scratch my back and I'll scratch yours. Any nation which ignores this little unwritten treaty is asking for economic trouble. A state like Washington, with its face turned west into the prevailing winds along the shipping lanes, dares not let it be ignored.

But international trade through Washington's busy ports has survived numerous irritations and aggravations. Consider, for instance, a sticky little incident before the turn of the century involving the famous Puget Sound sidewheel steamer *Eliza Anderson* and, of all things, its calliope.

When competition threatened on the run between Olympia and Victoria, British Columbia, Captain Wright of *Eliza Anderson* installed a steam calliope and turned it loose on "John Brown's Body" or something at least as violent when entering or leaving harbors.

As it happened, one Fourth of July *Eliza Anderson* lay along the dock in dignified Victoria. Moved by patriotism, Captain Wright ordered his calliope player to belch forth "Yankee Doodle" in honor of the day.

He did so. Once and again . . . and again.

Finally Canadian authorities, trembling a little, ordered the captain either to silence his calliope or leave the dock.

Captain Wright chose to leave the dock, anchored his vessel in the harbor and ordered his calliope player to serve up "Yankee Doodle" for the remainder of the afternoon.

It was done. Victoria vibrated painfully, but trade relations between the United States and Canada apparently didn't suffer seriously, a fact for which Washingtonians should be everlastingly grateful.

The growing port of Tacoma . Main terminal complex is at lower right, including huge dome designed to hold alumina. Open flatland above terminal is the port's industrial development district, consisting of more than 3000 acres.

SUGGESTED READING

Andrews, Ralph W, and A. K. Larssen; FISH AND SHIPS; Superior; 1959.

Birkeland, Torger; ECHOES OF PUGET SOUND; Caxton; 1960 (steamboating).

Johnson, Jalmar; BUILDERS OF THE NORTHWEST; Dodd, Mead; 1963 (Captain John C. Ainsworth).

Morgan, Murray; ONE MAN'S GOLD RUSH; University of Washington; 1967.

Morgan, Murray; SKID ROAD: AN INFORMAL PORTRAIT OF SEATTLE; Viking; 1960.

The Puget Sound steamer Eliza Anderson *is shown in a picture taken about 1885. Her calliope made international history.*

Chapter Eight ★

The Railroads
THE ADVENTURE OF ONE-EYED JIM

Jay Gould was one of the richest and most powerful Americans of his time but no matter; one day he had to look up from his desk to gaze on a "veritable gorilla of a man, with an abnormally long torso and abnormally short legs, with a prodigiously heavy chest and neck, with thick, sinewy arms, and limbs like granite columns. The great, dome-like head shook so vigorously that the long, tangled iron-gray hair and the bristling iron-gray beard tossed violently about; and the one good eye blazed like a living coal, until it seemed to bore and burn its way straight to the center of Gould's weazened soul . . . Then the beard burst asunder, the thick lips snarled back, and from between the huge teeth there came a succession of hoarse, growling barks."

James J. Hill wanted to build his railroad west from Minnesota, long-reaching across the prairies and the deserts and the mountains until it fetched up on the shores of Puget Sound. In order to do this, he needed a law passed by Congress allowing him to build across Indian reservations. He thought he had it all arranged; then the powerful Gould had blocked it. Gould owned the Union Pacific railroad at the time and didn't want Hill's line or anyone else's competing for the vast market of the West.

Jim Hill was relatively young when he paid his call on Jay Gould and hadn't much more than wet his feet in the railroad business but anyone who heard him speak to the much-feared Gould would never have guessed it.

"You've played the hog in this matter just as long as you're going to be permitted," rasped Hill. "Unless you call off your bushwhackers at once, I'll tear down the whole business . . . . I'll go to Washington and I'll

Jim Hill, Empire Builder, at Vancouver about 1911.

camp there until I nail every one of your crooks to the doors of the Capitol by their ears!"

Big Jim soon got his law. His biographer claims that the bill was passed because of "the pressure of public opinion." Not likely; he got his law because Jay Gould didn't feel up to bucking him in Congress.

Hill wasn't all rage and bluster, by any means, but it's not hard to understand why Montana kids of his day sang about him:

"Twixt Hill and Hell, there's just one letter;

"Were Hill in Hell, we'd feel much better."

There are those who insist that this legendary man, who never lived in the state of Washington, did more to develop Washington than any other person. His Great Northern railroad helped transform Seattle from a dismal little town reeking of fish and frustration into the reigning metropolis of the Pacific Northwest. With one stroke of business—the setting of low rates for lumber shipped to the east—he made a mighty timber industry possible in Washington. And it was Jim Hill who almost single-handedly stirred up Puget Sound's massive trade with the Orient. Children sang scandalous verses about him, but many adults from Bellingham to San Francisco called him "Empire Builder." There were those who swore by him; there were those who swore *at* him. So it must be, apparently, with most public figures.

Late in life Jim Hill said, "Most men who have really lived have had, in some shape, their great adventure. This railway is mine."

★

The adventure began along the Mississippi River, in a Minnesota settlement which had been known as Pig's Eye. Shortly before an 18-year-old named James J. Hill blew into town from Canada, the community had come down with an attack of dignity and turned itself into St. Paul. One-eyed Jim (he'd lost an eye as a child when struck by an arrow) didn't care what they called it, since he planned only to catch a ride on a Red River cart, then go north to join a fur trappers' brigade headed west into the Rockies. He intended eventually to work his way across the Pacific to India, where he meant to put Mississippi-type steamboats to work on the Hoogly and Brahmaputra rivers. He had even chosen a district between Delhi and Allahabad as the most promising for a beginner.

Idle daydreams? For most teen-agers, they would have been, but Jim Hill had no time for idle dreams. Had there been a Red River cart caravan leaving St. Paul soon after he got there, Jim Hill might well have become a transportation tycoon of India. History often hangs on coincidence; India's loss was Washington's everlasting gain.

Within 12 hours after hitting town in 1856, the 18-year-old had found a job as clerk for J. W. Bass & Company, steamship agents. He checked freight, watched over the warehouse, kept time for the roustabouts and when necessary, sweated on the levee like an ordinary dock-walloper. It was a fascinating education for a lad hooked on transportation and there is much evidence that Jim Hill soaked it all up hungrily and went looking for more. When the Red River carts started north in the spring of 1857, Jim Hill watched them go, then went back to work. His roots were down in St. Paul.

J. W. Bass & Company sold out to another outfit and Jim Hill went along with the deal. Soon he was virtually running the company and learning, always learning. Young Jim realized early that knowledge was the foundation of power and wealth and he set about getting all of it his capacious mind could hold. How did a steam engine work and how could it be made to work better? Why did some steamboat companies earn huge profits, others little or none? Why were some steamboat hulls fast and others slow? How could goods of all kinds be moved more rapidly, more efficiently, more profitably? Why did it have to cost so much to move a bundle of something from here to there?

There was an American novelist of the 19th century named Horatio Alger whose young heroes always triumphed through sheer virtue. Alger wrote a series of books about boys who began poor, as did Jim Hill, and ended up fabulously rich, as did Jim Hill. Alger heroes always accomplished their ends by working their heads and hands to the bone, studying nights until their eyes slammed shut, then rising clear-eyed after a few hours' sleep to enter business for themselves, whereupon, through a combination of thrift, honesty, hard work and blinding intelligence, they overcame all obstacles to gain fantastic wealth and world renown.

Jim Hill probably came as close to being a real life Alger hero as anybody. But Alger heroes, at bottom, were sickening prudes, with more stuffing in their shirts than in their mattresses. There was the Alger side of Jim Hill, all right, but there was another side, usually displayed when he went into one of his monumental rages. In temper, it was said that if Jim Hill's tongue didn't quite peel the paint from a wall, it did shake leaves from trees.

Once, late in life, Hill had occasion to ask the name of a clerk he had noticed in the head office of his railroad and when he found out that it was "Spittles," fired the man on the spot. Horatio Alger would have been horrified . . .

On another famous occasion, residents of Wayzata, Minnesota, complained that Hill's trains were spoiling hotel business in the lakeshore town because of their all-night ringing and whistling and clanking and squealing as they switched around the station.

Furious, Hill immediately ordered the station torn down and moved two miles up the line to Holdridge. It was said that the first train to enter Wayzata after the station was moved hurried through with so many sparks flying from the stack that the town water tank was set on fire. Horatio Alger would have clucked his tongue, at the very least . . .

Jim Hill wasn't born to get ulcers; he was born to give them, so soon he went into business for himself selling fuel. In 1877, he got into the railroad business; the course of his skyrocket was set and the fuse lit. With three partners, Hill bought the sick St. Paul & Pacific Railroad, the seed from which eventually grew the Great Northern Railways System. Hill and his partners quickly set the bankrupt St. Paul & Pacific back on its feet, drove the rails through to the Canadian border, then reorganized the line and called it the St. Paul, Minneapolis & Manitoba. Hill beat down Jay Gould's controlled Congressmen and won the right to push the Manitoba west.

No one before or since could push a railroad through as fast as Jim Hill. Lee Howard, who worked on a Hill track gang as the rails reached west, was quoted by Stewart Holbrook in "The Story of American Railroads": "During a sizable blizzard, Jim Hill came out in his special car to where a crew of us were trying to clear up the line. He didn't stay in his car, either. He grabbed my shovel and started tossing snow, telling me to go back to his car and I'd find a pot of coffee there. I did, and spent half an hour drinking coffee and resting. Mr. Hill spelled off first one man, then another. My, but he was tough! He must have shoveled snow two or three hours that day."

Jim Hill wasn't just building a railroad; he was giving life to ideas. He liked to say, "Land without population is a wilderness. Population without land is a mob." He wanted his railroad to prosper; he wanted the Pacific Northwest to prosper. He knew from the beginning that one wasn't likely to make it without the other.

So, in characteristic style, he did something about it. In those years, immigrants from Europe were flooding through New York. Hill offered a rate on the Great Northern of $10 per person to any immigrant who

Jim Hill could harangue a crowd with the best of them. This picture catches him in action at a spike-driving ceremony.

agreed to settle along the G.N. track. For only a few dollars more, he offered a family a whole freight car, in case they wanted to carry household effects or even a few animals.

The immigrants responded by the thousands. Old timers in the West, disturbed by the march of humanity into their wild, free land, called them "hunyockers," a term of contempt which probably came from "hunyak," a word applied earlier to Slavic immigrants who had settled in Dakota and Minnesota.

So Jim Hill, then at the peak of his strength and vigor, pushed his iron west. He said, "I visited and made personal inspection of various lines . . . examined the country and the soil, water and climate . . ."

Hill did more than survey on these trips; he usually managed to work in a little horse trading, too. He expected a community to appreciate him and his railroad and to demonstrate that appreciation in a substantial way. Spokane citizens found this out in 1892.

The Northern Pacific already had a line through Spokane to Puget Sound, but the citizens were unhappy with the high rates. When they heard that Jim Hill was scouting ahead of the new Great Northern line and would be stopping in Spokane to talk railroad, the citizens were delighted because Hill had a reputation for setting and holding low rates. It was assumed that Great Northern tracks would be laid through Spokane.

"Now," the leaders of the Spokane group exulted, "we'll show that cutthroat Northern Pacific outfit a thing or two!"

But Jim Hill had a surprise in store for Spokane . . .

"You have no idea," he said in an interview published in the *Spokane Review,* "how hard your city is to get in and out of . . ."

Hill went on to point out that the valley of the Little Spokane River north of the city really was much more inviting to a railroader who believed in low grades. He described in painful detail the terrible difficulties the Great Northern would face in trying to lay a line through Spokane.

Spokane's civic leaders turned pale and hastily called a meeting at which Jim Hill graciously consented to say a few words.

Hill pointed out that laying the five miles of track through Spokane would cost the Great Northern a cool million dollars, give or take a penny or two.

"Now what we ask of Spokane," he bellowed, "is that from the time we come to the city limits you will give us the right-of-way, so that the building of the road will not cost anything."

week later Jim Hill had his free right-of-way through Spokane.

Hill's eye had always been on the Pacific Northwest, particularly on
:ate of Washington. He said: "I found there nearly four hundred
n feet of standing timber, the best in the world. It had no domestic
et. Before our road was built the rate on lumber was ninety cents a
red pounds and that was practically prohibitory. They used to cut this
:r down and let it run out to sea to get rid of it. I called the
sentative lumbermen of the Pacific Northwest together. They told me
could ship their lumber east if we made them a rate of sixty-five cents
idred. I said that they could not move any large amount if they paid
than fifty cents. I offered them a rate of forty cents on fir and fifty
on cedar, and these rates went into effect. That built up a large trade,
ons of the lumber going even to the Atlantic Coast, but the great bulk
being distributed throughout the interior West, north of St. Louis and
)hio River."

ounds simple, as Jim Hill tells it. But simple or not, Washington
:nly had for itself an important lumber industry; it still has.

Hill's St. Paul, Minneapolis & Manitoba became the Great Northern
390. In January, 1893, the Great Northern reached Puget Sound at
ett.

At first the Great Northern had plenty of westbound freight but
ed too many empty cars east. So Hill created a new market for Oregon
Washington lumber in the Midwest and East. As this market ex-
ed, he found himself needing more freight to fill his westbound cars.
promptly created a market for American cotton and steel in China and
n and soon filled those empty cars running toward Puget Sound.

'I found," Hill said, "that if the people of a single province of China
ld consume an ounce a day of our flour, they would need 50,000,000
els of wheat per annum, or twice the Western surplus."

The Great Northern began to make enormous operating profits. Of
se; Jim Hill had planned it that way. He built his lines with low
es and as few sharp curves as possible so that his trains could operate
omically. A Hill railroad could operate at a profit with rates so low
the competition soon was gasping for breath. During financial panics
l in those days the bottom seemed to drop out of the economy every
years) a Hill-run railroad could cut corners and survive while the
oads run by Wall Street speculators died like flies.

As a result of one of these panics, Hill was able to buy control of the
thern Pacific, Washington's other transcontinental railroad. Then he
ht a famous battle with E. H. Harriman, Union Pacific president, to

get the Spokane, Portland & Seattle built from Spokane to Vancouver.

Railroad tycoons, once authentic American heroes, fell out of public favor and came to be considered little more than plundering pirates by millions of citizens. But Jim Hill's reputation escaped with as few smears as any. He remains the Empire Builder and the state of Washington, keystone of his empire, remembers him that way. Jim Hill was the only man who built a transcontinental railroad without subsidy or land grant from the federal government; maybe Jim Hill was the only man who could have.

In 1909, he was invited to be featured speaker at the Alaska-Yukon-Pacific Exposition in Seattle. His statue was cast in bronze, displayed on the exposition grounds, then given to Washington State University in Pullman, where it was put to rest on a base made of granite blocks from Japan, Canada, Minnesota and Washington. Canada was concerned because he had been born there; Minnesota cared because he lived and died there and made his start as a railroader there; Japan and Washington had to be represented because Washington was end-of-track for his railroad, Japan end-of-line for his steamships.

Hill died in St. Paul on May 29, 1916. Whether his soul departed his body and soared to heaven or whether it sank to the nether regions, it's a safe bet that within minutes after he got where he was going, he began to lay out a railroad between the two, a money-making railroad with low grades and no sharp curves.

THE LITTLEST TYCOON

Jim Hill had his way of running a railroad; Dr. Dorsey Syng Baker had his. Both, in their respective ways, were tycoons. Hill built his Great Northern railroad over thousands of miles and spent millions of dollars; Dr. Baker built his Walla Walla & Columbia River line over a mere thirty miles on little more than a shoestring. Yet both helped mightily in the

Jim Hill's railroad had to cross the Cascade Mountains the hard way during the early days. The name of the game was "switchback," four different levels of which are pictured here before the turn of the century. A seven-car passenger train is being pulled by two locomotives and pushed by another. A tunnel completed in 1900 made this switchback trip no longer necessary. Was all that felled timber eventually loaded and hauled to a mill? One wonders.

development of Washington and both deserve to be remembered.

People laughed in 1872 when Dr. Baker set out to build his railroad between Walla Walla and Wallula on the Columbia. They laughed even harder when he got it into operation three years later. Old Doc Baker had the last laugh in 1878 when he sold his busy little pike to the Oregon Railway & Navigation Company for a cool million dollars. (People in the old days seemed to get special enjoyment out of poking fun at struggling railroads and high-and-mighty railroad men. Even Jim Hill wasn't immune. Hill's Northern Pacific bought a branch line, the Pacific Railway & Navigation Company, which ran from Portland to Tillamook, Oregon. The line was called the "P.R.& N." by Hill; the passengers who had to put up with it called it the "Punk, Rotten & Nasty.")

Dr. Baker had gone westering with the gold rush crowd of '49, then settled down to business in Walla Walla. After the Civil War, the farmers around Walla Walla began to grow a great deal of wheat, which they had to ship slowly and expensively to a Columbia River landing by team and wagon. A railroad could haul the wheat at much lower cost; Doc Baker saw the opportunity and grabbed it.

A bond issue failed, so he had to finance construction out of his own pocket. To stretch his money as far as possible, he decided to use four-by-six timbers for rails, rather than iron or steel. To keep the wheel flanges from wearing the inside edges too rapidly, he attached two-inch strips of iron. (A short section of this rail is displayed at Cheney Cowles Museum, Spokane.) Sometimes the iron worked loose in places and wrapped itself around the axles and tore holes in the floors of the cars. The scoffers circulated the story that Doc Baker had tied his rails together with rawhide and that every winter, hungry coyotes ate his railroad to pieces. The railroad has come down through history with the tag, "Rawhide Railroad," even though the rawhide charge was a good yarn and nothing more.

Baker's line had other little innovations that Jim Hill never thought of. His engineers were bothered by stray cattle on the tracks so a sheep dog was trained to ride the train until trespassing cattle were sighted, whereupon the dog leaped off and ran ahead to bark the offending animals out of the way.

The first motive power on the Walla Walla & Columbia River pike was a couple of little locomotives which, by modern standards, were no more than wheeled teakettles. At first no passenger cars were provided but

Dr. Dorsey Syng Baker, his beard combed and his eye cocked, posed for this picture in 1885.

the line carried passengers just the same, often perching them on sacks of grain stacked on flat cars.

An Englishman named John M. Murphy took a ride on the Walla Walla & Columbia River when he visited the Pacific Coast in the 1870s and set down his reaction to what apparently was a memorable experience:

"The next stoppage was made at Wallula, a post town and shipping point claiming the distinction of supporting neither lawyer, physician, nor minister, and only one school-teacher. It is 240 miles from Portland, and may be called the head of navigation on the Columbia proper, as no other hamlet is met until Idaho is reached.

"I went ashore there, intending to go to Walla-Walla, in Eastern Washington Territory. On landing, I was informed that the stage had left in the morning, and that the only means of reaching my destination was to hire a farm waggon, or secure a seat in a goods truck attached to a miniature train that ran fifteen miles into the interior on a wooden line of rails. Having secured an interview with the president, secretary, conductor, and brakeman of the road, he informed me that he would book me as a passenger on the payment of 2 dollars, and that sum being paid, I was placed on some iron in an open truck and told to cling to the sides, and to be careful not to stand on the wooden floor if I cared anything about my limbs. I promised a strict compliance with the instructions, and the miserable little engine gave a grunt or two, several wheezy puffs, a cat-like scream, and finally got the car attached to it under way. Once in motion, it dashed on at a headlong speed of two miles an hour, and rocked like a canoe in a cross sea. The gentleman who represented all the train officials did not get aboard, but told the engineer to go on and he would overtake him in the course of an hour. Before I had proceeded half a mile, I saw why I was not permitted to stand on the floor of the truck, for a piece of hoop-iron, which covered the wooden rails in some places, curled up into what is called a 'snake head,' and pushed through the wood with such force that it nearly stopped the train. After this was withdrawn the engine resumed its course, and at the end of seven hours hauled one weary passenger, with eyes made sore from the smoke, and coat and hat nearly burnt off by the sparks, into a station composed of a rude board shanty, through whose apertures the wind howled, having made the entire distance of fifteen miles in that time. The route of this famous railway ran through a sandy alkaline desert, capable of producing nothing but rank wild sage and kindred useless shrubs; hence, houses were scarce, and those seen were perched on the banks of some stream. Life was active enough there, however, for immense prairie schooners, as the waggons are called, drawn by teams of seven or eight pairs of mules or horses, or ten of oxen, wound in long serpentine lines over its bluish surface; and some of their drivers had the temerity to challenge the president of the railway line to run a race with them in his old machine, but he scorned their insinuations and kept quietly walking beside his train."

★

In addition to his dandy little railroad, Dr. Baker established a bank in Walla Walla with John F. Boyer. The Baker-Boyer National Bank is still in business and now proudly bears the distinction of being the oldest bank in Washington.

At one point, the bank was managed by one of Dr. Baker's sons, Will, who at birth was christened "Walla Walla Willie Baker." For reasons of dignity, he later adopted the name of W. William Baker.

Will Baker was president of Baker-Boyer in 1929 when the financial crash caused banks to fail by the hundreds. During the crisis, he received a telegram from the president of Wells Fargo Bank of San Francisco, then and now one of the largest and strongest banks in the West.

"DO YOU NEED RESERVES?" the telegram asked. "LET ME KNOW IF I CAN HELP YOU."

Will Baker quickly wired back an echo of his sturdy, self-reliant father: "THANK YOU, NO. WE ARE SOLVENT AND OPEN TO BUSINESS AS USUAL. LET ME KNOW IF I CAN HELP YOU."

When the Northwest railroad boom began about 1880, the population of Washington, Oregon and Idaho was 282,494. When the transcontinental lines were firmly established around 1910, the area's population was 2,140,349—seven and one-half times as large. The railroads were mainly responsible for the fantastic growth.

In modern Washington, as elsewhere in the country, railroads have lost their transportation leadership. Their passenger traffic has faded to almost nothing; autos and airplanes now carry most of it. Trucks cut so deeply into freight traffic for a time that railroads were threatened but there have been recent signs that the iron horse may prosper again.

Railroads made the vast open spaces of the West less fearsome, less lonely, and supplied some of its romantic flavor. No Diesel truck snorting down a freeway can compare as a stirring sight with a mile-long Great Northern freight train emerging like a slithering monster from Cascade Tunnel.

Those faint, distant shouts of agreement surely arose from the ghostly throats of Jim Hill and Dorsey Baker, the big and little tycoons who ran Washington's big and little railroads.

SUGGESTED READING

Abdill, George B.; PACIFIC SLOPE RAILROADS; Superior; 1959.

Olson, Joan and Gene; OREGON TIMES AND TRAILS; Windyridge; 1965 (Hill vs. Harriman).

Reynolds, Helen Baker; GOLD, RAWHIDE AND IRON; Pacific Books; 1955.

Chapter Nine ✭

Agriculture
THE DAM AT THE END OF
THE RAINBOW

It is just possible that a few persons doing no more than standing and sweating and holding up signs on a dusty road in eastern Washington changed the face of the state forever and won a world war.

Before you scoff, consider these facts:

The year was 1934. The road led to the site of a low dam being built on the Columbia River near the huge, ancient trench known as Grand Coulee. The signs were blunt: "WE WANT THE HIGH DAM!"

That was all. A clear, simple, shot-in-the-eye message, impossible to misunderstand, intended for just two of the men who were scheduled to travel through the dust along the road on that summer afternoon.

The men were the 32nd president of the United States, Franklin Delano Roosevelt, and his Secretary of the Interior, Harold L. Ickes.

For a year and a half, Roosevelt's New Deal administration had been setting off dynamite under the country's terrible economic problems. As a candidate, Roosevelt had promised that he would take action to harness the Columbia River's enormous potential; Grand Coulee Dam would be started immediately and completed as soon as possible.

But once in office, the president had second thoughts, as politicians sometimes do. Four hundred million dollars seemed like a ridiculous amount of money for a single dam, even for a ridiculously large dam, even to a president who was trying mightily to spend the country out of the quicksand of the Great Depression. Besides, as part of his recovery program, Roosevelt was trying to hold down farm surpluses. Did it then make sense to turn a million acres of desert in the far reaches of the West into producing cropland? Not much, it didn't. And those persistent people from the state of Washington, people like Jim O'Sullivan, always wanted to talk irrigation rather than power production.

"Tell you what, boys," the president finally said to the dam boosters from Washington. "Let's build a low dam, for power production only. Then, maybe later on, we can raise it and get that irrigation you want."

The Bureau of Reclamation was ordered to start work on the low dam and the stage was set for the president's visit in the summer of 1934.

Jim O'Sullivan and his Columbia Basin friends hadn't labored for so many years only to settle for the wrong kind of dam. So the O'Sullivan people stood by the road when the president came to inspect the damsite, holding up their signs, breathing the dust as the motorcade passed . . .

★

A person who wants to say he did it can leap across the Columbia River at its source deep in Canada. Yet, at the river's mouth 1270 miles southwest, a powerful ferryboat had to chew at the current for a full hour to cross between Megler, Washington, and Astoria, Oregon. (The river won, incidentally; there's a spectacular bridge at the place now.)

A river may be measured in many ways.

In terms of volume of water moved, the Mississippi is larger than the Columbia but the Mississippi can't hold a candle to the Columbia in speed of flow. Compared to the Columbia, the Mississippi just meanders along. In case of flood on the Mississippi, one can write a letter to warn downstream villages of the danger. When the Columbia floods, send a telegram; it's safer. The great speed of the Columbia's flow is due to its phenomenal drop of 2619 feet between source and mouth. Standing on the shore of the Columbia, a person senses the stream's great impatience; here is a river that is in an all-fired hurry to get to the sea and it looks and sounds strong enough to brush aside any obstacle in its path. (It has brushed aside and knocked over and ground down more than a few in its day.)

Five hundred miles of the Columbia are in Canada. By the time the stream decides to become American, it is a major river already carrying five times the flow of New York's famous Hudson.

In another respect, the Columbia is a freakish sort of river. Most non-tropical streams run low during summer, the dry season. Not the Columbia. Because it is fed in Canada by melt from some of the largest

Grand Coulee Dam on the Columbia is one of the mightiest structures in the world.

snow and ice fields in the world, it carries more water in summer than in winter. Sooner or later somebody was bound to ponder on this summer flow and think seriously about what a dandy little irrigation ditch it would make. Several somebodies did, several citizens of the state of Washington: Rufus Woods, Nat Washington, Jim O'Sullivan and Billy Clapp, to name only the most prominent and stubborn leaders of a stubborn group.

A special feature of the bleak, craggy lava landscape made the Grant County site especially attractive for an irrigation dam—the immense gash in the earth called Grand Coulee. Once, centuries ago, an ice dam formed in the river's normal course. The water was turned aside and began to grind away at the soft earth. Grand Coulee was formed, two to five miles wide and fifty miles long. Then the ice dam melted away and the river resumed its normal course, leaving Grand Coulee empty and waiting for the dreamers who hankered to turn it into the biggest farm pond ever likely to be seen in the state.

What the dreamers and schemers wanted to do was pump water out of the huge lake formed behind a dam and dump it into Grand Coulee. (After plugging both ends of the coulee, naturally; every bathtub requires a stopper.) The water could be stored in the coulee until needed and it wouldn't be necessary to depend on the river's flow for irrigation. The dam would be used to make electric power, too, and in order to produce the juice, a tremendous amount of water would have to flow through the great turbines. Without stored water, the farmers in the Columbia Basin might be shorted on water by heavy power plant demands. With Grand Coulee full, there would always be enough water for both purposes. Not much imagination was required to come up with the now-common term: multi-purpose dam.

★

The seeds that grew into Grand Coulee Dam were planted in Ephrata, Grant County, in 1918. On a hot July day, Rufus Woods, publisher of the *Wenatchee World,* thumped into town in his typewriter-equipped Model T Ford and began to hunt for news—or what passed for news in this empty, quiet country. He was referred to a local attorney, Billy Clapp. Billy, Rufus Woods was told, might have "the biggest story you've ever written."

Billy Clapp had a story, all right. It was no less than a scheme for a

Before the water came to the Columbia Basin, many farm homes had to be abandoned, this one near Quincy as it looked in 1920.

40523

dam which would provide the water to transform the Columbia Basin from a snake-infested desert into an agricultural paradise.

There had been talk of such a project around Wenatchee and Ephrata for many years but now Clapp wasn't just talking; he had a report from the Grant County engineer, C. W. Duncan, which indicated that the thing was feasible; it could be done.

Soon the *Wenatchee World* trumpeted: "TWO MILLION WILD HORSES—FORMULATE BRAND NEW IDEA FOR IRRIGATING GRANT, ADAMS, FRANKLIN COUNTIES, COVERING MILLION ACRES OR MORE."

Thus began a battle that was to last for 17 years.

The Columbia, after all, wasn't the only river in Washington. One group wanted to pipe the waters of the Wenatchee River into the so-called "Big Bend" area. A Spokane group plumped for a canal-tunnel system which would draw water from Lake Pend Oreille in Idaho and channel it past Spokane to the Big Bend.

But the Grand Coulee scheme gained ground, year by year. Finally the opponents of Grand Coulee had to fall back to a last line of defense: the plan was simply TOO BIG.

At that point the project was sucked into the quagmire of national politics. Dams, harbors, bridges and similar public works were usually paid for with "pork" and pork, as any first-term congressman knows, comes from the pork barrel, that huge container of federal money into which politicians dip for political purposes. Politicians mend their fences in the home district not with wire, but with pork. States with the most voters stood first in line at the barrel; in those days, the state of Washington had little influence in the halls of national government. Many Easterners, in fact, weren't entirely sure where Washington was, except that it most certainly was well west of the limits of civilization.

A Republican congressman from New York described Grand Coulee as "a vast area of gloomy tablelands interspersed with deep gullies." He stated that there was no one in the region to sell power to "except rattlesnakes, coyotes and rabbits. *Everyone knows that.* There is no market for power in the Northwest . . . absolutely no market for the power in this section and will not be for many years to come."

That congressman missed the mark by a coulee country mile.

Another congressman wouldn't even concede the rattlesnakes. In a historic burst of hogwash, Grand Coulee was called the center of a land so forbidding that "even snakes and lizards shun it." The Grand Coulee itself, to this congressman, was nothing more than a "vast valley of rock and black wilderness inhabited by ghosts a hundred feet tall . . . The air you breathe is full of the dust of dead men's bones."

A pretty speech, that, but any Big Bend resident could quickly knock at least one hole in the truth of it. The area did, too, have rattlesnakes, plenty of them, and they all seemed delighted with the dry, wind-swept region.

And so reminded of the tender concern of the Eastern political powers, the citizens of the hopelessly blighted area merely shrugged their shoulders, fought their way through the hordes of snakes, wild beasts and savages, rubbed the windblown sand out of their eyes, slithered anxiously past the cactus and went to work.

Other leaders quickly emerged to help Rufus Woods and Billy Clapp. Nat Washington became the first president of the Columbia River Dam, Power and Irrigation Association, whose members quickly became known as "Coulee Communists," who, the Easterners said, surely were out to destroy the national economy with their fantastically expensive crackpot dam plot. (Now, of course, those early leaders are considered farsighted pioneers; so it goes.) Jim O'Sullivan boomed in from the East, bought land around Moses Lake and threw himself into the fight with all his Irish strength and fervor.

Up the Irish! With O'Sullivan's arrival, the scales began to tip.

For some of the dam's supporters, the dream was enough; they couldn't believe that it might really happen. O'Sullivan, an immensely able, practical and energetic man, insisted on reality or nothing. He pulled all the supporting groups together, operated a one-man propaganda factory and combed the desert for more converts, often taking a collection of a few dollars at one meeting to provide gasoline to get him to the next, borrowing office space from Billy Clapp in Ephrata and accepting living quarters and food from anybody who wanted to see Jim O'Sullivan stay on the job.

The struggle continued through the 1920s. Late in the decade, support began to fall away; some groups were almost ready to throw up their hands. O'Sullivan pleaded with them to keep the faith a little longer.

Finally, in 1931, a big break came with the issuance of the Army Engineer's landmark "308 Report."

The report recommended construction of Grand Coulee Dam!

It wasn't any puny little stick-and-mud structure that the engineers called for, either. Its pool level was to be 354.6 feet above low water; the resulting lake would stretch 151 miles to the Canadian border. It would be the largest concrete dam in the world; some would even call it the world's

largest manmade structure. With all its generators installed and humming away, it would produce more hydroelectric power than any other dam in the world. The sheer size of the project boggled the minds of its critics and must have shaken up even a few of its supporters. "Grand Coulee" has a majestic ring, but no name was likely to be as majestic as the dam itself.

But an engineers' report—even a ten-inch-thick report—wouldn't dam a river. This would take money, millions and millions of unadulterated money. With the country deep in the clutches of the Great Depression, money was as short as the tempers of the big private power interests which had always been bitter opponents of the big public power project in the barren coulees of Grant County.

Then an ironic twist of history suddenly produced a flood of dollars, more money than you could stuff into the mouth of a river . . .

In 1932, Franklin D. Roosevelt included Grand Coulee and Bonneville dams when he turned loose his flood of campaign promises. Elected president, Roosevelt launched his New Deal, a central feature of which was a multi-billion-dollar public works program—federal spending the likes of which the country had never seen. Suddenly the federal government was searching for huge projects which would provide work for many thousands of unemployed over a period of many years.

Grand Coulee Dam and its irrigation canals certainly qualified; no big spender could sneer at its estimated cost of 400 million dollars.

But the victory seemingly won now threatened again to slip away. When the plans were announced, they called for a low power dam which would provide no irrigation water for the Big Bend. O'Sullivan and his busy band had labored so long not for power, but for water on the land. Now it seemed that they would get a dam, all right—but the wrong one!

It was a stunning blow but O'Sullivan and the others shook their heads clear and called another meeting. They had come too far to quit.

Construction of the low dam began in September, 1933. In 1934, President Roosevelt and Secretary Ickes came west for a look at Grand

Grand Coulee Dam supplies water for small reservoirs like this in the Columbia Basin.

➡

Grand Coulee Dam is the foaming centerpiece of a powerful panorama. In the center distance is Banks Lake, major irrigation reservoir of the Columbia Basin, largest reclamation project in the world. Above the dam on the far shore are the great pipes through which water is pumped to Banks Lake. Roosevelt Lake backs up behind the dam.

Coulee and Jim O'Sullivan asked his people to make a few signs.

Secretary Ickes was first to change his mind. After taking a look at the great river, the craggy land, the far reaches of desert and the signs held by O'Sullivan people, Ickes announced, "We should have a high dam out there."

Nudged by O'Sullivan and Washington's congressmen, President Roosevelt soon became a convert to the cause. In June of 1935, the Bureau of Reclamation was told to throw away its plans and begin work on a high dam at Grand Coulee.

O'Sullivan had finally won his long struggle. The people of Washington had won, too, and in the process had set in motion a flow of events that would make a garden out of an immense desert, help mightily to win the worst of all wars and lay a foundation for a peacetime industrial empire based on airplanes and aluminum.

★

Thousands of workers swarmed to the scene, building and moving into new towns, and throwing up coffer dams to divert the river so that work could begin on the main dam. Then excavation down to bedrock was necessary to provide a firm base for the earth-breaking weight of the concrete. (There is enough concrete in Grand Coulee Dam to build a two-lane highway 22 feet wide and eight inches thick from Seattle to Miami, Florida, plus a three-foot sidewalk along its entire length.)

Building a dam the size of Grand Coulee is by no means a simple matter of dropping a block of concrete into the river. For instance, to polish the bedrock so that it would accept a strong bond with the concrete, it was necessary to set many men to work with soap and water and brushes. And whom did they hire for this work? Tombstone polishers!

A clay bank began to slide down a canyon wall toward the installations below. Every attempt to hold the slow-moving mass failed. When disaster seemed imminent, a young engineer had a bright idea.

"Freeze it," he said, and it was done. Refrigeration pipes were installed in the sliding clay and ammonia was sent in. Soon the mass was frozen; it stopped sliding. The work went on.

The same technique solved another problem. Drying concrete produces great heat; the concrete must cool before it is strong. If workmen had to wait for the giant mass to cool naturally, work would be delayed,

Water is pumped from behind Grand Coulee Dam through these monstrous pipes to Banks Lake, main irrigation reservoir.

some engineers said, for as long as 150 years. That would never do, so pipes were laid in the forms and cold river water run through. The concrete cooled in a month, then more cement was forced through the pipes into the joints, forming a solid mass. (Those 1700 miles of pipe are in the dam today.)

Great pipes called penstocks—18 feet in diameter, large enough to accept a railroad train—were installed to carry water down to the huge turbines which would power the generators. These 18 pipes can carry enough water to supply every person on earth with a gallon an hour; the superintendent of the dam requests that you bring your own bucket.

On October 4, 1941, the first power flowed from the great dam's generators. Two months later, the Japanese assault on Pearl Harbor plunged the U.S. into World War II.

Brute power, not irrigation, mattered most to a nation fighting for survival, and Grand Coulee bent its brawny shoulders to the task. Electric power born in Grant County—Coulee power—nourished the huge shipyards in Vancouver and around Puget Sound. Coulee power created Washington's massive aluminum industry. Boeing factories devoured the light, strong metal, then spewed it out as war-winning airplanes. Coulee power fueled the top-secret Hanford atomic works; Hanford plutonium was the angry heart of the doomsday bombs which dissolved Hiroshima and Nagasaki and ended the war.

With the war over, the dam was returned to peacetime work. In 1951, huge pumps took water from Franklin D. Roosevelt Lake back of the dam and lifted it to the ancient excavation once called Grand Coulee, now Banks Lake. On August 10, 1951, the first test water flowed from Banks Lake toward the Columbia Basin. On May 29, 1952, the first water was delivered to a project farm, that of 30-year-old Donald Dunn, selected by the Veterans of Foreign Wars as the nation's "Most Deserving Farm Veteran."

The valve which turned water onto Dunn's farm was opened by Mike Strauss, commissioner of reclamation, who said, "The world wants food. And here the world sees a project which means food for the hungry, food from farms which will never know drought, from land which guarantees abundance to those who work it wisely . . . Here this afternoon we celebrate the addition of the equivalent of a new state to the union. For out of the wisdom and the effort which have gone into this project our country

Serious irrigation in Washington began with this Sunnyside Canal, photographed in 1906 against a Mt. Adams backdrop.

is now about to reap harvest from the desert."

Now the life-giving water flows from Banks Lake through immense canals and siphons as far south as the Tri-Cities—Pasco, Kennewick and Richland. What once was windblown sand is now lush, green farmland where a crop failure is unknown. Towns like Ephrata, Moses Lake and Soap Lake—which once fought a year-to-year battle against dust and poverty and the hovering vultures of extinction—now boom and bloom along with the surrounding land.

The forlorn past has become the glowing present, but the past was not forgotten. On September 28, 1948, Washington's governor, several congressmen and the Secretary of the Interior gathered south of Moses Lake to honor an ailing 72-year-old man who had left a hospital bed to attend the ceremony.

Secretary of the Interior Julius Krug said, "He insists that Rufus Woods, Billy Clapp and many others deserve a major share of the credit. That credit is being given them today, Jim, but I want these people out here to remember the nickels and dimes given by thousands of persons during those dark days of the twenties when you spoke yourself voiceless time and again in begging for support for the project . . ."

Then the secretary dedicated an important new dam in the basin project—O'Sullivan Dam.

DOWN ON THE FARM

The fact that Columbia Basin qualifies as the largest farmland reclamation project in the world should prepare anyone to respect Washington agriculture. Yet, outside the state, ask someone about Washington and chances are you'll get an answer something like this: "Washington? Oh, sure, that's where they grow the big trees and make the big airplanes. Lots of fishing, too. Water sports and all like that. But they tell me it rains *all the time.* And don't they have that big dam?"

A few of those interviewed might think to mention apples. Even some Washingtonians may be surprised to learn that their state leads the nation in production of six crops: apples, late summer potatoes, dry field peas, hops, peppermint and spearmint.

The Palouse Hills present special farming problems and equipment manufacturers have had to design peculiar equipment to solve them. This harvester was an early solution.

More surprising may be the news that while Washington ranks only sixth in the U.S. in spring wheat and second in winter wheat, the state boasts the three top wheat-producing counties in the country: Whitman, Lincoln and Adams. The reason is the highest per-acre yield in the United States. Those weird-looking Palouse Hills produce wheat as if there were no tomorrow.

Washington apples, grown mostly in the central part of the state around Yakima, Ellensburg and Wenatchee, are eaten with juicy delight around the world. But not so well known is the fact that the state ranks second in the U.S. in production of pears, apricots and sweet cherries; third in asparagus, grapes, strawberries and alfalfa seed; fourth in cranberries and fall potatoes; and fifth in prunes and plums.

Within the state, not surprisingly, wheat leads in financial return to farmers. Milk, cattle and calves, apples, hay and potatoes follow in importance as money crops.

Like Gaul, farming areas in Washington are divided neatly into three parts. In the eastern dry lands, grain and cattle dominate. In the central section which is watered by Grand Coulee, fruits and diversified crops are grown. In the wet, lush valleys of western Washington, the major farm products are berries, poultry, vegetables and dairy products.

Without international trade, Washington agriculture would be in a bad way. Almost one-fourth of the state's production is sent out of the country, including a whopping 80 per cent of the wheat.

It has been mentioned that Washington leads the United States in production of six crops. Actually it leads in seven, if you count rhubarb.

SUGGESTED READING

Brumfield, Kirby; THIS WAS WHEAT FARMING; Superior; 1968.
Fish, Byron; ADVENTURING ON THE COLUMBIA; Superior; 1956.
Johnson, Jalmar; BUILDERS OF THE NORTHWEST; Dodd, Mead; 1963 (Jim O'Sullivan).
Morgan, Murray; THE DAM; Viking; 1954.

Chapter Ten ★

Labor
TOIL AND TROUBLE:
THE WOBBLIES

THE PREACHER AND THE SLAVE
(Tune: "Sweet Bye and Bye")

Long-haired preachers come out every night
Try to tell you what's wrong and what's right;
But when asked how 'bout something to eat
They will answer with voices so sweet:

(CHORUS)
You will eat, bye and bye,
In that glorious land above the sky;
Work and pray, live on hay,
You'll get pie in the sky when you die.
　　　　　　　　—Joe Hill, I.W.W. Songbook

★

On the evening of December 30, 1905, a man named Frank Steunenberg opened his garden gate in Caldwell, Idaho, and in the next instant was blown to kingdom come.

The monstrous blast of snow-buried dynamite signalled the beginning of a quarter century of labor-management uproar in the Pacific Northwest and exploded the nickname "Wobbly" into headlines around the country. The state of Washington was fated to be the scene of some of the bloodiest encounters in the warfare to come and the names "Wobbly" and "Washington" now ride tandem across the violence-torn pages of history.

A Wobbly was a member of the Industrial Workers of the World, a union formed in Chicago only a year before Steunenberg's echoing death. ("Wobbly," the story goes, first came from the lips of a Chinese member, who, wishing to say "I.W.W.," could manage only "Eye Wobbly Wobbly." Wobblies they became and Wobblies they remain.) Soon after the death of Steunenberg, who had earned labor's enmity as governor of Idaho, police arrested one Harry Orchard, who quickly confessed a series of bombings and shootings. Orchard said that he had been paid for his killings by three I.W.W. leaders: Charles Moyer, George Pettibone and Big Bill Haywood. The trial of Haywood, head man of the Wobblies, turned him into a national figure. By the time of his acquittal on July 28, 1907, "I.W.W." and "Wobbly" were part of the American language and the Wobblies were off to a noisy start, borne on a flood crest of publicity. (Moyer was acquitted, too. Charges against Pettibone were dropped. Orchard was sentenced to life imprisonment.)

Wobbly halls opened in Seattle, Tacoma, Spokane and other lumbering centers to enlist loggers and sawmill workers in what came to be called the "One Big Union." Woods and mill workers tramped in by the hundreds, then by the thousands, to pay their dues and acquire the little "Red Card" which marked them as Wobblies. A soaring membership and a full war chest were needed badly because the Wobblies were aiming high and far; they had set no small goals for their infant organization. Any doubt on this score is removed by the first two paragraphs of the preamble to their constitution:

"The working class and the employing class have nothing in common. There can be no peace so long as hunger and want are found among millions of working people and the few, who make up the employing class, have all the good things of life.

"Between these two classes a struggle must go on until the workers of the world organize as a class, take possession of the earth and the machinery of production, and abolish the wage system . . ."

Among many of the I.W.W. leaders—and Big Bill Haywood, in particular—this was not just big talk ballooned up with empty words; it was a solid plan of action. Small wonder, then, that capitalists began to writhe sleeplessly in their beds as I.W.W. membership rose rapidly and as loud, blunt Wobblies began to climb onto their street corner soapboxes and harangue the crowds.

"Radical" is a fearsome, rankling word today. But the I.W.W. was radical, without question, and what's more, was button-bursting proud of it. Among its members were Communists, Socialists and anarchists and no one made any bones about it. The I.W.W. had no intention of merely rocking the boat; it wanted to overturn it and drown the occupants, if such action would help the One Big Union wipe out the wage system and topple the capitalists from power.

Haywood and his hearty crew had stirred up a strong brew and much of the strength came from the West, particularly from the logging camps of Washington. When Eastern leaders of the union tried to soften I.W.W. methods and substitute ballots for bullets, it was usually the Washington faction which urged continued use of force as a weapon against management. Loggers were migratory; they seldom stayed in one place long enough to vote, hence their preference for a weapon that would work against the Northwest timber barons.

Why such radical notions and violent emotions? A reasonable person must admit that the Wobblies had a point; U.S. working conditions at the turn of the twentieth century were generally terrible. Wobbly goals and methods were extreme but so were the provocations.

During the last quarter of the nineteenth century, a few tycoons like J. P. Morgan and John D. Rockefeller, operating through vast economic octopuses called "trusts," snatched near-complete control of American business. By 1904, for instance, Rockefeller's Standard Oil Company controlled about 85 per cent of the U.S. petroleum trade and a full 90 per cent of the export trade. Competition, that mighty force which holds wages up and prices down, had almost ceased to exist in some industries.

Working conditions were sickening. Children as young as 10 worked 60-hour weeks in factories and mines. In the 1890s, $13 per week was considered the minimum on which a family could be raised, yet almost one third of the men employed in factories and mines earned less than $10, the women less than $6. Safety precautions hardly existed. Approximately 300 workers were killed each year in the steel mills of Pittsburgh and 2000 more were injured. Conditions in the mines and factories were even worse.

The textile industry came to public attention when flames chewed through New York City's Triangle Shirtwaist factory in March, 1911. Nearly 150 women and girls died. Some of them suffocated in an attic because doors had been bolted to keep out union organizers. Others crashed to their deaths in the streets after leaping from windows to escape the onrushing fire. There was a public outcry; sympathy was gained for the workers' cause; more angry citizens acquired their little Red Cards.

In the West's logging camps and mines and farm fields, workers rambled from job to job, drudging for 10 or 12 hours a day for a few days, then moving on. One logging camp boss said, "We got three crews: one coming, one going and one working." A migratory worker wrote: "Camp conditions were basically unchanged from fifty years before. Food was

poor, crudely prepared, dished up in tin utensils. Living quarters were still of the traditional pattern—crudely built bunkhouses with rude double-deck bunks, infested with bedbugs and sometimes lice. There were no washhouses or dryhouses, no recreation facilities. Men still packed their own blankets between camps." One logger said of the food in his camp, "The meat is so tough you can't stick a fork in the gravy." A common story insisted that worn-out ox teams were butchered for the loggers' table.

To these rootless workers, the direct action and no nonsense promised by the I.W.W. had immediate appeal.

So the Wobblies talked, they shouted, they sang—usually at the top of their lungs. Throughout the West, they mounted soapboxes. They enlisted members, they organized, they slapped the face of management again and again, harder and harder.

To no one's surprise, management reacted angrily. A series of "free speech" battles throughout the West was kicked off in Spokane; the first one was a dandy.

Perhaps it was such a humdinger because a fiery female was involved —Elizabeth Gurley Flynn, whose name looms large in I.W.W. history. Then young and attractive, Elizabeth blew into Spokane with the brim of her cowboy hat flipped up in front to expose her handsome face to admiring eyes. A scarf—red, of course—adorned her lovely throat as she began to talk a blue streak on the street corners, day and night.

"Rise up!" she cried to the workers on Trent Avenue. "Shake off your chains! Fight for free speech!"

So Spokane police arrested the girl and flung her into jail, after first breaking her loose from the lamppost to which she had chained herself.

This was a mistake, as it turned out. Spokane might have absorbed a thousand Wobblies but it couldn't handle the many thousands of angry hoboes who panted in when the I.W.W. press bellowed to the nation that a fair lady had been mistreated in the Far West. "Tools of Timber Barons Jail Rebel Girl!" trumpeted the Wobbly press, whereupon loggers left the woods in herds and pointed their calked boots toward Spokane to join their eastern brethren in marching up and down the streets far into the night and in singing vulgar songs and in being thrown into jail by a police force which was beginning to look a little haggard.

The jailhouse and a quickly converted schoolhouse soon were

Crowded bunkhouse conditions were only one of many just grievances of loggers which gave strength to the Wobbly movement. Note in this 1892 photo the pipe-smoking skull on the stove door.

crowded. Jammed into small cells, the Wobblies suffered. As official tempers grew short under Wobbly heckling, they suffered more. They were forced into hard labor on a bread and water diet. They were taken out of jail, beaten, hosed down with icy water, then thrust back into their unheated cells. Pneumonia killed three of them, but the confined Wobblies continued to make trouble as the weary winter months wore on.

A decision finally came with the advent of spring. The battle had been joined in early November, 1909; it ended on March 10, 1910, when Spokane taxpayers, drained dry by the cost of feeding almost 600 Wobblies over the winter, put pressure on elected authorities.

Quietly Spokane city fathers surrendered.

Jail doors squeaked open and exultant Wobblies stomped out. Most of them quickly left town, following the lead of Elizabeth Gurley Flynn, who promptly went east to stir up further trouble in the textile towns of Lawrence, Mass., and Paterson, N.J. The remaining Wobblies remounted their soapboxes in Spokane; the One Big Union had won its first big battle against authority in the West.

(Incidentally, Miss Flynn was not the only famous woman Wobbly. One mustn't forget "Mother" Jones, an Irish lady born in County Cork, who had become a living legend by 1905. Bill Haywood wrote: "Whenever trouble broke out against the miners, Mother Jones went there. When a bridge was patrolled by soldiers she waded the river in winter. When trains were being watched the train crew smuggled her through." It was her habit to organize armies of women during mining disputes to harass strikebreakers with mops and brooms and dishpans. "It's the old mother with her wild women!" the mine owners would cry in horror when faced with her advancing force. Mother died in 1930 at the age of 100. No doubt she took a swipe at the Grim Reaper with her broom.)

Wobbly fortunes took a sharp upward swing during the decade which followed the Spokane victory. The dream of "One Big Union" took on more solid outlines with each passing year and the Wobbly philosophy of industrial unionization began to make more sense. Previously unions had taken in members of only a single craft or trade. The Wobblies weren't so particular. Under the Wobbly banner were to march members of all crafts and trades and even those common laborers with no craft or trade at all and with no restrictions as to sex, race, religion or nationality. To qualify for membership in the I.W.W., it was required only that a person consider himself a member of the working class.

Outright violence became a Wobbly tool after the 1908 convention in Chicago, when a group of Western loggers dominated the convention and voted an important policy change: Wobblies hereafter were to forget about political action and concentrate instead on strikes and sabotage.

Soon after that fateful convention, strikes, riots and sabotage crippled production in most logging and mill centers of the Northwest. It was the beginning of a decade of trouble in the lumber industry as the Wob symbol of sabotage, a wickedly grinning black cat, appeared frequently on stickers pasted to doors and windows of lumber firms marked for harassment.

In self defense, management stiffened its back, hired more Pinkerton strikebreakers and dug in. Now the Wobblies and the bosses were on a collision course and neither showed the least disposition to turn aside. Mass murder was inevitable.

It came first in Everett, on the afternoon of Sunday, November 5, 1916. Under a bright sun, the Everett Massacre thundered into history.

But the trouble did not come out of a clear sky; there was background. The I.W.W. had stirred up trouble during a shingle mill strike at the Puget Sound town. Authorities ran about 40 Wobs out of town, no big thing in itself, but they chose to force the men to run between two lines of huskies bearing pick handles on their way out; some Wobbly blood flowed.

The Seattle I.W.W. cried out for revenge and announced angrily that it would sail to Everett en masse on the following Sunday and a picnic was not on the agenda. On that day, almost 300 Wobblies boarded the steamers *Verona* and *Calista*. Bellowing songs from the Wobbly songbook, the men on the *Verona* were in high spirits as their ship left Seattle harbor ahead of the *Calista* and steamed toward Everett. Some of them were singing their last songs . . .

Police and vigilantes waited on the wharf at Everett, their mission plain: keep the Wobs from landing.

Firing broke out; men screamed. (Police said the first gunshots came from the *Verona;* the Wobs said they came from the wharf; the truth probably will never be known.) The water around the ship soon went red with the blood of the dead and wounded.

When the firing stopped, the skipper of the *Verona* frantically backed his ship out of range, then turned and ran at full steam for Seattle, meeting the *Calista* along the way. Told of the Everett battle, the *Calista*'s captain swung his craft and followed the *Verona* back to Seattle.

Five Wobblies and two vigilantes had died in the brief outburst of murder. Almost 60 men were wounded. (The names of the Wobbly dead say something about the take-all-comers character of the organization:

Felix Baran, a Frenchman; Hugo Gerlat, a German; Gustav Johnson, a Swede; John Looney, an Irishman; and Abraham Rabinowitz, a Russian Jew.)

Seventy-four Wobblies were arrested off the ships at Seattle, despite the fact that police found no firearms on the ships, only clubs and packages of red pepper. (It would have been easy, of course—and wise—for the Wobblies to throw their guns into Puget Sound.)

An important Washington Wobbly, Tom Tracy, was first to go on trial for the Everett Massacre. During a two-month hearing, his lawyers argued that it was impossible to tell who had fired the first shot; they pointed out, too, that the two dead vigilantes might well have been shot by their own kind during the wild scramble on the pier. Tracy went free, as did the other 73 Wobbly defendants. No one was ever tried for killing the five Wobblies. The Everett Massacre, when all was said and done, was a publicity bonanza for the I.W.W. As was their habit, they milked it dry.

But big, new trouble for the Wobblies was just around the corner.

The I.W.W. had been loud in its opposition to U.S. entry into World War I. When the U.S. declared war against Germany, it would have been wise for the Wobblies to simmer down. They didn't, of course. Instead they urged Wobblies to refuse service in the armed forces and staged crippling, frustrating strikes in war industries.

Outraged howls rose from the middle class around the country. War fervor combined with fear of Wobblies to set off many ugly episodes. Open season was declared on Wobblies. The Los Angeles *Times* snorted: "A vast number of I.W.W.s are non-producers. I.W.W. stands for 'I won't work' and 'I want whiskey' . . . The average Wobbly, it must be remembered, is a sort of half-wild animal. He lives on the road, cooks his food in rusty tin cans . . . and sleeps in 'jungles,' barns, outhouses, freight cars . . . They are all in all a lot of homeless men wandering about the country without fixed destination or purpose, other than destruction."

The Wobblies didn't help matters one bit by printing sarcastic bits of verse in their newspaper, *Industrial Worker,* such as the following:

I LOVE MY FLAG

I love my flag, I do, I do,
Which floats upon the breeze.
I also love my arms and legs,
And neck and nose and knees.
One little shell might spoil them all
Or give them such a twist

They would be of no use to me
    I guess I won't enlist.

I love my country, yes, I do,
I hope her folks do well.
Without our arms and legs and things,
I think we'd look like hell.
Young men with faces half shot off
Are unfit to be kissed,
I've read in books it spoils their looks;
    I guess I won't enlist.
        ANONYMOUS, *Industrial Worker*
            April 14, 1917

And so the wild Wobblies forced the hand of the federal government. In September, 1917, five months after the declaration of war, federal agents swooped down on I.W.W. offices around the country and confiscated evidence against the union. The next year, in Chicago, 100 Wobbly leaders were tried on charges of obstructing the war effort. They were found guilty on all counts and sentenced to long terms in Leavenworth Prison.

The Wobblies didn't know it (or wouldn't admit it) but they were finished as a major force in America. They stirred up a general strike in Seattle in February, 1919, and made it sound like a revolution a-borning but it accomplished little more than to set thousands of inconvenienced citizens permanently against the I.W.W. On the first day of the strike, 60,000 workers stayed home. Mayor Ole Hanson threatened to use troops, then never did. The strike committee had set no terminal date for the strike, so it limped along. The committee couldn't end it without seeming to give in to management. Strikers began to sneak back to work and soon the strike which had been advertised as the kick-off of a national revolution had all the drama and excitement of a dead, red herring. What had begun with a roar ended with a whimper.

But no one really expected the I.W.W. to go out with a whimper, not in Washington nor anywhere else. That which lives in violence often dies in violence and the last great outpouring of blood was to take place in Centralia, Washington.

There are three paramount Wobbly heroes: Joe Hill, Frank Little and Wesley Everest. All died martyr's deaths. Hill was a Swedish immigrant who wrote stirring words for the Wobbly songbook. Hill was executed in Utah in 1915 for allegedly killing a Utah grocer during a robbery. He

may have deserved execution, but Wobblies will always believe that his death was ordered by the copper mining kings. Little, half-Indian and proud of it, was a master organizer. Masked men lynched Frank Little in Butte, Montana, in 1917, after first dragging him, his previously broken leg in a cast, by a rope behind a car.

Wes Everest was neither poet nor organizer; he merely happened to be sitting in the I.W.W. hall in Centralia, Washington, on Armistice Day, 1919. Yet Wes Everest's name rings out as loud and clear as any in the Wobbly Valhalla.

As 1919 wore on, lumbermen in Centralia decided that the time had come to rid Centralia of Wobblies once and for all and they so warned the I.W.W. through advertisements in local newspapers. They chose a veterans' organization, the American Legion, to accomplish their aim. (The Legion in Centralia had previous experience with the Wobblies, had, in fact, invaded the union hall earlier in the year wielding pipes and rubber hoses.)

The union fortified the hall and the stage was set for the Centralia Massacre.

On November 11, 1919, the Legion marched, armed with pipe and hose. They passed the Wobbly hall and perhaps they stopped in front of it. At any rate, somebody, somewhere, fired a gun and then another.

Who fired first? Each side, of course, said the other had. Neither proved its point; perhaps it doesn't really matter. Both sides could have; both sides wanted to. At any rate, the Legion felt called upon to break its parade formation and storm the building.

Wes Everest was inside the building, wearing his army uniform. (Not all Wobblies refused military service; Everest had served in France.) The army had taught Everest how to use guns. When the Legionnaires entered, Everest rose and emptied his rifle into the advancing horde, then dropped the rifle, snatched out a pistol and ran for the woods, pursued by a bellowing mob.

The fugitive waded to his waist in the Skookumchuck River. Then, feeling the wild current and realizing that he was about to drown, he stopped and turned to face his tormentors and offered to submit to police arrest.

It wasn't enough to stop the mob, which plunged into the water after

Wesley Everest, Centralia logger, must have looked much like this on the day of his death. In this photo, taken a few months before he was lynched, he wears his World War I uniform.

him.

Wes Everest fired his pistol four times before it jammed. He snapped the trigger again and again. Finally the gun fired and killed Dale Hubbard, nephew of one of the lumbermen who had organized the march on the I.W.W. hall.

His gun empty, Everest fought the mob with his fists, but soon was overpowered.

Everest raged, "You don't have the guts to hang a man in the daytime!"

He was right, for what little it was worth.

They tied Everest to a car's bumper and dragged him back to Centralia and through Centralia. Then they had him locked in jail.

Evening came to Centralia. Lifesaving lights blinked on, lights which Wes Everest knew would protect him. Perhaps, gentle citizens prayed, the horror had ended.

Then lights went out all over town. Figures moved through the blackness and soon beat at the jailhouse door.

They wanted Wes Everest and they got him, threw him onto the floor of a car and drove to the Chehalis River bridge.

They hanged him there and riddled his body with bullets.

Only Wobblies were tried for the Centralia Massacre. No one tried to bring Wes Everest's killers to justice. The American Legion raised $11,750 to pay $4 per day to 50 Legionnaires in uniform to occupy the front seats of the courtroom where the Wobblies were tried. Three witnesses who testified that Legionnaires attacked the Wobbly hall before a shot was fired were arrested for perjury as they left the stand; it was that kind of trial.

After 15 years in prison, the Wobblies were paroled. No one spent as much as one day in prison for murdering Wesley Everest. The story ends . . .

Where did the Wobblies go wrong? Their idea of organizing labor on an industry-wide basis was taken over by the Congress of Industrial Organization in the 1930s and made to work; it works to this day. Why didn't it work for the Wobblies?

Well, for one thing, many of their leaders were revolutionists. Like most revolutionists, they weren't good for much but revolution. The Wobblies attracted members by the droves and shook the employer class to its boots but they proved generally unable to translate this power into solid benefits for the membership. And so they died . . .

For another thing, their reckless use of riots and sabotage to gain their goals brought a harsh and deadly reaction from an angered, frightened federal government. And so they died . . .

In a sense, though, the I.W.W. succeeded too well for its own good. Its activities and propaganda threw a spotlight on disgusting working conditions in many industries. Rapid improvement often resulted. So, as time trickled by, there was less and less for workers to revolt about. Riots and revolts grow out of last-ditch desperation. The better years came and passed and killed the sprouting seeds of desperation.

Technically, the I.W.W. is not dead. A few dusty little offices remain scattered around the country. The Wobbly newspaper, *Industrial Worker,* is still published. A few old-timers still lounge around the offices smoking pipes under the pictures of Joe Hill and Frank Little and Wes Everest. To them, the One Big Union is anything but dead.

So be it. Anyone passing the haunted halls of the I.W.W. in the dark of a modern night should not be shocked to hear the old-timers softly singing the Wobbly anthem to the tune of "John Brown's Body":

> "It is we who plowed the prairies; built the cities
> where they trade;
> "Dug the mines and built the workshops; endless miles
> of railroad laid.
> "Now we stand outcast and starving, 'mid the wonders
> we have made
> "But the union makes us strong,

> "Solidarity forever!
> "Solidarity forever!
> "Solidarity forever!
> "For the union makes us strong."

"CHINABOY, GO HOME!"

The radicalism and violence which swirled around the Wobblies in Washington should surprise no one who has read history; the birth throes of organized labor in the state were anything but smooth and peaceful.

Some of the fiercest battles fought by Washington workers were not against cruel bosses but against a race of incredibly durable laborers who took the hard, dirty jobs that no one else wanted, then performed the work better for lower wages and with fewer complaints. These were the Chinese imported by the thousands (some against their will; they were literally

"Shanghaied") to work in the mines of California, then to build railroads throughout the West.

But when the railroad building and mining slacked off, Washington's Chinese were shot at, beaten, dragged from their homes and finally driven from the state. Washington's first important labor union, the Knights of Labor, had much to do with the expulsion of the coolies.

Thousands of Chinese were brought into the Northwest after 1860 to work in gold mines. When the boom ended, they turned to other menial work. Many others worked on the railroads. With the completion of the Northern Pacific and the Canadian Pacific, that work fell off sharply, too.

Suddenly there were more workers than jobs. White men who had looked down their noses at "coolie work" now were willing to fight for it. But the Chinese who held the jobs were willing to work for less than whites and could do more work under worse conditions. It was hardly surprising that their white employers were reluctant to let them go.

Inevitably someone soon screamed, "Drive them dirty furriners out!"

In autumn, 1885, a mob in Wyoming killed a few Chinese coal miners. This was all the spark required to set off coolie-haters in Washington.

Since the largest Chinese communities were in Tacoma and Seattle, the riots of 1885–1886 centered in these towns.

A full two-thirds of the workmen who hacked out the roadbed and laid the rails for the western division of the Northern Pacific railroad were Chinese. N.P.'s western terminus was Tacoma; one might say that the railroad owned the town. Chinatown in Tacoma had been built on land donated by the railroad.

But the railroad was finished and unemployment became a problem. Citizens of Tacoma formed a committee which saw its duty and did it. The Chinese were given 30 days to get out of town. When the time was up, 300 men moved into Chinatown and forcibly removed the coolies, loading their possessions on wagons, burning their houses and driving the coolies to the Northern Pacific station. There the Chinese were forced to spend a cold, wet night in the open. At least one died of exposure.

But Tacoma got rid of its Chinese. So did Seattle, in much the same way, except that the vigilantes of Seattle, instead of railroading the coolies, loaded them on boats bound for San Francisco.

To the credit of the citizenry and some public officials, committees

Chinese coolies built much of the Northern Pacific railroad in Washington; here they work near the summit of the Cascade Mountains.

quickly formed to protect the Chinese. The work of these "law and order" groups, usually undertaken at great personal risk, may well have kept the death toll among the coolies from being much higher than it was.

The thing was pretty silly, really, unless you happened to be Chinese, in which case it must have been terrifying. If the coolie had ever been a serious threat to the white workingman, by the fall of 1885 he no longer was. The Chinese Exclusion Act of 1880 prevented more from entering the country. By 1885, there were only about 3000 Chinese in all of Washington and a fair number of these had left by fall, when the agitation began. It was one of the sorriest episodes of Washington history and it helps not at all to be reminded that the same sort of thing happened throughout the West.

The Knights of Labor were capable of better things. In 1886, their platform in the territorial elections advocated a bureau of labor statistics, postal savings, industrial compensation laws, graduated income taxes and weekly payment of wages. None of these proposals seems the least bit radical today.

Before the turn of the century, the American Federation of Labor had largely replaced the Knights; labor unionism had painfully entered adulthood. After 1903, labor legislation in Washington led the nation in many important aspects. Acts were passed restricting the employment of women, requiring safety devices in factories, establishing the eight-hour day for public employees and providing for a permit system for workers between ages 12 and 14. A state bureau of labor was created in 1905.

Labor unrest, sparked by Wobblies, flared and died, then flared again. The brutal depression of the early 1930s sent workers back to the ramparts and gave rise to such interesting organizations as Spokane's "Order of the Forgotten Man," which quickly attracted 11,000 members. The Teamsters Union, led by David W. Beck of Seattle, began to expand in 1934. During the next quarter century, the Teamsters became one of the largest and most powerful unions in the country. (But not without sliding under a cloud; both Beck and his successor, James Hoffa, were sentenced to federal prisons.)

Seattle has long been known as a strong union town. One way or another, Seattle and Washington have managed over the years to make national news on the labor front.

Washington's labor force in 1969 was concentrated in manufacturing,

There was women's work at Boeing in the early days, too, such as sewing fabric on wings.

with aerospace (spelled "B-O-E-I-N-G") and lumber-wood products leading the way. Aerospace hired almost 102,000 workers; lumber and wood products 46,000. Total manufacturing employees were 287,000.

Next largest employer was government, with almost 234,000 persons on the public payrolls. Transportation-communication-utilities hired 72,500; agriculture supplied work for 41,000.

Men doing Washington's work and fighting for improvement of their lot supplied a bright splash of color in the panorama of Washington history. There always have been immense jobs to do in Washington— some of the world's greatest dams to be built, wide swaths to be cut through mighty forests, the sea's bounty to be gleaned, a wild river to be tamed so that more than a million acres of desert could bloom, aerospace machines to be built by the thousands for war and peace. Immense jobs . . . and men of matching size to do them.

SUGGESTED READING

Lens, Sidney; WORKING MEN: THE STORY OF LABOR; Putnam's; 1960.
Meltzer, Milton; BREAD—AND ROSES; Knopf; 1967 (labor history).
Renshaw, Patrick; THE WOBBLIES; Doubleday; 1967.
Sung, Betty Lee; MOUNTAIN OF GOLD; Macmillan; 1967 (Chinese immigration).
Werstein, Irving; PIE IN THE SKY; Delacorte Press; 1969 (Wobblies).

Chapter Eleven ★

Aviation
BOEING: GIANT OF THE SKY

Groggy after an overnight flight from Seattle, Well-wood Beall, chief engineer of the Boeing Airplane Company, hurried into the office and slumped into a chair. When he saw Echols's face, he knew what was coming: the U.S. Air Force was ready to fish or cut bait on the B-29, Boeing's superbomber design.

Battered and reeling on all fronts in the first months of World War II, driven out of Europe into Africa and virtually wiped out in the Pacific, the United States needed such a plane in the way a blind man needs eyes. Only such an aircraft could mount an attack against Japan across the vast watery distances of the Asian oceans; only such an aircraft could deliver the awesome weapon being tested during this grim spring of 1942 at Alamogordo, New Mexico.

The Air Force needed such a plane, but did it specifically need the B-29? Boeing's B-17, the almost indestructible Flying Fortress, was rapidly proving itself but the B-29 was a vastly different airplane, a leap into the future. Beall knew that the Air Force had doubts about the remote control guns on the Superfortress. Would they work in combat? But Boeing engineers knew that the usual gun blisters and turrets were little more than speed-killing lumps in the airstream and couldn't be used on the B-29 if the plane were to have the range and swiftness required for an assault on the Japanese home islands. A 400-mile-an-hour airplane had to be slick and smooth. Slick and smooth like the XB-29 ("X" for "Experimental") Superfortress now taking shape behind tight walls of secrecy in Plant Two, Seattle.

Developing a good combat airplane demands long days, months, years of research, planning, testing. Boeing employees had spent many thousands of hours on the B-29 and the plane still had not left the ground.

But war, the cruelest of masters, insisted that time be telescoped. A war-winning weapon usually is designed before war begins. Wellwood Beall was convinced that Boeing had designed such a weapon in the B-29 but now, facing General Oliver Echols, Air Force engineering chief, he feared that the Air Force was not convinced. Eventual victory in the great war might well be hanging in the balance.

"The United States government," said Echols, "is about to spend more money on one project than on any other single project of the whole war. The B-29. We haven't even flown the airplane. The risk is tremendous. It may not pan out. Now, you are the chief engineer of the Boeing Airplane Company. We want to know—and the survival of the country may depend on this—we want to know what you really believe in your heart. Is that a good airplane? Or isn't it?"

Beall breathed deeply. Here it was, finally, the huge question dropped into his lap. How could he say with absolute certainty that the B-29 could do the job? And if the B-29 didn't work, there might not be time enough to design a better airplane.

So now Echols had decided to test Beall's personal faith in the big, beautiful machine. Beall had watched the great plane grow from a sketch on drawing paper. It wasn't hard for him to believe in it. In addition, he had faith in the 1900 persons in the Boeing engineering department. He knew that those 1900 believed in the B-29. In the moment of decision, it was that simple.

Beall lifted his head and said strongly, "Yes, General. It's going to be a good airplane. Give us first priority on test facilities. Let us do all the testing we want to do, when we want to do it, flight testing, systems testing, all kinds of testing. Assign us the airplanes to do this and I guarantee you B-29s that will be successful in operation."

Echols left to talk to General Hap Arnold, chief of the Air Force. When he returned, he said, "We'll do what you ask."

The gigantic production program would cost three billion dollars. The B-29 would be built in plants in Renton, Washington; Marietta, Georgia; Omaha, Nebraska; and Wichita, Kansas.

In General Echols's office on that fateful day in 1942, Beall was confident that Boeing was ready to meet its great responsibility. After all, Boeing Airplane Company was no Johnny-come-lately. It had been preparing for this dramatic moment since 1915.

★

The engine of Terah Maroney's Curtiss hydroplane hung between two muslin-covered wings which in turn were supported on shafts attached to a float. It was a gawky apparatus, a plumber's nightmare. The propeller was a pusher; that is, it spun behind the wings, not in front.

This conglomeration of struts, wires and startling appendages was supposed to fly. Its appearance warned that the first serious wisp of wind would tear it apart. But it was this fragile machine which was to provide young William Boeing's first airplane flight on July 4, 1914.

The wealthy young Seattle bachelor settled himself into the seat beside Maroney on the front edge of the bottom wing and held on. The Curtiss gathered speed and thundered across the water and finally accomplished a rough and noisy takeoff.

Maroney held the plane below 1000 feet. As Seattle and Puget Sound unrolled its beauty in panorama below Bill Boeing, he relaxed and began to feel comfortable in the air. Suddenly it seemed right and proper for man to fly.

There were more flights with Maroney. Then one day Boeing announced to a friend, Conrad Westervelt, "There really isn't a whole lot to that machine of Maroney's. We could build a better one."

"Of course we could."

Westervelt, a Navy engineer, began to inquire into airplane technology. They talked to Herb Munter, a Seattle exhibition flyer, who was building a new plane.

"Is the public interested in flying?" asked Boeing.

Munter grinned. "They come out mostly to see me crash. So I dive straight down and then pull up close to the ground. It's not really dangerous, in a plane this slow, but it gives 'em the thrill they came for."

Boeing pondered Munter's words. Surely there was more to aviation than that. All of Europe was at war and it seemed likely that the United States would be drawn in. The nations at war were working hard on combat airplanes. Could the United States afford to lag behind?

Boeing and Westervelt talked Munter into joining them, then began work on two airplanes. B & Ws, they would be called, for Boeing and Westervelt. Two shipyards were put to work on the wings, fuselage and pontoons. Meanwhile, Boeing went to Los Angeles to learn to fly under pioneer aviator Glenn Martin.

A great day arrived: the first B & W sat in varnished splendor on the Lake Union ramp. Its wings spanned 52 feet; its engine boasted 125 horsepower. The first test flight was made by Bill Boeing, who barely lifted the craft off the water. When Herb Munter's turn came, Boeing warned him not to fly it until he was thoroughly familiar with the controls. Munter dutifully taxied the plane for a few days. When boredom got the best of him, he snatched the control stick back and sent the biplane soaring high. After he landed, he had to face his boss.

Glowering, Bill Boeing said, "Don't ever do that again unless I authorize it." Then he turned to look proudly at the airplane. A grin flickered. He asked, "How was it?"

"Good. It was just fine."

The month was June; the year 1916.

Bill Boeing was in the airplane business and the seed of Washington's major industry had been planted.

★

Two young men named Phil Johnson and Claire Egtvedt joined Boeing's design department in 1917, not long after the United States entered World War I. Both were to play major roles in development of the company; both were destined to serve as chief executive of the firm at various times.

The work rattled along at the brisk pace demanded by war. The Navy dragged its feet on acceptance of a new Boeing design called "Model C" but gave the struggling young factory contracts for construction of planes designed by other firms.

But the war ended in November of 1918 and with its end came the cancellation of military orders. The Boeing company quickly found itself groping for a peacetime direction.

On March 3, 1919, William Boeing and Test Pilot Eddie Hubbard fought snowstorms and heavy winds to fly the Model C to Vancouver, B.C., and back to Seattle with sixty letters—the first international air mail.

Needing orders to keep a growing factory busy and solvent, the top Boeing team of Johnson, Egtvedt and Ed Gott continued to seek government business. Off the design tables and out of the factory flew the PW-9, a pursuit plane (now it would be called "fighter"), the NB-1 and NB-2, Navy trainers, and the Model 40 mail plane. Model 40, operated by a subsidiary company, Boeing Air Transport (later to become United Air Lines), made history on the Chicago-San Francisco mail and passenger runs. As mail-passenger transports, the all-metal, low-wing, single-engine

William E. Boeing, with mail pouch, and Eddie Hubbard come ashore after carrying 60 letters from Vancouver, B.C., to Seattle in 1919, thus completing the world's first international air mail flight. The plane is the Boeing C-700.

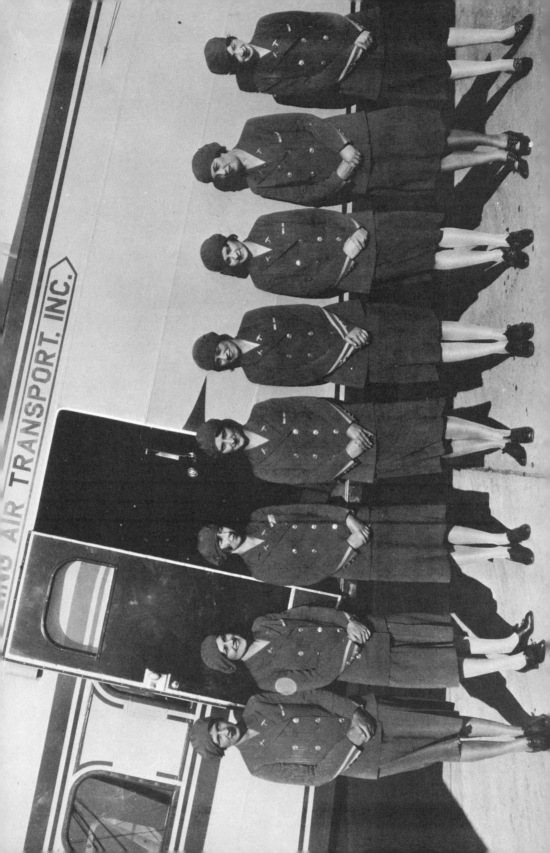

Monomail and the twin-engine 247 were the big news for Boeing in the 1930s. The mighty B-9 bomber and the P-26 pursuit proudly represented the Boeing name in military competitions.

Then the Air Force announced in 1933 that it wanted a new long range bomber, a mighty plane that would carry a ton of bombs and fly 5000 miles, five times as far as the B-9.

What it got from Boeing was B-17, the Flying Fortress, which was to blaze a path of glory through the world's war-torn skies and earn an unchallenged place in aviation history for itself and Boeing Airplane Company.

★

On December 14, 1941, one week after the Japanese attack on Pearl Harbor, Captain Hewett Wheless was leading his bomber crew off Formosa in an attack against Japanese shipping. His plane, a B-17 Flying Fortress, had escaped the heavy Japanese raids on Clark Field in the Philippines on December 8; now his crew was flying night and day as part of the vastly outnumbered and all-but-destroyed American forces in the Far East.

On their fateful day, trouble began for Captain Wheless and his crew when bad weather separated them from the two other B-17s in their formation. Wheless decided to attack the Japanese ships alone.

As he committed the Fortress to its bomb run, no less than 18 Japanese fighter planes knifed through the clouds with their guns spewing flame and hot metal as they bore in on the lone B-17. The turret guns on the Fortress chattered angrily; almost immediately one of the attacking fighters flew apart.

"You're getting 'em!" Wheless roared into the intercom. "You're getting 'em!"

But the score evened moments later when Private Killin died in the belly turret. Navigator Meenaugh, swearing revenge, immediately took his place.

Captain Wheless stubbornly held the Fortress to its bomb run, because any attempt at evasive action would ruin accuracy. The attacking fighters thus were given a cruel advantage but for a bomber commander, there could be no alternative.

A shout of triumph rattled through the intercom and another Japanese plane rolled away in a smoke-trailing spin, but both waist gunners

These are some of the first airline stewardesses. They had to be registered nurses then, not beauty contest winners.

had been wounded by the hot enemy metal which now ripped into the plane from all sides. Sergeant Gootee, wounded in the right wrist, aimed a gun with his left hand and continued to blast at attacking fighters.

Two fighters hanging on the B-17's tail were doing terrible damage but Captain Wheless couldn't veer from his bomb run to give his waist gunners a crack at them. (Early Fortresses had no tail gun.)

Finally the exultant shout came from Bombardier Schlotte in the nose:

"Bombs away!"

Immediately Wheless whipped the plane into a skidding turn to give the waist gunners a chance to knock the fighters off their tail. Schlotte came back to help Gootee at a waist gun. Uproar surrounded them now, the heavy chatter of their own .50 caliber machine guns, the snarling engines of the enemy fighters as they swept past in attack after attack, the sharp warnings in the earphones as a plane swept in from a new direction, the straining thunder of the Fortress engines.

The belly gun of the B-17 was no longer in operation. Gootee picked off another fighter, but jammed his gun in the process. And still there were 14 of the enemy, boring in harder now as they sensed the approaching death of their prey.

Now No. 1 engine failed on the Fortress and soon thereafter, the other waist gun went out of action. Its fuselage ripped and scarred and mangled, the badly bloodied plane shrugged off its wounds and flew on.

Then it was reported to Captain Wheless that all the guns were out of action. He knew the end was near. Defenseless, they would soon be blown out of the sky. Even as valiant an airplane and crew as this one had its limits and those limits had been reached.

More dismal reports came to him as he gripped the control wheel, fighting a losing battle for precious altitude. At least half of the control cables were useless. The oxygen system was gone. The tail wheel had been shot away. The front tires were riddled. The radio no longer operated. A fuel tank had been torn open. Air screamed through a thousand gashes in the fuselage. Their time had almost run out . . .

Suddenly Captain Wheless became aware that the sounds of battle had faded. He stared out through his shattered window at a Japanese fighter plane flying close alongside the limping B-17. The pilot of the fighter was staring, too, his jaw hanging in disbelief.

Then Wheless understood. *They were out of ammunition.* A Flying Fortress had absorbed the ammo loads of 18 Japanese fighter planes and still flew!

The fighters turned away and disappeared into the clouds. Wheless grimly nursed the B-17 along at low altitude as daylight waned. Their ordeal was far from over. They had to reach the Philippines before dark to have a chance of survival.

Suddenly he saw land through the mist and rain—Mindanao! The Philippines!

Wheless turned the shuddering aircraft toward a small airfield close to the beach and let it sink. Then, after committing the plane to its landing approach, he saw barricades on the field and a great weight pressed down on him; a groan came from the depths of his soul. To have come so far, to have suffered so much, only to die in a flaming heap against a friendly barricade . . . it was too much to bear. It was unthinkable.

Like a projectile, the B-17 plowed through the barricade without collapsing, then trundled for 200 yards on flat tires until its wheels locked. Then, like a dying beast, the great plane tipped forward onto its nose, threatened for an instant to flop onto its back, then slammed its belly to the ground and lay still while dust settled around it.

Seven American airmen climbed out with wonder in their eyes as they stared at the wreckage which had brought them home. To a man, they patted some part of the B-17 and fondly muttered something like, "You great ol' gal . . . you doggoned great ol' gal."

★

On April 28, 1942, President Franklin D. Roosevelt said in a radio fireside chat: "Our planes are helping the defense of the French colonies today, and soon American Flying Fortresses will be fighting for the liberation of Europe. This is the story of one of our Flying Fortresses operating in the western Pacific. The pilot of this plane is a modest young man, proud of his crew for one of the toughest fights a bomber has yet experienced."

Then the president told the story of the B-17's battle against the 18 Japanese fighter planes.

"The name of that pilot," he continued, "is Captain Hewett T. Wheless of the United States Army. He comes from Menard, Texas, population 2375. He has been awarded the Distinguished Service Cross. I hope he is listening."

Nine days later, 18,000 Boeing employees at Plant No. 2 in Seattle laid down their tools and gathered on the concrete in front of the factory. Press and radio were there.

So was Captain Hewett T. Wheless of Menard, Texas.

"It wasn't so bad," Wheless drawled into the microphones. "When we got down on the ground in Mindanao, my first gunner said, 'Captain, we were just getting on to the knack of shooting 'em down when we had to leave and go home.' The men operating the planes don't want all the credit. I want to thank you for myself and a lot of other pilots who owe their lives to your design and workmanship. Continue the good work and together we can't lose."

★

A heavily-loaded B-29 Superfortress labored off the crushed coral runway on Tinian Island in the ominous dark at 2:45 A.M. The date was August 6, 1945. The great plane flew alone through the blackness, then into the dawn, over 1600 miles of ocean to the Japanese home island of Honshu. Shortly before 9:15 A.M., the B-29 *Enola Gay* arrived at high altitude over the quiet, unsuspecting city of Hiroshima.

The B-29s had been over the Japanese home islands many times in recent months, had, in fact, virtually burned out Tokyo, Nagoya, Osaka and Kobe with fire bombs.

But the mission of *Enola Gay* was no ordinary one . . .

At 9:15 A.M., the bomb slithered away from the B-29's underside and fell toward the center of sprawling Hiroshima. Wearing hastily-donned green goggles, crew members watched almost breathlessly for fifty seconds as the bomb whistled through the peaceful air.

When it finally came, the purplish-white flash was brighter than any they had ever seen, brighter than the sun, brighter than many suns. Despite the colored glasses, they had to turn away for a moment.

When they turned back, they watched in frozen horror as the weird glow grew at a fantastic rate to become a swirling, rising, seething ball of fire. A shock wave rocked the plane. A column of smoke spewed out of the center of the dying fireball and leaped into the sky beneath a mushroom cap, reached the altitude of *Enola Gay* in what seemed like only a few seconds, then soared to 50,000 feet before halting its climb and hanging in the air to form one of the most awesome spectacles man had ever witnessed.

In Hiroshima, 75,000 persons died, many of them instantly, as the

A flight of Boeing Flying Fortresses laces the sky with vapor trails on a World War II raid over Europe.

core of the city was devastated.

President Truman immediately asked the Japanese military government to accept surrender terms.

The government refused.

A second atom bomb was dropped from a B-29 on Nagasaki. The dead: 35,000.

On September 2, 1945, the Japanese surrendered formally aboard the battleship *Missouri* anchored in Tokyo Bay. World War II, the most widespread and intense war in man's bloody history, had finally ended. Use of the atom bombs had made an invasion of Japan unnecessary. It had been estimated that such an invasion would have cost one million American casualties. It was this grim prophecy which led President Truman to order his B-29s into the air with their terrible loads.

There was celebration in Boeing plants when the war ended, but the cancelling of war orders brought the company to the point of crisis again. This time, however, Boeing was remembered for its war record. It was a war the U.S. had to win and Boeing had helped mightily. Postwar tabulations showed that B-17 Flying Fortresses had hauled 46 per cent of total bomb tonnage dropped in Europe and had knocked out of the sky 66 per cent of the enemy fighter planes destroyed by American bombers. B-29 Superfortresses, the planes which ended the war, had dropped a monumental 96 per cent of the bombs on Japan. No American aircraft company had more stars in its wartime crown.

Boeing directors chose William Allen, Seattle attorney, to lead the company through peacetime pitfalls into the jet age. His long tenure began in September, 1945, and Boeing prospered as never before. The Boeing B-47, a medium bomber, thrust the U.S. Air Force into the jet age. It was a completely new kind of airplane, perhaps the first truly beautiful one, best described by Harold Mansfield in his excellent Boeing book, "Vision: A Saga of the Sky:"

"Long, tapered body, trailing off into the parting flare of sweptback fin and stabilizers; wings that were slender as a fine steel blade, sweeping out and back and gently down, relaxed and poised for beauty of flight, jet engines leaping forward from those wings with open mouths. 'Give us sky,' those engines seemed to be saying, 'we'll show you what we can do.' "

The B-47 "Stratojet" first flew in September, 1947, and was followed by the B-52 "Stratofortress," giant intercontinental bomber, which first flew in Seattle on April 15, 1952. Mansfield describes the moment:

A Boeing B-47 leaps into the air with the noisy help of its built-in JATO (Jet-Assisted-Take-Off) units.

Boeing Parade of Progress

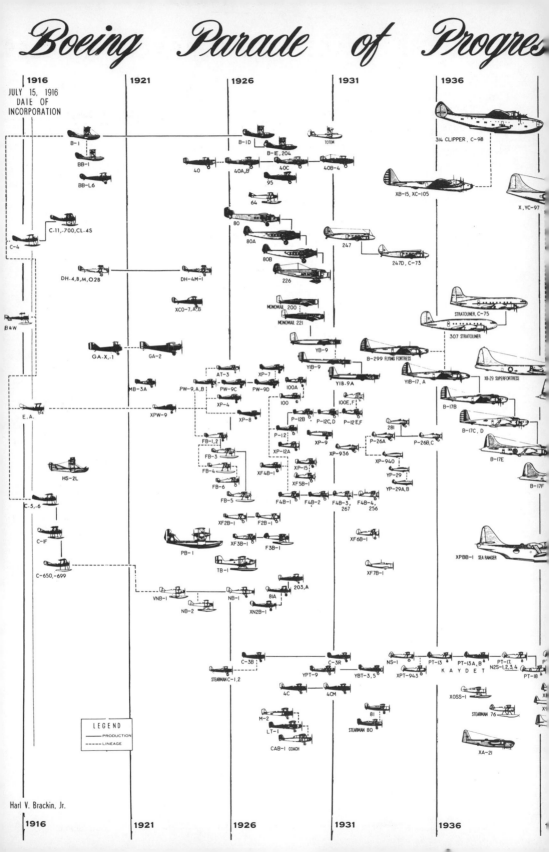

1916   **1921**   **1926**   **1931**   **1936**

JULY 15, 1916
DATE OF
INCORPORATION

B-1

BB-1

BB-L6

C-4

C-11,-700,CL-4S

DH-4,B,M,O2B

DH-4M-1

B & W

XCO-7,A,B

GA-X,-1   GA-2

MB-3A

XPW-9

E.A.

HS-2L

C-5,-6

C-1F

C-650,-699

B-1D

B-1E, 204

40

40A,B

40C

40B-4

95

64

80

80A

80B

226

MONOMAIL 200
MONOMAIL 221

10TEM

247

247D, C-73

YB-9

Y1B-9

Y1B-9A

AT-3   XP-7

PW-9,A,B   PW-9C   PW-9D

XP-4   100A

100

XP-8

FB-1,2

FB-3

FB-4

FB-6

FB-5

XF4B-1

P-12B

P-12

XP-12A

XP-15

XF5B-1

F4B-1

XF2B-1   F2B-1

XF3B-1   F3B-1

PB-1

TB-1

VNB-1   NB-1

NB-2   XN2B-1

81A

203,A

100E,F

P-12C,D   P-12 E,F

XP-9

XP-936

F4B-2   F4B-3, 267   F4B-4, 256

XF6B-1

XF7B-1

28I

P-26A

P-26B,C

XP-940

YP-29

YP-29A,B

B-299 FLYING FORTRESS

Y1B-17, A

314 CLIPPER, C-98

XB-15, XC-105

X, YC-97

STRATOLINER, C-75

307 STRATOLINER

XB-29 SUPERFORTRESS

B-17B

B-17C, D

B-17E

B-17F

XPBB-1 SEA RANGER

C-3B

STEARMAN C-1,2

C-3R

YPT-9   YBT-3,5

NS-1   XPT-943

PT-13   PT-13A,B   PT-17, N2S-1,2,3,4

KAYDET

PT-18

4C   4CM

M-2

LT-1

CAB-1 COACH

81

STEARMAN 80

XOSS-1

STEARMAN 76

XA-21

LEGEND
—— PRODUCTION
- - - LINEAGE

Harl V. Brackin, Jr.

1916   **1921**   **1926**   **1931**   **1936**

AIRBORNE, SPACE AND SURFACE VEHICLES

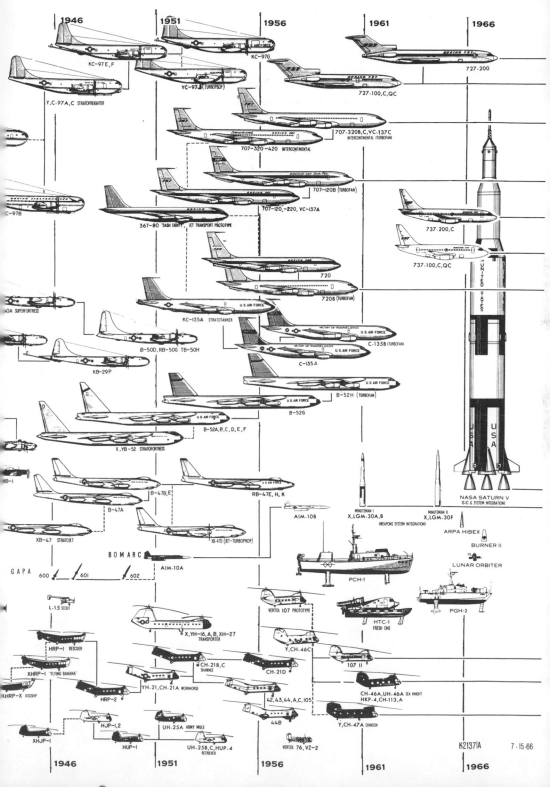

"Tall, rangy 'Tex' Johnston, who'd worn his Texas boots on every important flight since he won the Thompson Trophy race in 1946, would pilot the intercontinental giant . . . The day was bright. General Mark Bradley, Air Force director of procurement and production, was at the plant. Bill Allen and Beall went with him over to the field. The product of an effort now seven years old, its eight jet engines sweeping forward out of sweptback wings, its sharklike tail fin jutting four stories high, was going to reveal in a few minutes whether it would qualify as America's deterrent to enemy aggression. It was poised at the north end of the 10,000-foot runway.

"People crowding office windows, the ramp, the roof, waited in suspense. The roar of jet thrust filled eardrums and hearts. The airplane began to move. Slow, like a ship under sail, at first. How could it be so slow, wondered Allen, standing on the ramp. He leaned forward, urging it. Tex was lumbering toward them, gaining momentum, thundering with power, deafening power going past them.

" 'Pour it,' Allen shouted, his fist following after the ship in a haymaker sweep. 'Pour her on!' The Stratofortress was accelerating rapidly now, as a jet does once its own speed adds power to its power, and was lifting easily, even lightly, into the air.

"Tex went on up, circled and raced back over the field, saying with a sky-cracking roar that the airplane was O.K., doing great."

★

Another major triumph was ahead for Boeing: there was a 707 in its future. On July 15, 1954, the yellow, brown and silver prototype of America's first jet transport roared skyward from a runway near its birthplace, the Boeing factory in Renton. It was destined to become one of the most successful planes in the history of commercial aviation and would gain Boeing the solid foothold in civil aviation that it had long sought without success. With the acceptance of the beautiful 707, Boeing began to dominate civil aviation as it had long dominated military aviation.

But if there was any fear that success had softened Boeing Airplane Company or watered down its spirit of adventure, Test Pilot Tex Johnston proved otherwise not long after the 707's introduction. A huge crowd gathered around Seattle's Lake Washington for the Gold Cup hydroplane

The first 747 rolls out of the Boeing plant at Everett in 1968. The huge aircraft was expected to help Boeing dominate civil aviation as it has long dominated military flying.

races suddenly looked to the sky as a giant aircraft screamed in at low altitude, zoomed up in a graceful reach for the sky and curled into a lovely slow roll, a maneuver only stunt planes were supposed to attempt.

This was no stunt plane; this was Boeing's only flying sample of the new commercial jet transport, the 707, and the pilot, apparently gone mad, was Tex Johnston.

To the gasping astonishment of the crowd, Johnston performed the maneuver a second time.

The next morning, Johnston was asked to appear on the carpet of Boeing President Allen. What Allen wanted to know was: just exactly what did Johnston have in mind in pulling such a stunt with a company plane worth 15 millions of dollars?

"I just had to," Johnston is said to have replied. "I was flying the greatest airplane ever built and with all those people watching, I just HAD to. Besides, any airplane you cain't slow roll just ain't safe to fly."

The 707 reaped a harvest of publicity out of the incident. It is conceivable that President Allen wasn't as unhappy about the affair as he appeared to be.

In 1968 Boeing worked hard to make the 707 obsolete with the supersonic SST, one block long and designed to fly from the U.S. to Europe in a couple of hours, and the 747, a plane rather like a 626 m.p.h. flying apartment house, designed to carry 490 persons and make future air travel as common (and perhaps as inexpensive) as present bus travel.

The first 747 rolled out of its monstrous Everett assembly plant in late 1968 and was flown in early 1969. While the first of the new generation airplanes was a-building, one often heard the word "incredible" around Everett. And why not? Consider the fact that the 747's fuselage is twice as long as the entire length—120 feet—of the Wright brothers' first flight! The pilot's perch is three stories high; the rudder towers as tall as a five-story apartment building. Some 50,000 persons in 49 states and six foreign countries worked on the 747.

If the hatched bird is incredible, its nest is only slightly less so. An area about the size of New York's Central Park—780 acres—was cleared for the Everett factory. The 10-story assembly building has 63 acres under a single roof.

Only an industrial colossus could dream such gigantic dreams, could hope to hatch such incredible birds. Boeing had become such a colossus: the world's largest aerospace company, the state of Washington's largest industry and major employer, the keystone and bulwark of Washington's economy.

In late 1968, Boeing went to the moon. The first stage of the Saturn 5 rocket which propelled three astronauts away from the earth toward the first circumnavigation of the moon was Boeing-built.

The word "incredible" comes to mind again when one remembers that it all began as recently as 1916 because a young man named Bill Boeing wanted to build a stick-and-wire airplane for no other reason than that he thought it could be done better.

Claire Egtvedt had called it "honesty of purpose." He insisted that Boeing Airplane Company must always design and build the best airplane it could, even though its customer of the moment might be willing—even eager—to buy a cheaper, shoddier machine, or a rehash of an old model. Egtvedt's philosophy caused the company to take greater risks than it would have had to take, to reach farther into the unknown than it needed to reach.

Why did Boeing Airplane Company become great? In looking for the answer, one could do worse than to start with "honesty of purpose."

WINGS ACROSS THE SEA

The small group had waited all night at the Wenatchee airport but the expected airplane had not winged in out of the dark. Then, soon after 7 A.M., they saw it flying at low altitude toward the field.

As it neared, someone gasped, "Look, the wheels are gone!"

The fact soon became painfully plain: the approaching monoplane had lost its landing gear but it would attempt a landing anyway. Those on the field watched breathlessly as the plane's bare metal belly sank danger-ously close to the ground, then touched the runway, squealed and screeched along it, rose ominously on its nose, then settled and disappeared in a great dust cloud until it slowed and finally stopped with its left wingtip leaning against the dirt with the resignation of a crippled bird.

Clyde Pangborn had come home. In the process, he had completed with Hugh Herndon the first non-stop flight over the Pacific Ocean. The date was October 6, 1931. The tense group watching the controlled crash which passed for a landing at Wenatchee consisted of Pangborn's mother, brother, friends and a reporter for the *Wenatchee World.*

Ironically the record-setting flight was something of an accident. Pang-born and Herndon had intended to try for a new around-the-world mark when they left New York in their Bellanca monoplane on July 28, 1931. They crossed the Atlantic Ocean and Europe, then decided after reaching

Siberia that the existing record—eight days, 15 hours and 51 minutes—was out of reach.

A Japanese newspaper had offered $25,000 for the first non-stop flight across the Pacific. As a consolation prize, it was attractive, so Herndon and Pangborn took off for Tokyo without even so much as a map of Japan. Moments after they landed near Tokyo, their plane was seized and they were arrested and charged with spying.

A Japanese official found Herndon's camera on the plane and developed the film in it. *Banzai!* There were pictures of what appeared to be military fortifications on the Japanese island of Hokkaido.

After several weeks' detainment, Pangborn and Herndon were fined $2500 (paid by Herndon's rich relatives in the U.S.), then released. On October 3, they coaxed their Bellanca into the air from a sandy beach near Tokyo and pointed its blunt nose across the Pacific, toward Wenatchee, almost half a world away.

Excess weight threatened to bog down the plane, so they dropped the landing gear. Then ice on the wing nearly plunged them into the Pacific. At another point, their engine coughed and stopped, sending the monoplane into a glide that promised to end in open ocean. A gasoline tank had run dry. Before they could complete the switch to another, Pacific waves were lapping hungrily at them.

But the Bellanca stayed in the air and finally Queen Charlotte Islands loomed in the murk and then the glow of Seattle's lights appeared in warm welcome. They circled Mount Rainier and banked toward Wenatchee, where they struck earth in resounding style.

In the 1920s and 1930s, Wenatchee's Clyde Pangborn made aviation history, setting record after record, winning prize after prize. Without doubt, he was Washington's premier pilot. Wenatchee's Pangborn Air Field honors his name and marks his passage through Northwest skies.

But Pangborn's was not the only trans-Pacific flight to end in Washington. In June of 1937, Russia got into the act. Three Heroes of the Soviet Union—Chekaloff, Baidukoff and Beliakoff—took off from Moscow in a single-engine ANT-25 with a remarkable 125 feet of wingspread and set out for the U.S. west coast.

They were aiming for Oakland, California, and were willing at one point to settle for Eugene, Oregon, but sticky weather there turned them back north. They landed at Pearson Airpark in Vancouver, Washington,

Clyde Pangborn's trans-Pacific monoplane looked like this after pancaking to a landing at Wenatchee.

having flown 5288 miles in 63 hours and 17 minutes.

It was a remarkable achievement and it was fitting that it ended on the soil of Washington. If a few Washingtonians yawned, it was understandable.

After all, they had watched for years the exploits of Washingtonians Bill Boeing and Clyde Pangborn.

SUGGESTED READING

THE AMERICAN HERITAGE HISTORY OF FLIGHT; American Heritage; 1962.

Bowers, Peter M.; BOEING AIRCRAFT SINCE 1916; Aero Publishers; 1966.

Mansfield, Harold; VISION; Duell, Sloan and Pearce; 1956 (Boeing history).

Roseberry, C. R.; THE CHALLENGING SKIES; Doubleday; 1966 (aviation history).

Webber, Bert; RETALIATION: Japanese Attacks and Allied Countermeasures on the Pacific Coast in WW-II; Oregon State University Press, 1975. (Believe it or not, the state of Washington was attacked by the Japanese at least 28 times during World War II. This remarkable book finally tells the full story of offshore submarine actions and the weird paper balloons which dropped bombs on the state.)

Chapter Twelve ★

ICE, LAVA AND A SPACE NEEDLE

If any human animal lived in what is now Washington during the Proterozoic era, he had one huge advantage over modern Washingtonians: he didn't have to join an African safari to hunt crocodiles and hippopotamuses; he had only to scramble out of his Blue Mountain cave and trot down to the warm beach.

From his front stoop, Proterozoic Washingtonian, in the unlikely event that there was such a creature, had a superb view of a saltwater sea with a tropical shoreline complete with palm trees. Those who are supposed to know about such things tell us that Proterozoic Washington consisted mostly of saltwater lapping against what we now call the Blue Mountains in the far southeast corner.

Much of this is no more than an educated guess. After all, this period is called "prehistoric" for a good reason; it was "before history." But persons with high-sounding titles like "geologist," "anthropologist" and "paleontologist," after decades of digging, have managed to paint at least a fuzzy picture of what happened way back when in this scarred and craggy land called Washington.

How many years ago? A thousand? Ten thousand?

Nonsense. Ten thousand years is no more than the tick of a clock compared to the vastness of prehistoric time.

All right then; a *million* years. A good strong million . . .

Guess again. *Hundreds of millions* of years is more like it. The straining reach incredibly far back into time boggles the mind and numbs the senses.

From the Proterozoic, let's slide as gracefully as possible into the Palezoic. (Be thankful; it's easier to spell.) The great sea had begun to fill up with silt during many periods of drying out and flooding. If descendants of Proterozoic Washingtonian still occupied the family homestead in the Blue Mountains, they might well have found that their ocean view had disappeared (resulting, no doubt, in a dismal drop in real estate values).

Should we now skip lightly into the Mesozoic? This era, by itself, might well have lasted for one hundred million years. Time enough, at any rate, for Washington real estate to assume still different positions, such as standing on end. It was during the Mesozoic era that the land suffered ups and downs and took on the highly unlikely, though interesting, shape it holds today. Toward the end of the period, hot rocks thrust their scalding way through the earth's crust and began to form the mountains now called Olympics and Cascades. (The Mesozoic was the age of reptiles; dinosaurs were cocks of the walk.)

But if the reptiles thought the Mesozoic was interesting, they should have seen the Cenozoic, the most recent era.

Rivers of black, steaming lava oozed over much of central Washington to a depth of 6000 feet, melting all but the largest lumps on the landscape and forcing streams to seek new routes. (This is one reason for the Columbia River's drunken meanderings.) The western part of the state remained underwater, except for the highest peaks of the Olympic Mountains. But the floor of the great sea gradually lifted and the Olympics were joined to the mainland.

Lava flow over fallen ginkgo trees formed one of Washington's most interesting cemeteries—Ginkgo Petrified Forest in Grant County. (The world's only remaining native ginkgo trees grow in China.)

The lava cooled, the lakes and rivers were formed and rich soils were laid down in the valleys. But don't think for a minute that the excitement was over; never a dull eon; there was still to come the Quaternary period of the Cenozoic era and everyone knows how lively they are.

First the mountains blew up, vomiting great gouts of cinders, ashes, molten rock and stinking gases. Cones were formed; these peaks are now called Baker, St. Helens, Adams and Rainier. Without these snow-covered eminences, Washington's modern photographers would be hopelessly handicapped. Mt. Rainier, at 14,410 feet, is Washington's tallest (only four more in the continental U.S. are taller) but it could really have looked down on lesser peaks in the Cascades if it hadn't blown its top during one of many angry moments in a long history of irritability. The fit cost the surly mountain 2000 feet of peak.

Mount St. Helens, Washington's ice cream cone in the sky, is adorned by a topping of cloud.

The volcanic fireworks eventually simmered down but the show was far from over. A feature act, the Ice Follies, took over center stage. Canada is friendly today but in the Quaternary period it chilled and sent glaciers creeping into the northern half of Washington. Ice formed dams which diverted the rivers and sent the Columbia off on another of its periodic rambles. One of eastern Washington's most spectacular scars, Dry Falls, was formed when the Columbia was forced out of its old bed by an ice dam. Many of the remarkable coulees of east-central Washington are the spectacular footprints of the wandering Columbia. Unromantic fact insists that construction of Grand Coulee Dam was begun during the administration of Franklin Delano Roosevelt; a geologist might well argue that it was begun forty million years ago. Grand Coulee, the huge irrigation reservoir of the Columbia Basin Project, was carved by the impetuous river during one of its ancient vacation trips.

As it has a habit of doing, ice melts. The Columbia returned to its old course. Dry Falls went dry, as did Grand Coulee.

The glaciers retreated to the north, leaving interesting mysteries behind like the Tenino Mounds, hummocks and hills that look almost manmade.

The land called Washington had come of age. Salt water flowed into Puget Sound through gaps in the Olympic and Cascade Mountains. These two ranges thrust greedy fingers into rain clouds rolling in from the ocean and tumbled out the moisture, leaving western Washington very wet and eastern Washington very dry. They remain so to this day. The process is simple: warm air can hold more water than cold; air close to the earth is warmer than high altitude air; water-soaked clouds drift in, strike rising currents of air against the west wall of the Olympics, lift, cool and lose much moisture; it rains. Heavens above, how it rains! Wynooche, north of Aberdeen, soggily boasts of one of the highest annual rainfall averages in the U.S.: 150.73 inches. But the Olympic Peninsula doesn't own the one-year record; that was held by Cougar, on the Lewis River in southwest Washington: 171.88 inches. Then Hawaii joined the Union. Mt. Waialeale, on the island of Kauai, registered 471.68 inches, highest in the world. One hopes that western Washington now will just let Hawaii have its dripping crown.

Having dumped a load of water on the west slope of the Olympics, marine air moves inland, sucks up more water passing over Puget Sound, rises at the foothills, gives the west slope of the Cascades a good dunking,

At this diggings, flooded in 1969, were found the remains of Marmes Man.

then allows its drained clouds to coast empty into eastern Washington. Around the Tri-Cities of Richland, Pasco and Kennewick, annual rainfall might be less than nine inches. The difference is the difference between rain forest and desert, between mosquito marshes and dust storms.

But through all these geologic convulsions, where was man? *Homo sapiens?* Or even John Smith?

A good question. Through most of this exciting time, so far as we know now, he was missing. Earth seems to have evolved long before he did . . . which is a pretty good arrangement, when you stop to think about it. For millions of years, the steaming, hissing planet was populated by fishes, birds and reptiles. (It still is; it might not hurt man to think about that a bit.) Man is a newcomer, a raw recruit. No one knew how new, how raw, until 1968, when a team of scientists from Washington State University identified the remains of a human being at the bottom of a 13-foot excavation on the Roland Marmes ranch near the junction of the Palouse and Snake rivers. The bones, it now appears, will enter anthropological records as "Marmes Man," some of the oldest human remains yet found in the Western Hemisphere.

Geologist Roald Fryxell, professor of anthropology at Washington State, was one of those credited with the discovery.

"The skull pieces were partially charred and the long bones split on the ends," Fryxell said, "indicating that the person either was cremated or cooked and eaten by his fellows."

A relatively new radio-carbon method of dating indicates that Marmes Man is 10,000 years old, a mere tick of the geological clock. The land modern Washingtonians live upon is much, much older.

Early in 1969, the Marmes excavations were flooded by water backed up behind the new Lower Monumental Dam on the Snake River. Archaeologists worked frantically to remove as many artifacts as possible before the flooding. The Corps of Engineers built a coffer dam in a last ditch attempt to defeat the advancing tide but water seeped under the structure faster than it could be pumped out. Soon the diggings, considered by some archaeologists to be the most significant in the United States, were covered by more than 500 feet of water. It was estimated that three-fourths of the artifacts remain undiscovered.

And lost forever? In geological terms, there is no forever. Manmade objects like dams are only temporary. Two thousand years from now, when the dam has dissolved, archaeologists may return to pry further into

Mount Rainier, as seen from Paradise, displays a few of its many glaciers.

VANCOUVER ISLAND

SAN JUAN

LOPEZ

S

SHA

DECATUR

STUART

WALDRON

ORCAS

BLAKELY

CYPRESS

GUEMES

Anacortes

Marmes Man's affairs.

⭐

The geological convulsions have left eye-popping tracks in Washington's topography. The great glaciers retreated but the rear guard was trapped. Discount upstart Alaska and Washington has more glaciers than all other states combined; Mt. Rainier alone has 26. The Olympic Peninsula has 60 more, many of these extending to a remarkably low elevation due to great snowfall and cool marine air which slows melt. Total glacier area in Washington is 135 square miles; Oregon, next most glaciated of the mainland states, has only eight square miles.

The volcanic peaks thrusting snowcaps majestically into Washington's skyline appear to be dead but don't get too close; Mr. Rainier and Mt. Baker were erupting as late as 1870, which is barely yesterday in geological time.

But pointing out volcanic peaks and great glaciers is merely a beginning in the account of wonders in the land called Washington. From corner to corner and end to end, the observer's eye is startled and beguiled.

Beguiling is the only word for the far northwest corner, San Juan County. San Juan is one of only two counties in the United States composed entirely of islands, about 80 of them, comprising a watery, forested world that is rated next door to heaven by boaters and fishermen. (Many published accounts have put the number of islands at 172. Floyd Schmoe, whose book about the area was published in 1964, took the trouble to consult hydrographic charts and counted every lump of earth or rock that appeared at low tide. He concluded that there were actually only about 80 islands.)

The ferryboats which paddle faithfully among the islands are operated by the state ferry system, largest in the world. Some of the stately, comfortable craft which slide sedately through the San Juans and pick their way among the straits, channels and bays of Puget Sound formerly graced San Francisco Bay, thus providing a colorful link with the past. The San Juans would be charming without ferryboats; with them, northwest Washington gains an unique attraction for those among us who would rather float at a

A ferryboat representing the Washington State Ferry System, largest in the world, cruises the San Juan Islands.

◄

The San Juan Islands reach from Anacortes toward Vancouver Island, Canada.

relaxed and graceful 15 knots between Anacortes and Friday Harbor on the ferry *Klickitat* than zip-zap between Seattle and Portland at 600 miles an hour aboard a screaming jet. (For one thing, ferry passengers disembarking at Friday probably can lay hands quickly on their luggage, no small advantage in this era of electric toothbrushes.)

Another wonder of western Washington is the Olympic Peninsula. Olympic National Park, with the aforementioned glaciers, is considered something very special by touring Americans for more reasons than sliding ice fields. What's special about it?

Well, for one thing, more different species of thoroughly gigantic trees grow here than anywhere else in the world. It must be admitted that California's redwood forests have taller trees but they don't have the variety that the peninsula boasts. Tropical rain forests have more kinds of trees but they don't grow to such enormous size. Olympic trees average 200 feet tall!

"Perhaps the most awesome part of the remnant virgin forest in America," writes Ruth Kirk in "The Olympic Rain Forest." ". . . a green and padded realm where nature seems compelled to fill every cubic inch with leaf and twig."

What's special about it? Well, even the tourist brochures describing it tend to slip into poetry: "Bigleaf maple, red alder, and black cottonwood grow near the streams. Moss-covered vine maple forms an understory beneath the giant conifers. Mosses softly carpet the forest floor and upholster tree trunks and fallen trees, while draperies of clubmoss hang from the branches. Ferns mingle with the mosses and delicate flowers on the forest floor and accompany the mosses to the upper branches of some of the trees. The forest appears to be filled with warm, green light."

What's special, you still ask? Olympic is the only national park in the U.S. which can claim both snow-capped mountains and ocean beaches. It boasts Lake Crescent, too, more than 600 feet deep, with its bottom below sea level.

One can't have rain forest without rain. Weather records for the town of Forks in Clallam County on the dripping side of the Olympic Mountains proclaim damply that every single month for a period of 30 years had measurable rain.

Wet, wet, wet it unquestionably is on the ocean side of the Olympics but mild it also is. Tatoosh Island, the tiny blob of land off Cape Flattery,

Hurricane Ridge in the Olympic Mountains offers startling vistas winter and summer.

has a 306-day growing season, even though its latitude places it north of Nova Scotia.

Believe it or not, the town of Sequim on the same Olympic Peninsula is the driest spot on the Pacific Coast north of Los Angeles. At Sequim, one shouldn't expect more than about 16 inches of rainfall each year. Sequim, Port Angeles and Port Townsend, among other towns, are in a "rain shadow" east of the mountains. Clouds off the ocean already have risen and dumped their loads before reaching these towns.

Outsiders tend to think of Washington as a green, dripping jungle of Christmas trees, the largest, prettiest rain barrel in the world. Anyone living in Washington east of the Cascades might have a hard time getting through with his story of heat and dust and irrigation. The outsider would be thinking that bringing irrigation water to Washington is very much like carrying coals to Newcastle.

If there is a constant element in Washington's climate, it would have to be wind. In the west, winter storms marching in from the North Pacific like hurrying platoons of angry soldiers bring wet gusts sweeping over the land and not subsiding until they strike the western walls of the mountains. A marine storm is a hair-raising sight to see, but for most, once is enough.

In summer, the wind over western Washington turns benign. Sun-heated air rises over the land in mid-afternoon; cool ocean air slides eastward to replace it. Result: natural air conditioning from a brisk and dependable breeze.

In the great open spaces east of the mountains, wind is a fact of life winter and summer, as it must be wherever few natural obstacles exist to blunt its force. In central Washington, there are a few oldtimers who insist that the desert zephyrs blow night and day, year in and year out, and never once have been known to stop. But the general dryness of the air, making both winter cold and summer heat easier to bear, appeals to many. While a western Washingtonian in January might well have his head in fog and his feet in a puddle, his eastern Washington cohort often can manage a pleasant slouch against the sunny side of a building under an endless blue sky. (Ear muffs probably wouldn't be a bad idea, however.)

In rebuttal, western Washingtonians can point out that in 1870 Ezra Meeker prepared for a trip east by gathering 52 varieties of flowers found blooming on his farm near Tacoma during the first week in December. He

Denny Hill in Seattle was removed by steam shovel and horse cart during the remarkable regrading process. This picture was taken in 1906.

gave the flowers to Horace Greeley, famous editor of the *New York Tribune,* who then remarked in his newspaper upon Washington's mild climate.

A high percentage of Washington's population has always lived in the busy, prosperous area around Puget Sound and present growth figures suggest that the pattern isn't likely to change. Seattle—muscular, energetic and handsome—is the focal point. Since 1962, its skyline has been punctured and dominated by the slim 600-foot tower called "Space Needle." Built for a highly successful world's fair, the Needle has become Seattle's prime tourist attraction. Its heart-stopping outside elevators, rotating restaurant and observation deck draw throngs the year around.

Seattle's hills make it very much an up-and-down town but once it was much more so. Possibly taking a cue from the state's violent geologic upheavals, city fathers decided before the turn of the century to cut those pesky hills down to size. In one of the most drastic efforts ever undertaken to alter the earth to suit a city, major work at "regrading" began in 1898 and continued into the 1920s. Historic Denny Hill was carted away completely, with much of the material being removed to the tideflats. Most of the steepest slopes in an area bounded by First and Seventh streets, Jackson Street and Denny Way were cut down to a reasonable size. The work began with men shoveling into horse carts and ended a quarter of a century later with power shovels and conveyor belts. In all, 50 million cubic yards of dirt and rock were picked up one place and dumped another. One wonders how many erupting volcanoes can claim as much.

★

The San Juans, Puget Sound and the Olympic Peninsula—enough of natural wonder for any state. But Washington only begins in the west. Looming to the east is the mountain barrier called Cascade, but beyond, across as much as 400 inches of snow in Snoqualmie, Stevens and Stampede passes, lies the rocky, sandy, sunny, windswept Inland Empire, a defeated desert spotted with oases bearing the unlikely names of Wenatchee, Yakima, Spokane, Pullman, Walla Walla, Richland, Pasco and Kennewick, to name just a handful.

The throbbing, whirring concrete heart of the region is Grand Coulee Dam but Coulee is not alone in its bold attempt to tame and then enslave the Columbia River. Chief Joseph Dam, Bonneville, McNary, The Dalles,

Bonneville is the oldest power dam on the Columbia. In the near channel are a powerhouse and lock; in the far channel is the spillway dam.

Rocky Reach, John Day, Priest Rapids, Wanapum, Wells, Rock Island—their combined muscle has already turned the once-turbulent Columbia into a slackwater lake for much of its length, perhaps the longest lake in the world.

One wonders if the Columbia, which in its day has dealt with lava and ice and earthquakes, won't also deal one day with the arrogant slabs of concrete which man has thrust across its ancient path.

But the mighty river and the cocky dams are not the only wonders of eastern Washington. There is lonely Lake Chelan, stretching for 57 miles into alpine wilderness. There is that wilderness itself, the North Cascades, proclaimed a national park in 1968.

There are the honestly-named Scablands in Lincoln, Adams and Franklin counties, reaching in barren splendor west to the Columbia. Here the ancient lava flow, left naked of windblown soil, bares the scars of eons of erosion. Here the earth reminds one of an animal divested of flesh, its body fat and skin and muscle wasted away, its skeleton revealed.

There are more civilized and comfortable wonders in the spacious expanse of eastern Washington. There is large, still-growing Spokane, a busy, no-nonsense city of 187,000 citizens spotted in a most unlikely fashion among the empty, flowing hills of yellow and black. To an onrushing stranger carried to its environs, there must be something dreamlike about metropolitan Spokane.

Drive south of Spokane, into the heart of the wheat country; cast your eyes north and south and east and west; then admit that wonders, in Washington, may never cease. What you see, as far as the eye can range, is the Palouse Hills, giant mounds of windblown soil on a lava base, a small grain factory for the world. The hills look like nothing more nor less than solid sand dunes. A Midwest prairie farmer would glance at the angle of the slopes and write them off as hopeless but eastern Washington farmers for decades have sent their great machines snorting and grinding over these old hills, then dumping the golden harvest into trains and ships and barges which haul it to a hungry world.

★

All of this is Washington—its exciting past, its bustling present, its hopeful future. In the 1960s, Washington's population grew by leaps and bounds, as did the economy which feeds and houses the population. Without question, there was quantity.

Lake Chelan reaches far back into the mountain wilderness.

Can there continue to be quality as well? Can there be a good life as well as a prosperous life?

Fish in the clean streams . . . trees in the forest seeming to touch the sky . . . air flowing with the green, fresh scent of pine . . . space for a man to stretch his arms, then his spirit.

Perhaps only a greedy person would dare to ask that all this be saved forever. No dollar signs can be placed upon these virtues, yet, for many of us, they remain virtues. Those old ones, the pioneers, they understood and they yearned and they came west, to Washington. They endured great hardship but they expected a reward: a better life in every way for themselves and their children, for the children who followed their children, for the generations to come.

The generations to come . . .

Ruth Kirk, writing in "The Olympic Rain Forest," said: ". . . man cannot make airplanes and newsprint and lumber and electricity and boating lakes and farms out of one remaining fragment of original forest —and also keep it natural. If man decides to tame a wilderness, he can. Or he can cherish it, not for what he could *make* of it, but for what it *is*."

The late Western historian, Bernard DeVoto, cared enough to request that his ashes be strewn over the Lolo Trail. DeVoto said: "I have no urge to be active in the wilds, but I agree with the outdoorsmen—life would be intolerable if I could not visit the woods and mountains at short intervals. I have got to have the sight of clean water and the sound of running water. I have got to get to places where the sky-shine of cities does not dim the stars, where you can smell land and foliage, grasses and marshes, forest duffs and aromatic plants . . ."

All of these splendid things still exist in Washington but only continued care and concern will preserve them.

New generations must keep faith with the old. There is no other way for those now living on the land to repay the debt owed to those buried in it.

SUGGESTED READING

Moser, Don; THE PENINSULA; Sierra Club; 1962.

SUNSET TRAVEL GUIDE TO WASHINGTON; Lane; 1968.

Thompson, Bob (ed.); BEACHCOMBERS' GUIDE TO THE PACIFIC COAST; Lane; 1966.

Warren, Jim; PICTORIAL HISTORY OF SEATTLE; Warren; 1964.

Zim, Herbert S., and Dodge, Natt N.; THE PACIFIC NORTHWEST; Golden Press; 1959.

Washington Facts and Figures

Total area: 69,127 square miles (20th largest in U.S.)

Population: 3,292,420 (1968 estimate)

State capital: Olympia

Counties and county seats: Adams (Ritzville); Asotin (Asotin); Benton (Prosser); Chelan (Wenatchee); Clallam (Port Angeles); Clark (Vancouver); Columbia (Dayton); Cowlitz (Kelso); Douglas (Waterville); Ferry (Republic); Franklin (Pasco); Garfield (Pomeroy); Grant (Ephrata); Grays Harbor (Montesano); Island (Coupeville); Jefferson (Port Townsend); King (Seattle); Kitsap (Port Orchard); Kittitas (Ellensburg); Klickitat (Goldendale); Lewis (Chehalis); Lincoln (Davenport); Mason (Shelton); Okanogan (Okanogan); Pacific (South Bend); Pend Oreille (Newport); Pierce (Tacoma); San Juan (Friday Harbor) Skagit (Mount Vernon); Skamania (Stevenson); Snohomish (Everett); Spokane (Spokane); Stevens (Colville); Thurston (Olympia); Wahkiakum (Cathlamet); Walla Walla (Walla Walla); Whatcom (Bellingham); Whitman (Colfax); Yakima (Yakima)

Elevation: Sea level to 14,410 (Mt. Rainier)

Major industries: Manufacturing, agriculture, tourism, lumber-wood products

First provisional government: 1843

Territorial status: 1853

Statehood: 1889

State motto: "Al-Ki" (Indian for "in times to come" or "bye and bye")

State flower: Rhododendron Macrophyllum

State bird: Willow goldfinch

State tree: Western hemlock

State song: "Washington Beloved"

Selected Bibliography

Abdill, George B.; THIS WAS RAILROADING; Superior; 1958.

American Guide Series; WASHINGTON: A GUIDE TO THE EVERGREEN STATE; Binfords & Mort; 1950.

Anderson, Eva Greenslit; CHIEF SEATTLE; Caxton; 1943.

Andrews, Ralph W.; HISTORIC FIRES OF THE WEST; Superior; 1966.

Avery, Mary W.; WASHINGTON: A HISTORY OF THE EVERGREEN STATE; U. of Washington; 1965.

Barker, Burt Brown, L.L.D.; THE DR. JOHN McLOUGHLIN HOUSE; McLoughlin Memorial Ass'n; 1949.

Bidwell, John, Hubert Howe Bancroft and James Longmire; FIRST THREE WAGON TRAINS; Binfords & Mort; n.d.

Binns, Archie; SEA IN THE FOREST; Doubleday; 1953.

Brier, Howard M.; SAWDUST EMPIRE; Knopf; 1958.

Burns, Robert Ignatius, S.J.; THE JESUITS AND THE INDIAN WARS OF THE NORTHWEST; Yale; 1966.

THE COLUMBIAN (Vancouver); various issues.

Corning, Howard McKinley (ed.); DICTIONARY OF OREGON HISTORY; Binfords & Mort; 1956.

Cowan, Dr. Charles S.; THE ENEMY IS FIRE!; Superior; 1961.

Cullen, Allan H.; RIVERS IN HARNESS; Chilton; 1962.

Douthit, Mary Osborn (ed.); THE SOUVENIR OF WESTERN WOMEN; Anderson & Duniway; 1905.

Drotning, Phillip T.; A GUIDE TO NEGRO HISTORY IN AMERICA; Doubleday; 1968.

Drury, Clifford Merrill; ELKANAH AND MARY WALKER; Caxton; 1940.

Dryden, Cecil P.; GIVE ALL TO OREGON!; Hastings; 1968.

FAMOUS INDIANS: A COLLECTION OF SHORT BIOGRAPHIES; U.S. Dept. of Interior; 1966.

Frazier, Neta Lohnes; FIVE ROADS TO THE PACIFIC; McKay; 1964.

Freeman, Otis W., and Howard H. Martin (eds.); THE PACIFIC NORTHWEST; Wiley; 1954.

Friedman, Ralph; NORTHWEST PASSAGES; Pars; 1968.

Goddard, John W.; WASHINGTON: THE EVERGREEN STATE; Scribner's; 1942.

Heckman, Hazel; ISLAND IN THE SOUND; U. of Washington; 1967.

Highsmith, Richard M., Jr. (ed.); ATLAS OF THE PACIFIC NORTHWEST; Oregon State U.; 1968.

Hixon, Adrietta Applegate; ON TO OREGON!; Signal-American Printers; 1947.

Holbrook, Stewart H.; BURNING AN EMPIRE; MacMillan; 1943.

Holbrook, Stewart H.; JAMES J. HILL; Knopf; 1955.

Horan, James D.; THE GREAT AMERICAN WEST; Crown; 1959.

Howard, Helen Addison; NORTHWEST TRAIL BLAZERS; Caxton; 1963.

Jessett, Thomas E.; CHIEF SPOKAN GARRY, 1811–1892; Denison; 1960.

Johansen, Dorothy O.; EMPIRE OF THE COLUMBIA; Harper & Row; 1967.

Johnson, Jalmar; BUILDERS OF THE NORTHWEST; Dodd, Mead; 1963.

Kirk, Ruth; EXPLORING THE OLYMPIC PENINSULA; U. of Washington; 1967.

Kirk, Ruth; THE OLYMPIC RAIN FOREST; U. of Washington; 1966.

Laut, Agnes C.; THE CONQUEST OF THE GREAT NORTHWEST; Musson, n.d.

Mansfield, Harold; VISION; Duell, Sloan & Pearce; 1956.

McDonald, Lucile; WASHINGTON'S YESTERDAYS; Binfords & Mort; 1953.

McKee, Ruth Karr; MARY RICHARDSON WALKER: HER BOOK; Caxton; 1945.

Mintonye, Edna A. (compiler); THEY LAUGHED, TOO; Naylor; 1968.

Montgomery, Richard G.; THE WHITE-HEADED EAGLE; MacMillan; 1934.

Morgan, Murray; THE COLUMBIA; Superior; 1949.

Morgan, Murray; THE DAM; Viking; 1954.

Morgan, Murray; THE NORTHWEST CORNER; Viking; 1962.

Morgan, Murray; ONE MAN'S GOLD RUSH; U. of Washington; 1967.

Morgan, Neil; THE PACIFIC STATES; Time; 1967.

Murphy, John M.; RAMBLES IN NORTH-WESTERN AMERICA FROM THE PACIFIC OCEAN TO THE ROCKY MOUNTAINS; Chapman and Hall; 1879.

THE NEGRO IN THE STATE OF WASHINGTON 1788–1967; Washington State Library; 1968.

Neils, Selma M.; SO THIS IS KLICKITAT; Metropolitan; 1967.

Olson, Joan and Gene; OREGON TIMES AND TRAILS; Windyridge; 1965.

OREGON HISTORICAL QUARTERLY; various issues.

THE OREGONIAN (Portland); various issues.

Pyle, Joseph Gilpin; THE LIFE OF JAMES J. HILL; Doubleday; 1917.

Quiett, Glenn Chesney; THEY BUILT THE WEST; Appleton-Century; 1934.

Renshaw, Patrick; THE WOBBLIES; Doubleday; 1967.

Reynolds, Helen Baker; GOLD, RAWHIDE AND IRON; Pacific Books; 1955.

Roseberry, C. R.; THE CHALLENGING SKIES; Doubleday; 1966.

Ruby, Robert H., and John A. Brown; HALF-SUN ON THE COLUMBIA; U. of Oklahoma; 1965.

Salisbury, Albert and Jane; TWO CAPTAINS WEST; Bramhall; 1950.

Schmitt, Martin F., and Dee Brown; THE SETTLERS' WEST; Scribner's; 1955.

Schmoe, Floyd; FOR LOVE OF SOME ISLANDS; Harper & Row; 1964.

Scofield, W. M.; WASHINGTON'S HISTORICAL MARKERS; Touchstone; 1967.

SEATTLE POST-INTELLIGENCER; various issues.

THE SPOKESMAN-REVIEW (Spokane); various issues.

Stevens, James; PAUL BUNYAN; Garden City; 1925.

THE STORY OF THE COLUMBIA BASIN PROJECT; U.S. Dept. of Interior; 1964.

SUNSET; various issues.

TIME; various issues.

TRANSACTIONS OF THE OREGON PIONEER ASSOCIATION; various issues.

Trotter, F. I., F. H. Loutzenhiser and J. R. Loutzenhiser (eds.); TOLD BY THE PIONEERS; State of Washington; 1937, 1938.

Weisberger, Bernard A., "Here Come the Wobblies!" AMERICAN HERITAGE; June, 1967.

Wheeler, Thomas C. (ed.); A VANISHING AMERICA; Holt, Rinehart & Winston; 1964.

WITH PRIDE IN HERITAGE: HISTORY OF JEFFERSON COUNTY; Jefferson County Historical Society; 1966.

Index to Persons and Places

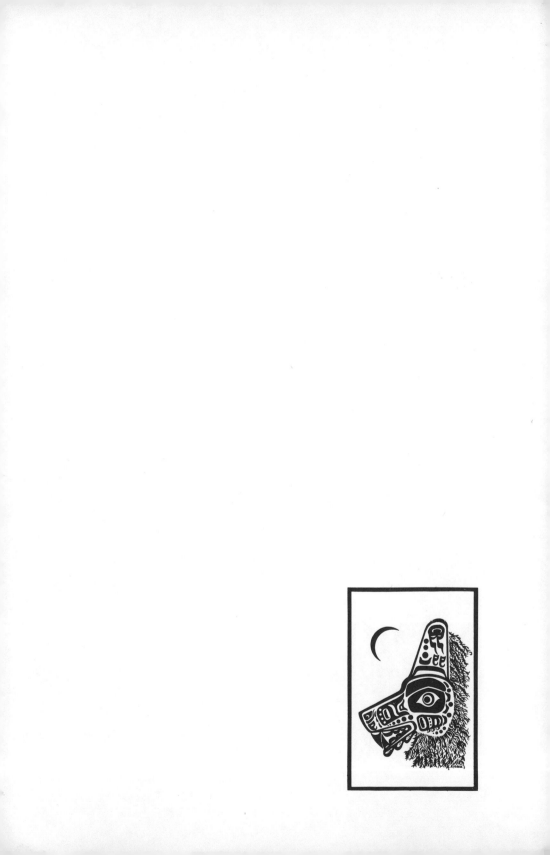